# The Remarkable Beatrix Potter

Other titles by Alexander Grinstein, M.D.

*The Index of Psychoanalytic Writings*
*Sigmund Freud's Writings*
*On Sigmund Freud's Dreams*
*Freud's Rules of Dream Interpretation*
*Freud at the Crossroads*
*Conrad Ferdinand Meyer and Freud: The Beginnings of Applied
   Psychoanalysis*
*Understanding Your Family,* with Editha Sterba

# The Remarkable Beatrix Potter

by

## Alexander Grinstein, M.D.

INTERNATIONAL UNIVERSITIES PRESS, INC.

Madison        Connecticut

INTERNATIONAL UNIVERSITIES PRESS and IUP (& design) ® are registered trademarks of International Universities Press, Inc.

**Library of Congress Cataloging-in-Publication Data**

Grinstein, Alexander, 1918-
    The remarkable Beatrix Potter / by Alexander Grinstein.
      p. cm.
    Includes bibliographical references and index.
    ISBN 0-8236-5789-2
    1. Potter, Beatrix, 1866-1943—Criticism and interpretation.
2. Women and literature—England—History—20th century.
3. Children's stories, English—History and criticism. 4. Animals
in literature. I. Title.
PR6031.072Z586 1995
823'.912—dc20                                                                 95-16173
                                            CIP

Manufactured in the United States of America

*To Adele*
*With all my love and appreciation for your*
*inspiration and invaluable collaboration on this book*

# Contents

# List of Abbreviations

| | |
|---|---|
| *Americans* | *Beatrix Potter's Americans: Selected Letters.* ed. J. C. Morse. Copyright © 1982 The Horn Book, Inc. Boston: The Horn Book, Inc., 1982. |
| *Children* | *Letters to Children from Beatrix Potter*, collected & introduced by J. Taylor. Beatrix Potter's original book illustrations and new reproductions of them copyright © Frederick Warne & Co. London: Frederick Warne & Co., 1992. |
| FC | Beatrix Potter (1929), *The Fairy Caravan.* Copyright © 1929 Frederick Warne & Co., renewed 1957. London: Frederick Warne & Co. New edition 1951, reprinted 1957, 1987. |
| FW | Letters owned by Frederick Warne & Co. |
| JM | Letters owned by Rosalind Moscrop. |
| *Journal* | Beatrix Potter (1966), *The Journal of Beatrix Potter 1881–1897*, rev. ed., foreword J. Taylor. London: Frederick Warne & Co., 1989. |
| *Letters* | *Beatrix Potter's Letters*, selected & introduced by J. Taylor. Beatrix Potter's original illustrations copyright © Frederick Warne & Co. London: Frederick Warne & Co., 1989. |
| NJ | Letters owned by Nigel Jee. |

NT          Letters owned by the National Trust.
SA          Beatrix Potter (1932), *Sister Anne*. Philadel-
            phia: David McKay Company.

# Acknowledgments

The writing of this book continues my lifelong professional interest in endeavoring to understand some of the highly complex determinants of the personalities of creative individuals.

Beatrix Potter combined the talent of a highly gifted artist with a vivid literary style. The result of her work was both intensely personal and universally appealing.

After studying her work and the biographies about her, I still wanted to learn more. To accomplish this goal I approached Judy Taylor, the preeminent authority about Beatrix Potter. Understanding the sincerity of my dedication and scholarly efforts, she kindly consented to help me. It is to her that I acknowledge my deepest appreciation and gratitude.

Sally Floyer made it possible for me to obtain photocopies of the Beatrix Potter letters in the Frederick Warne Archive. Subsequently, she granted me permission to use material copyrighted by Frederick Warne and Company.

My correspondence and contact with people who knew Beatrix Potter or had information about her, or were in possession of her letters, was a most rewarding experience. People willingly sent me photocopies of her letters, often with additional comments and personal remarks which were extremely helpful.

I wish to acknowledge with thanks the following people who have sent photocopies of Beatrix Potter's letters for me to study.

Anne S. Hobbs, Archive of Art and Design, who painstakingly photocopied and annotated more than 65 letters from the collection of the Victoria and Albert Museum.

Felicity Barker, Elizabeth Battrick, Hunter Davies, Betty Hart, Brigadier John Heelis OBE, Jean Holland, Bruce Logan, Rosalind Moscrop, Robert W. Moscrop, Rosalind Rawnsley, Constance Rigby, and Lady Elizabeth Willink.

Nigel Jee kindly sent me copies of his collection of letters from Beatrix Potter to Louie Choyce and gave me permission to quote from the correspondence. After my manuscript had already been completed, the entire correspondence was published.

In addition, various institutions and organizations were very cooperative about sending photocopies of their Beatrix Potter letters to me. This was accomplished through the efforts of: Karen Lightner, Reference Librarian (The Free Library of Philadelphia); Susan Denyer, Historic Buildings Representative (The National Trust); Lisa Backman, Manuscript Specialist (The Denver Public Library); Dana Tenny, Librarian (Osborne Collection of Early Children's Books, Toronto Public Library; John Gavin, Chairman (The Armitt Trust); Margaret Courtney, Archivist (The Girl Guides Association); Colin Harris (The Bodleian Library, University of Oxford); Patience-Anne W. Lenk, Special Collections (Colby College Library); Special Collections Librarians (The National Library of Scotland); David M. Bowcock, Assistant County Archivist (Cumbria Record Office).

In addition to photocopies of letters, Kenneth G. Hecht sent prints and negatives of snapshots which his grandfather, Charles George Yates King, had taken of Beatrix Potter. One of these is reproduced as the frontispiece.

Ann Malmquist made her bibliographic work on Beatrix Potter available for study.

## Acknowledgments

Christine Jones of Penguin USA found copies of works on Beatrix Potter that had been published by Frederick Warne but were not readily accessible to me.

Judge Saul Nosanchuk was helpful in obtaining copies of legal documents from England for study.

Pamela MacKintosh, Director, Becky Sorenson, Research Specialist, and other members of the staff of the Michigan Information Transfer Service, The University of Michigan, Ann Arbor, researched obscure references as well as notable ones with remarkable discernment and precision.

Patricia Siegel, Renata Propper, Lois Vaisman, graphologists, made a careful study of Norman Warne's handwriting sample.

Dr. Margaret Emery, Editor-in-Chief of International Universities Press, Inc., has been unfailingly encouraging and helpful throughout the entire undertaking.

In addition, I want to acknowledge my gratitude to Jacqueline Olivanti, my secretary for many years. She participated in all the stages of this project from its initial inception and research, contributed significant suggestions based on her thorough familiarity with the complex material, and used her considerable judgment and editing skills in preparing the manuscript for publication. Hers was a labor of diligence and dedication, an expression of her own admiration for Beatrix Potter.

Alexander Grinstein, M.D.

Portions of *Beatrix Potter's Americans: Selected Letters,* Copyright © 1982, are reprinted by permission of the Horn Book, Inc.

In addition, I am grateful to: The National Trust, London, for permission to use extracts from the letters of Beatrix Potter; Rosalind Moscrop and Robert W. Moscrop for permission to quote from Beatrix Potter's letters of June 14, 1926, April 11, 1929, January 22, 1930, May 26, 1930, March 25, 1936, February 25, 1937, January 9, 1940, January 18, 1941, February 26, 1942, June 11, 1942; the Denver Public Library for permission to quote Beatrix Potter's letters of November 19, 1930 and July 12, 1936; Lady Elizabeth Willink for permission to quote Beatrix Potter's letter of April 20, 1933; Nigel Jee for permission to quote from Beatrix Potter's letters of December 13, 1922, May 2, 1925, and May 10, 1939, which now have been published by the Beatrix Potter Society in *The Choyce Letters: Beatrix Potter to Louie Choyce, 1916-1943,* Copyright © 1994 The Beatrix Potter Society, Nigel Jee, Judy Taylor and Frederick Warne & Co.

# *Foreword*

I was brought up on Beatrix Potter, and my family lived not far, as the crow flies, from the mansion owned by the Potters that was destroyed during World War II—to her total lack of regret. It was the gloomy repository of a most unhappy childhood that was reenacted, according to Dr. Grinstein, in many subtle, dynamic ways throughout her writing, and helped to shape some of her remarkable attributes. The creatures of her imagination dominated many middle-class nurseries, although by the time my own children were being read to, other writers for children had entered the field with dressed-up animals whose adventures carried them far and wide, but who always returned to their cozy little homes where anxious parents awaited them. These animal books and comics seemed more in keeping with the expectations of newer generations of children, *except* for the undeniable fact that they lacked the exquisite illustrations and the undercurrent of deeper anxieties that propelled Miss Potter's stories willy-nilly into the hearts and minds of the younger set. Something in her style—and the style here is very much the lady, direct, unsentimental, intelligent, and humorous—made her eminently readable and "listenable," and it is clear, to me at least, that the matching of her stories with her psyche, as explicated for us by Dr. Grinstein, gave her this easy and compelling accessibility to her readership.

As I followed the author's detailed account of this "remarkable" woman, I found myself assimilating his combination of sympathy, understanding, and empathy that, speaking as a child analyst, reminded me of the attunement that I try to achieve with my patients. This attunement is possible if I am able to stay in touch with my own childhood and remember that past world of animism, disturbing fantasy, omnipotence, and ferocious drives.

When I first received the manuscript, I thought to myself, what has an analyst from Detroit got to do with an Englishwoman who wrote animal stories for young children. But then I remembered Bettelheim's sense of "enchantment" with fairy tales, Greenacre's absorption with Lewis Carroll and Swift, and my own abiding interest in Hans C. Andersen, and I was at once ready to be enthralled by the linking of childhood experience and the adult's creative reminiscence. At the end of my reading, I had the distinct feeling that Miss Potter would not have resented this insightful effort at bringing her life and achievement together in the way that she deprecated Graham Greene's "Freudian School of criticism" leveled at her. Dr. Grinstein is generally and refreshingly free from jargon and "wild" analysis. What he has done is to help us understand the central mystery of the writer's life—her lasting ability to engage the child's mind when she herself had no childhood worth anything, had no childhood friends apart from her brother, had no children of her own, and did not, in general, get on with children who found her somewhat brusque and schoolmarmish.

Her story-telling seems to have been self-curative, and as one follows her through her career with Dr. Grinstein, one is struck by the changes in the narratives as she allows herself increasing access to her troubled feelings and affects. She becomes impatient with the namby-pamby characterizations, and, against her publisher's expostulations, wants more angry reality to emerge, coupled with people not metaphorical creatures. She became ready for loving and ready for marriage. As she exhausted her own inner resources and "storied" herself out (one can only go so far creatively with a "repetition compulsion"), she openly and honestly cribbed from other fabulists on the grounds that "there is nothing new under the sun, and in the making of my books." It was hard not to be "plagiaristic" or to simply illustrate the works of Aesop and others, even though her publisher struggled to preserve her "originality."

In my own study of Andersen, what impressed me was, once again, the deplorable childhood, the lifelong fear of going insane like his father and grandfather, the loneliness, the inability to relate to women, the persistent guilt feelings, and the resort to fantasy and the writing of playlets to deal with the intense anxieties over growing up. As a man, and a famous man, he was to say that writing his fairy stories and shaping the outside terrible realities, kept him from going mad. I cited him as one of those resilient children who overcome early adversities and make themselves, without therapeutic help, "invulnerable." The story of the remarkable Beatrix Potter is another striking example of creativity in the service of resilience.

E. James Anthony, M.D.

Dr. Anthony is the Blanche F. Ittleson Emeritus Professor of Child and Adolescent Psychiatry, Washington University, St. Louis, and is a Training and Supervising analyst at the Washington Psychoanalytic Institute, Washington D.C. He is currently Director of Child and Adolescent Psychotherapy at Chestnut Lodge Hospital in Rockville, Maryland.

*Beatrix Potter (1913)*
Photograph by C. G. Y. King

# Introduction

Beatrix Potter (1866–1943) achieved international fame as the author of *The Tale of Peter Rabbit* and other stories for children. In England, she is also known as a major benefactor of the Lake District because of her donation of thousands of acres of land to the National Trust.

During her lifetime, because of her own adamant insistence on privacy, there was relatively little known about her as a person. After her death in 1943, however, the situation changed. Many scholarly publications about her life and work appeared. Among these are excellent works by Margaret Lane, Leslie Linder, Judy Taylor, Jane Cromwell Morse, Joyce Irene Whalley, Anne Stevenson Hobbs, Elizabeth M. Battrick, and others. In addition, there have been many television and radio programs dealing with her life story and adaptations of some of her stories for children. The celebration of the one hundredth anniversary of the writing of *The Tale of Peter Rabbit* in 1993 evoked a tremendous amount of world-wide attention to and interest in the life and works of Beatrix Potter.

The scholarship about Beatrix Potter has relied on a number of different sources. Primarily, there is the material directly derived from her own writings. Between the years of 1881 and 1897 she kept a journal, written in code. In 1958 Leslie Linder succeeded in breaking the code and transcribed her entire journal for publication. This work has provided invaluable information about her life during those sixteen years.

After she became famous, she wrote several reminiscences about her early life in response to various inquiries. In these accounts Beatrix Potter gave some of the background of her childhood, a period preceding the entries in her journal.

In addition to these primary sources of information there are her letters. The earliest letter, undated, is one she wrote to her father when she was a child, and the last, to Joseph Moscrop, her shepherd, was written ten days before her death. Actually we have no idea how many letters she wrote because, unfortunately, many of them have been destroyed. Some of them she destroyed herself, but many others were destroyed after her death by her husband, William Heelis, and, following his death, by members of his family. Still, a large number of her letters have been preserved and many of these have been published in *Beatrix Potter's Letters* with an introduction by Judy Taylor and in *Beatrix Potter's Letters to Children*. Other letters, selected by Jane Crowell Morse, are to be found in *Beatrix Potter's Americans: Selected Letters*. Some of Beatrix Potter's unpublished letters that are in private collections are occasionally made available for study. Through the kindness of their owners, I have been able to read a good many of them.

Her letters often had the character of free associations, so we are able to appreciate the nature of her ideas and her struggles, and to obtain glimpses of her life through her mature years from the 1890s to the early years of World War II.

These primary sources of material have been augmented through the efforts of scholars who have interviewed and corresponded with persons who knew Beatrix Potter or had some personal contact with her. Studies about her work have centered around the identification of the people she used as a basis for her characters and places, especially those in the Lake District, that she drew on for the illustrations in her books. The results of some of this research have been published in several biographies, in the quarterly newsletter sponsored by the Beatrix Potter Society, and in a recent book, "*So I Shall Tell You a Story . . .*" *Encounters with Beatrix Potter* (1993), edited by Judy Taylor.

There is another source of information about Beatrix Potter that remains to be explored in some detail, and that is her work itself and how it fits in with what is known about her life. It is my intention to study this area in the present work. It is hoped that this will throw additional light on her personality and especially some aspects of her inner life. This study has not been conceived as a biography in the usual sense, nor does it attempt to explain her abilities as an artist and writer. Various aspects of her life and her work have been thoroughly discussed by others, so it is not my wish, nor does there seem to be any necessity, to reiterate what others have already said so well, and have done so thoroughly, other than to put my findings in the proper context of her development.

I recognize that there are major difficulties and problems inherent in such an undertaking. Whatever conclusions are drawn from the content of an individual's creative or scientific work are inevitably subject to verification. Whenever we endeavor to apply our clinical understanding to an individual who is no longer living, who can neither confirm nor dispute our suppositions and constructions, we are always subject to the criticism of being speculative. This is especially true with regard to the individual's artistic product, where there are innumerable factors about which we have little or no knowledge that determine its selection and elaboration by its creator (the artist). We may be reminded, however, of Freud's (1930) comments in his paper about Goethe in which he wrote:

> When psycho-analysis puts itself at the service of biography, it naturally has the right to be treated no more harshly than the latter itself. Psycho-analysis can supply some information which cannot be arrived at by other means, and can thus demonstrate new connecting threads in the "weaver's masterpiece" spread between the instinctual endowments, the experiences and the

*3*

works of an artist. Since it is one of the principal functions of our thinking to master the material of the external world psychically, it seems to me that thanks are due to psycho-analysis if, when it is applied to a great man [or person], it contributes to the understanding of his great achievement [p. 212].

Freud went on to admit, however, that in the case of Goethe he had not succeeded very far because Goethe was "not only, as a poet, a great self-revealer, but also, in spite of the abundance of autobiographical records, a careful concealer" (p. 212).

   This assessment applies to Beatrix Potter as well. And yet, the situation is not entirely so bleak, for Freud himself wrote almost thirty years earlier, in 1901:

When I set myself the task of bringing to light what human beings keep hidden within them . . . by observing what they say and what they show, I thought the task was a harder one than it really is. He that has eyes to see and ears to hear may convince himself that no mortal can keep a secret. If his lips are silent, he chatters with his finger-tips; betrayal oozes out of him at every pore. And thus the task of making conscious the most hidden recesses of the mind is one which it is quite possible to accomplish [1905, pp. 77–78].

   In a footnote to his article on Beatrix Potter, Graham Greene (1933) wrote that after its publication he had received a "somewhat acid letter" from her in which "she deprecated sharply 'the Freudian school of criticism' " (p. 111). It is my belief, however, that rather than using psychoanalysis as a basis for "criticism" we can profitably utilize a psychoanalytic approach to provide another dimension for understanding Beatrix Potter. Even though she was reticent about personal matters in the British tradition, yet, being "mortal," she revealed more in her writings than she probably intended or realized. The repetition of certain themes and the inner consistency of such material, although expressed in various ways and motivated by literary, artistic, or even economic considerations, lends credence and confirmation to our constructions.

4

*Introduction*

Following her marriage to William Heelis in 1913, Beatrix Potter made it clear that henceforth she was to be known as Beatrix Heelis, or Mrs. William Heelis, in all aspects of her personal life. She continued to use the name Beatrix Potter for her books, and signed this name to some of her letters to children. Although I truly intended to adhere to her wishes, this distinction became too cumbersome and unwieldly. Some biographers faced with the same problem have opted to use her first name, but I felt that I could not allow myself that kind of familiarity. For the sake of clarity, therefore, I have chosen to refer to her as Beatrix Potter throughout the entire book.

While most of Beatrix Potter's stories are well known, summaries have been included to provide a basis for understanding their pertinence to her dynamics. The reader's conclusions and interpretations of the data, however, may differ from that of this author.

I want to emphasize that a knowledge of the artist's inner life and its pertinence to the artist's work in no way detracts from an appreciation of the person, or from an understanding and enjoyment of the final artistic product. In actual fact, it enhances it. In this instance, it has added immeasurably to my admiration for Beatrix Potter and her remarkable achievements.

Alexander Grinstein, M. D.<br>September 1993

Chapter 1

# Beginnings

About a year before her death in 1943, Beatrix Potter wrote: "It is immaterial to give the address of my unloved birthplace. It was hit by shrapnel in the last war; now I am rather pleased to hear it is no more!" (*Americans*, p. 213). The house in London, England, at 2, Bolton Gardens, Kensington, was destroyed by a German explosive on October 10, 1940. Beatrix Potter's comment succinctly expresses the intensity of her feelings about the house in which she lived for almost half a century, from her birth to her marriage. Her words sum up her pain and bitterness during those years, displacing her feelings from the people who were the closest to her to the inanimate structure of bricks and mortar.

From the information in her biographies and from her own record in her *Journal* we know a great deal, and can piece together even more, about those eventful years of her life.

Beatrix Potter summarized her background in a letter published in *The Horn Book*, May 1929. She wrote with obvious pride: "I am descended from generations of Lancashire yeomen and weavers; obstinate, hard headed, *matter of fact* folk. . . . As far back as I can go, they were Puritans, Nonjurors, Nonconformists, Dissenters. Your *Mayflower* ancestors sailed to America; mine at the same date were sticking it out at home; probably rather enjoying persecution" (*Americans*, p. 207).

7

In the same article she wrote that she believed in the importance of genetics. She said: "I am a believer in 'breed'; I hold that a strongly marked personality can influence descendants for generations. In the same way that we farmers know that certain sires—bulls—stallions—rams—have been 'prepotent' in forming breeds of shorthorns, thoroughbreds, and the numerous varieties of sheep" (p. 207).

In the early life of Beatrix Potter, as with every individual, her parents and parent substitutes were the dominant figures.

Her father, Rupert Potter, the second son of Edmund Potter and Jessy Crompton Potter, was born in 1832. Rupert's father was a highly successful businessman who made his fortune in textiles and in the printing of calico. He was active in politics and in 1861 was elected Liberal Member of Parliament for Carlisle (Taylor, 1986, p. 14).

Edmund Potter was a Dissenter, a strong Unitarian who campaigned for religious equality and toleration. Lane (1946) describes him as: "A Radical, a freetrader, a humane magistrate, a delighted spectator of the progress of science [and], an amateur of the arts" (p. 18). His wife, Jessy Crompton, was also a Unitarian. Lane (1946) describes the Cromptons as "an arrogant lot and given to extravagant expressions of opinion in politics and ethics" (p. 20).

A good student, Rupert Potter was awarded prizes for his accomplishments in the classics and in ancient history. In 1851 he received a Bachelor of Arts degree from Manchester New College, being the first member of his family to achieve this distinction. Rupert did very well in his studies at Lincoln's Inn, and was called to the bar on November 17, 1857, at the age of 25. Although Rupert was a barrister, he did not pursue the practice of law. Substantial money had been settled upon him by his parents which enabled him to live the life of a gentleman. For a number of years Rupert Potter did a considerable amount of drawing and sketching. From his work that has been preserved, it is obvious that he was very talented. Later, he became a skillful photographer.

On August 8, 1863, at the age of 31, Rupert Potter married 24-year-old Helen Leech, daughter of John Leech and Jane Ashton Leech. John Leech, a prosperous cotton merchant, was a Unitarian and friend of the Potter family. His daughter Helen, like Rupert, was also artistically talented as is evidenced by her surviving work.

Three years after their marriage, Helen Potter became pregnant and the Potters moved to 2, Bolton Gardens in Kensington. Their daughter, named Helen Beatrix Potter, was born in this house on July 28, 1866.

As was befitting the wealth of her parents, Beatrix Potter was reared with all the attendant advantages and problems of the monied class. The house at Bolton Gardens was large and required a good-sized staff of servants to manage it.

Both Lane (1946) and Taylor (1986) describe in a general way the early circumstances and arrangements of Beatrix Potter's childhood. Taylor (1986) remarks that although much had been written "about the strictness of her childhood," she believes that the Potters were no more overbearing than any other middle-class parents were at the time. She states that: "Children were seen and not heard; they were looked after almost exclusively by their nannies and governesses and were brought downstairs to see their parents only on special occasions or to say goodnight" (pp. 17–19). She indicates that Mrs. Potter would only visit the nursery occasionally. Much went on there that she knew nothing about (p. 19).

While it is certainly true that nineteenth century parents of their class followed a similar pattern with their children, the consequences of those practices were, without a doubt, different in each instance. Constitutional differences in the children, the complex interactions between parent, or parent substitute, and child, all exert a tremendous influence on the development of the child. But, in addition to these factors, no child's mind is a tabula-rasa upon which only external stimuli have an effect. Children have their own emotional lives, their own fantasies, their own responses to internal forces which modify external influences, resulting in manifold variations of character and personality development.

Ultimately, the fact does remain, and comes through forcefully in the biographies of Beatrix Potter, that her childhood years spent in that "unloved" birthplace at Bolton Gardens were exceedingly lonely. According to Lane (1946): "The Potters did not entertain at Bolton Gardens, and indeed it is hard to imagine what would attract visitors to that particular house, described as it has been by an irreverent Potter cousin as 'a dark Victorian mausoleum, complete with aspidistras' " (p. 34). And yet we learn that when they did entertain, their dinners were sumptuous and lavish (Taylor, 1986, p. 14).

Lane writes further that Beatrix Potter:

> [K]new no neighborhood children, and was given no opportunity of knowing any. Even cousins (and she had her share of these, notably Kate and Blanche Potter, a little older than herself and much livelier and prettier) though they sometimes came to Bolton Gardens with their parents, never became intimates. She neither shared her parents' life nor mixed with other children [p. 28].

And further, "One result of these strange years of seclusion was that [Beatrix Potter] became exceedingly shy, and was tongue-tied and *farouche* on the rare occasions when she found herself in company" (p. 28).

Beatrix Potter was 6 years old when her brother Walter Bertram Potter was born. In time, they became close companions. Not only did they play together but, as they grew older, they explored various aspects of nature together. Apart from him, however, she had no other friends.

Every year in April, the Potters spent two weeks in various seaside hotels in the West country while their house was undergoing a spring housecleaning. Then, from the end of July until sometime in October, the entire household went up North to Dunkeld in Perthshire, Scotland. Beginning in 1871, when Beatrix was 5 years old, and for about 11 years they leased Dalguise House, a mansion near the river Tay.

Beatrix Potter did not attend school. Reminiscing about her education in later years, she wrote: "The reason I am glad I did not go to school; it would have rubbed off some of the originality (if I had not died of shyness or been killed with over pressure). I fancy I could have been taught anything if I had been caught young; but it was in the days when parents kept governesses, and only boys went to school in most families" (*Americans*, p. 209). Her brother was sent to school but had serious difficulties there.

In the letter to Bertha Mahony Miller, published in part in *The Horn Book* (May 1929), Beatrix Potter revealed a number of her childhood memories. Her "peculiarly precocious and tenacious memory" she felt was an important factor in inspiring her to write children's books. She explained: "I have been laughed at for what I say I can remember; but it is admitted that I can remember quite plainly from one and two years old; not only facts, like learning to walk, but places and senti-ments—the way things impressed a very young child" (*Americans*, pp. 207–208).

Another source for her inspiration was "having spent a good deal of [her] childhood in the Highlands of Scotland, with a Highland nurse girl, and a firm belief in witches, fairies and the creed of the terrible John Calvin (the creed rubbed off but the fairies remained)" (*Americans*, p. 207). Taylor (1986) identifies this nurse as Miss McKenzie, who had begun caring for Beatrix Potter when she was an infant. Taylor writes that she "had sole charge of Beatrix and looked after her with strict and spartan attention. She fed her, dressed her, coaxed her to crawl and to walk, taught her her first words—and introduced her to fairies" (p. 20).

In describing her childhood Beatrix Potter recalled:

> I had a horrid large print primer and a stodgy fat book—I think it was called a "History of the Robin Family," by Mrs. Trimmer. I know I hated it—then I was let loose on "Rob Roy," and spelled through a few pages painfully; then I tried "Ivanhoe"—and the "Talisman"—then I tried "Rob Roy" again; all at once I began

to READ ["fluently and voraciously," she added in a letter to a woman on November 19, 1930] (missing the long words, of course), and those great books keep their freshness and charm still. I had very few books—Miss Edgeworth and Scott's novels I read over and over. [*Simple Susan* by Edgeworth was a special favorite.] [*Americans*, p. 208].[1]

Years later, on March 30, 1939, when Beatrix Potter was at Woman's Hospital in Liverpool awaiting surgery, she remembered, in a letter to Marion Frazer Harris Perry, that as a small child her nurse read *Uncle Tom's Cabin* to her—"Eliza springing across the ice on the Ohio River" (*Americans*, p. 95).

Reminiscing about her early interest in books, Beatrix Potter wrote that the books that she liked best were: "trash, from the literary point of view—goody goody, powder-in-the-jam, from the modern standpoint! I liked silly stories about other little girls' doings" (Taylor, 1986, p. 20).

But in addition to these, we learn from her response (November 19, 1930) to a questionnaire from an unnamed woman ("Dear Madam"), that among the books she enjoyed as a child were:

1. *Alice's Adventures in Wonderland* and *Through the Looking Glass*, Carroll.
2. *Black Beauty*, Sewell.
3. *Grimm's Fairy Tales*.
4. *Ivanhoe*, Scott.
5. *The Last of the Mohicans*, Cooper.
6. *The Little Lame Prince*, Mulock.
7. *Little Women*, Alcott.
8. *Water Babies*, Kingsley.
9. *Wonder-Book and Tanglewood Tales*, Hawthorne.

---

[1] This quotation is excerpted from Beatrix Potter's essay in 1942, published in *The Horn Book*, a magazine dedicated to children's books and reading. The essay was a portion of her letter to the editor and founder, Bertha Mahony Miller, who had requested biographical and literary information.

Yet, almost as an afterthought she added other titles to the list in this letter.

I cannot *quite* think that some of these unacquainted books can be so stirring or so well written as 1 Samuel 17 [the story of David and Goliath], *Pilgrim's Progress,* or that finest fairy tale of all, *A Midsummer Night's Dream?* [Unpublished letter. Denver Public Library, italics added].

As a small child Beatrix Potter discovered that she could draw and this provided her with a way to cope with her loneliness. About the time she was around 8 years old her parents recognized that her drawings demonstrated unusual talent and began to encourage her artistic abilities. The subjects of her drawings, taken from the world about her, were executed meticulously. Bertram was also artistically gifted and shared her interest in nature. As she and her brother grew older, they made detailed drawings of animals, using corpses of animals for their models. On one occasion they skinned a dead rabbit, boiled it until only the bones remained, and then articulated the skeleton.

Beatrix Potter's formal education began when her parents engaged a Miss Hammond as her governess. Evidently she "happily allocated a generous portion of the timetable to art without neglecting the basic necessities of 'reading, writing and arithmetic' " (Taylor, Whalley, Hobbs, and Battrick, 1987, p. 13). When Beatrix Potter was 12, a Miss Cameron was engaged as her drawing teacher and remained for five years (see also Taylor, 1986, p. 32). Beatrix Potter wrote: "I have great reason to be grateful to her, though we were not on particularly good terms for the last good while. I have learnt from her freehand, model, geometry, perspective and a little water-color flower painting" (Taylor, 1986, p. 32).

Although her progress in her artwork gave her a great deal of satisfaction, it did little to affect her basic feelings of loneliness and isolation. Taylor (1986) writes that:

[W]hat Beatrix really missed at this time of her life was a friend, someone other than her brother—of whom she was extremely fond and with whom she shared much but to whom she could hardly pour out her heart. . . . Beatrix's relationship with her mother was growing more difficult every day, and both her parents had always discouraged their children in close friendships with others, fearing exposure to germs and bad influences [pp. 33–34].

## Chapter 2

# The Journal of Beatrix Potter: 1881–1897

Beatrix Potter kept a journal from the time she was about 14 years old until she was 31. Exactly when she began writing in this journal is not known because she evidently destroyed some of her earlier entries. An undated entry, given as "London 1881," seems to be a kind of introduction. The subsequent entries, dating from Friday, November 4, 1881, are quite regular and systematized. The last entry is dated Sunday, January 31, 1897. An additional undated entry about her memories of Camfield Place (her paternal grandparents' home), presumably written around 1891, is also included in the published edition.

The entries were written in a private code of Beatrix Potter's own design which was not deciphered until Leslie Linder was able to do so in 1958. He relates the details of how he came to break the code on the evening of Easter Monday, in the introduction to his transcription of the *Journal* (pp. xvii–xxiii).

According to Linder, not even Beatrix Potter's closest friends knew of the existence of her journal. Approximately five weeks before she died, however, Beatrix Potter mentioned it in a letter to Caroline Clark, saying that it was: "apparently inspired by a united admiration of Boswell and Pepys." She went on:

When I was young, I already had the itch to write, without having any material to write about (the modern young authors

15

are not damped by such considerations). I used to write long-winded descriptions, hymns(!) and records of conversation in a kind of a cipher shorthand which I am now unable to read even with a magnifying glass. . . . They were exasperating and absurd compositions [*Journal*, p. xvii].

Not only did her *Journal* gratify her "itch to write," in a sense, it served as her companion and friend.

In addition, the *Journal* was a safe place where she could express her thoughts freely without the threat of criticism or rebuke. Thus, at the age of 18, after writing in code that "no one will ever read this," she proceeded to criticize a work of Michelangelo. "I say fearlessly that the Michelangelo is hideous and badly drawn; I wouldn't give tuppence for it except as a curiosity" (Saturday, November 15, 1884, *Journal*, p. 117).

The keeping of diaries or journals is by no means uncommon during adolescence. The underlying purpose of such literary efforts is not only to record specific events or impressions and to provide their authors with the opportunity of expression that they feel would be denied them otherwise; it also serves to keep a portion of their lives, their thoughts, ideas, dreams, and fantasies sequestered from the prying eyes of the adults. While less inventive and resourceful persons may simply keep their diaries locked or hidden, it is by no means unusual for adolescents to write in codes or cryptograms or in some exotic language known to their intimate friends but not to their parents or other authority figures. The custom of keeping a diary may then be continued well into adult years. Viewed from an adult vantage point, the adolescent entries are often exceedingly banal in character or, as Beatrix Potter wrote, "exasperating and absurd compositions."

Read sequentially, Beatrix Potter's *Journal* provides a detailed picture of the events of her life and her personal impressions about what she saw, as well as what was taking place politically and socially in Great Britain at the time (such as riots). Because her father had many acquaintances in the political world, Beatrix Potter had the opportunity to meet a number

*16*

of important people. She wrote about William Gladstone, his lengthy political career, and the great uproar in England about home rule for Ireland. Also duly noted in her *Journal* was the fact that Andrew Carnegie, the Scottish-American steel manufacturer and philanthropist, received more than 50 blackballs when he attempted to join her father's club, the Reform Club, whose membership consisted of prestigious Liberal sympathizers. Other entries included anecdotes about Disraeli, comments about the Conservatives' advocate, Sir Randolph Churchill, and remarks about the rise of the labor movement. Sometimes she simply stated her father's opinion of them but at other times, she expressed her own views. In addition to this, the *Journal* contains her candid impressions of art exhibitions that she and her father attended together.

Despite her careful attempts to keep her communications quite sanitized, even in code, every so often Beatrix Potter records a very personal thought, feeling, or incident. Thus we are able to view some aspects of her intrapsychic life with all its conflicts and turmoil. As the selection of material that Beatrix Potter wrote about in her *Journal* was determined by powerful conscious as well as unconscious forces, we are able to understand and to follow some of the progression of her psychological development. Moreover, as some themes seem to be repeated with relative frequency, we are able to appreciate their significance in her psychic life.

Obviously in a work such as this we cannot consider all the subjects that Beatrix Potter discusses in her *Journal*. We will, however, choose several themes that are pertinent to an understanding of her inner problems and provide a few illustrations of these.

Viewed solely from the number of entries, the most frequently mentioned person in Beatrix Potter's *Journal* is her father, Rupert Potter. There are well over a hundred references to him, so it is evident that he was a most important person in her life. Photographs of him reveal a man with a stern and unsmiling visage. Lane (1946) writes that from Beatrix Potter's *Journal* "it is clear that his irascible temper was a burden" (p. 142). On August 8, 1894, apropos a drive on the Northumberland moors, Beatrix Potter wrote: "I should have enjoyed it more without papa and the flies" (*Journal*, p. 334).

She chronicled their numerous trips to art exhibitions and commented on his opinions. A skillful artist in his own right, he had a "good eye," so that his critical remarks were of great educational value to her. He became engrossed in photography and, as Beatrix Potter grew older, he taught her a great deal about it so that she became very proficient in this medium. They went on many photographing trips together taking pictures of scenery, buildings, archaeological and geological objects as well as people (see Taylor et al., 1987, for examples of their photographs). Many of his photographs, each meticulously documented, have proved to be of great value to historians and scholars.

Rupert Potter and Sir John Everett Millais[1] (1829–1896) were very close friends. At Millais' request, he photographed many scenes and subjects which the painter wished to study or to incorporate into his paintings.

On Sunday, November 3, 1895, after visiting the Paget[2] family, where she had seen Sir William Flower[3] who did not recognize her, presumably because he was absent minded, Beatrix Potter wrote wistfully: "I wonder if people know the pleasure they may give a person by a little notice . . . Must confess to crying after I got home, my father being as usual deplorable, and beginning to read Gibbon's *Decline and Fall* from the beginning again . . . " (*Journal*, p. 408).

The connection between her wanting to be noticed by Sir William Flower and her crying after she got home, followed by her comment about her father being "as usual deplorable," reveals how hurt she must have felt because of her father's

---

[1] A founding member of the Pre-Raphaelite Brotherhood of painters.
[2] Friends and neighbors of the Potter family in London.
[3] English zoologist and anthropologist.

attitude toward her. This is but one of many instances of a similar nature that she mentioned in her *Journal*.

When her father was troubled by "gravel," Beatrix Potter notes her concern about his health. She "fretted so wearily" that she went privately to see his physician, a Dr. Aiken, who had evidently told her father to go abroad for five months of the year. Although she did not disagree with the recommendation, she expressed her anxiety that her father would refuse to move before he was ill. "I am anxious to do my best," she wrote, "but I really cannot face going abroad with him" (December 11, 1895, *Journal*, p. 411). We will bring up other information about her father from her *Journal* in subsequent chapters.

In contrast to the many references to her father in the *Journal*, there are remarkably few (only about twenty-five) to her mother, née Helen Leech (1839–1932). It is particularly impressive that while favorable impressions of other women are noted, for example, of both her grandmothers and her Aunt Sidney, there is hardly a positive line about her mother in the entire *Journal*.

On Tuesday, February 23, 1886, Beatrix Potter and her mother went to lunch at her "Aunt Sidney's" (Louisa Kay Potter [1806–1898] who was married to Sidney Potter [1806–1875]). Beatrix Potter described her Aunt Sidney, who was almost 80 years old at the time, as being of "middling height, erect, broad but not exactly fat . . . her hair is silver, neatly braided each side of her cap. The cap is white gauze, with broad streamers down her back" (*Journal*, p. 188). Beatrix Potter described her aunt as "mentally in perfect vigour . . . particularly clear and animated when speaking of old times. . . . I never saw a kinder, sweeter old lady" (*Journal*, p. 188). The entire description of her Aunt Sidney stands out in marked contrast to Beatrix Potter's remarks about her mother.

Some six years after this entry, Beatrix Potter reported in her *Journal* on Friday, August 19, 1892, that in the afternoon she had been "laid up [with] a sick headache" (p. 255). She was "still somewhat indisposed" the next day but, after lunch, went to a flower show complaining that she had "been rather exhausted with strong medicine" (p. 256).

She goes on in this entry to report that when her mother was:

[C]oming out of Miss Anderson's shop, [she] caught her heel and came down. She cut her elbow badly, to the bone. Went with her to Dr. Culbard, who was kind and very fat and snuffy. I did not distinguish myself, indeed retired precipitately into the garden, and had some difficulty in avoiding whisky. However, we all had tea by the way of a compromise. . . .

I felt much ashamed of myself, but upon my word I felt faint at the flower show; we will put it down to castor oil and seidlitz powder. How mamma managed to cut open her arm without even scrubbing her dress sleeve I cannot imagine [p. 256].

The following day, Sunday, August 21st, she wrote that her mother's arm was sore and uncomfortable, but not bruised. "Her arms are very fat, and I incline to think the sharp blow between the edge of the step and the elbow bone caused the flesh to crack as it were" (p. 257).

The factual description of the incident is almost painstakingly precise. But her account of her reaction to her mother's injury is presented in a somewhat puzzling manner as Beatrix Potter intersperses her description of her emotional reactions with remarks attributing them to her taking "castor oil and seidlitz powder."[4] Both drugs are cathartic and their combination is bound to produce dehydration. Thus, her feeling faint at the flower show could certainly have had something to do with the medication she had taken. But the intensity of her emotional reaction revealed by her recording that she "retired precipitately into the garden and had some difficulty in avoiding whiskey" and that she felt "much ashamed" of herself and "felt faint," undoubtedly was more than a response to the medication.

---

[4]Seidlitz powder is a combination of sodium bicarbonate, potassium sodium tartrate, and tartaric acid.

We may readily understand the intensity of her reaction as having been brought about by the surge of her guilt about her powerful negative feelings toward her mother. Her belief that her hostile impulses toward her mother could come to fruition frightened her.

On Tuesday, September 11, 1894, Beatrix Potter's entry in her *Journal* is even more expressive about her negative feelings toward her mother:

> I must confess to having been in an excessively bad temper being rather tired and very much vexed [at her mother] that I could not have the Hutton girls. There is only one spare bedroom, and that so dirty that no one will sleep therein (experto crede[5]), but the sting of my annoyance was the knowledge that this was regarded as a convenient excuse. I am afraid that it would have resulted in rubs, but I would so very much have liked to have Caroline, and I am afraid they rather expected to be asked.
>
> I was also today much provoked because my mother will not order the carriage in the morning or make up her mind, and if I say I should like to go out after lunch I am keeping her in, and if she does not go and I have missed the chance of a long drive, it is provoking [pp. 344–345].

A year later, on Monday, October 11, 1895, Beatrix Potter wrote:

> Mamma was taken very ill, sick from eight on Monday morning till three next morning. If it had gone on longer I should have been frightened as there began to be haemorrhage, but it stopped as suddenly as it began. She was upstairs nearly a fortnight, mending, without any shock, but I had a weary time, bother with the Servants as well.
>
> There is supposed to be some angelic sentiment in tending the sick, but personally I should not associate angels with castor oil and emptying slops. . . [p. 407].

While the entries in her *Journal* reveal a depth of feeling about both of her parents, the thinly veiled hostility toward her

---

[5]Take this on the word of one who has tried.

mother is especially evident. Later, when we discuss the material of Beatrix Potter's literary productions we will be able to appreciate this more fully.

Lane (1946) writes that the Potters were inevitably displeased with whatever arrangements were made while they were away on their spring or summer holidays. " 'It is somewhat trying,' Beatrix wrote in cipher in a rare moment of exasperation, 'to pass a season of enjoyment in the company of persons who are constantly on the outlook for matters of complaint' " (p. 54).

In contrast to the negative attitude expressed toward her mother, Beatrix Potter's *Journal* reveals her very warm, positive, adoring relationship with her grandmother, Jessy Potter, who lived at Camfield Place, Hertfordshire. Beatrix Potter writes on Wednesday, July 2, 1884, that she:

> Never saw grandmamma looking better, or livelier, talking about everything, enjoying the jokes, playing whist with her accustomed skill.
> How pretty she does look with her grey curls, under her muslin cap, trimmed with black lace. . . . So erect and always on the move, with her gentle face and waken, twinkling eyes. There is no one like grandmamma. She always seems to me as near perfect as is possible here—she looks as if she had as long before her as many of us but she is eighty-four [p. 96].

Beatrix Potter had a close relationship to her brother, Walter Bertram, six years her junior. Her *Journal* contains more than fifty references to him. While she does not say directly that she loved him, her geniune concern for him is clearly indicated, especially when it became apparent that he had serious emotional problems.

On Saturday, June 28, 1884, she wrote:

> Mamma and papa went to Eastbourne to see Bertram. He is top of third Class. Papa seems to think him rather quiet, better that than talk nonsense. I wonder how he will turn out? Sometimes I am hopeful, sometimes I am feared. He has an absorbing interest, which is a very great help in keeping anyone straight.

The best upbringing has sometimes failed in this family, and I am afraid that Bertram has *it* in him. Heaven grant it is not so, but I am afraid sometimes [p. 96].

The "it" to which she refers was a tendency toward alcoholism.

In addition to the members of her family, there were a number of other people who figured prominently in Beatrix Potter's early developmental years. We have already mentioned Miss McKenzie, the nurse from the Highlands of Scotland (chapter 1, p. 11). Later, there was a Miss Hammond, who remained for a number of years. In a letter to Mr. Samuel H. Hamer of the National Trust, written on May 27, 1930, Beatrix Potter wrote, most probably referring to this woman:

When I was a small discontented little girl with a governess, she set me an essay "spring time in London." I remember only one sentence of what must have deserved to be an immortal work— "The Sweet Smell of House-Painting pervades the air." My Governess had neither imagination nor sense of humour. She gave me three bad XXXs! which have rankled through five and fifty years [NT].

Beatrix Potter must have been 9 years old at the time.

Judy Taylor (1986) relates that sometime before she was 17, Beatrix Potter's governess, "Miss Hammond, to whom she had become deeply attached, had reluctantly admitted that her pupil was quickly overtaking her in academic prowess and that she could offer no more. Miss Cameron [her art teacher] had left the month before" (p. 39).

On Wednesday, April 18, 1883, Beatrix Potter writes that her mother had decided to engage Annie Carter as a new governess (*Journal*, p. 39). Beatrix Potter was not happy about this, and a week later (on Aprl 25, 1883) wrote: "If they said I must, I'd do it willingly enough only my temper'd be very nasty—but father wouldn't force me" (*Journal*, p. 38).

What Beatrix Potter objected to most was that the education would encroach upon her time for painting. She wrote:

"Only a year, but if it is like the last it will be a lifetime—I can't settle to any thing but my painting, I lost my patience over everything else. There is nothing to be done, I must watch things pass—Oh *Faith—Faith*" (pp. 38–39).

Annie Carter, however, remained for about two years. She left in June of 1885 to marry Edwin Moore. On Friday, July 10, 1885, Beatrix Potter recorded:

> My education finished 9th July. Whatever moral good and general knowledge I may have got from it, I have retained no literal rules. I don't believe I can repeat a single line of any language. I have liked my last governess best on the whole—Miss Carter had her faults, and was one of the youngest people I have ever seen, but she was very good-tempered and intelligent [p. 154].

Beatrix Potter and Annie Carter remained lifelong friends.

A few months after Annie Carter had been engaged, Beatrix Potter was taken to Mrs. A[6] for twelve drawing lessons. On Wednesday, November 21, 1883, Beatrix Potter recorded:

> Can have no more because Mrs. A's charge is high. . . . Of course, I shall paint just as I like when not with her. . . . I may probably owe a good deal to Mrs. A as my first teacher. [Yet] I am convinced [that] it lies chiefly with oneself. Technical difficulties can be taught, and a model will be an immense advantage. We shall see [pp. 56–57].

Several days later, on Saturday, November 24, 1883, she reported more about her lessons with Mrs. A. "Believe, though I would not tell any one on any account, that I don't much like it, which is rather disappointing. Wish it did not cost so much, is the money being thrown away, will it even do me harm?" (p. 57). She wondered:

> It is a risky thing to copy, shall I catch it? I think and hope my self-will which brings me into so many scrapes will guard me here—but it is tiresome, when you do get some lessons, to be

---

[6]The identity of Mrs. A has not been established.

taught in a way you dislike and to have to swallow your feelings out of considerations at home and there. Mrs. A. is very kind and attentive, hardly letting me do anything. . . . my temper has been boiling like a kettle, so that things are as usual. I do wish these drawing lessons were over so that I could have some peace and sleep of nights [p. 58].

On Thursday, November 29, 1883, she wrote that things were "going on worse. Do not like my drawing lessons" (p. 58).

Her dislike for the lessons increased and on December 5, 1883, she wrote that she would not allow herself to be influenced in the least by Mrs. A, "being a nice confession after all this money" (p. 58).

By January 6, 1884, she wrote that she didn't feel that she had learned much (p. 63). Beatrix Potter's dissatisfaction with her art lessons went deeper than her relationship with Mrs. A because it was connected with her underlying feelings of low self-esteem.

After viewing an exhibition at the Bodleian Library at Oxford with her father, she wrote on Wednesday, June 25, 1884, that the:

[P]ictures [were] mostly poor except as portraits. . . . Papa was particularly struck by their poorness. They were dreadful, certainly some of them, but I am sure he has not the least idea of the difficulty of painting a picture. He can draw very well, but he has hardly attempted water-color, and never oil. A person in this state, with a correct eye, and good taste, and great experience of different painters, sees all the failures and not the difficulties. He has never stared at a model till he did not know whether it was standing on its feet or its head.

Then, seeing Mr. Millais paint so often and easily, would make a man hard on other painters. It prevents me showing much of my attempts to him, and I lose much by it. When I go to a gallery I always avoid mentioning defects out loud, (to myself I say what I like), however plainly I see them [p. 94].

There are a number of aspects to this communication. Beatrix Potter and her father shared a negative assessment of the quality of the art in the exhibition, but she is more charitable in her criticism and only views "some of them" as dreadful. Although admitting that her father had a "good eye," Beatrix Potter decries the value of his artistic criticism by noting his lack of experience in executing a painting, and even depreciates the worth of his judgment of painters. Following these remarks, however, she states that because of her own fear of his criticism, she refrains from showing him her artistic endeavors, even though she admits that she loses "much" by not doing so. In this way she reveals a determinant for her negative opinion of her own artistic abilities. By a process of internalization she adopts her father's view of her abilities and becomes as critical of her own work as she feels he would be.

We learn more about Beatrix Potter's attitude toward drawing from her entry of Saturday, October 4, 1884.

> It is all the same, drawing, painting, modelling, the irresistible desire to copy any beautiful object which strikes the eye. Why cannot one be content to look at it? I cannot rest, I must draw, however poor the result, and when I have a bad time come over me it is a stronger desire than ever, and settles on the queerest things, worse than queer sometimes. Last time, in the middle of September, I caught myself in the back yard making a careful and admiring copy of the swill bucket, and the laugh it gave me brought me round [p. 109].

From these remarks it is apparent that Beatrix Potter was able to alleviate her feelings of depression and diminished self-worth by utilizing her creative drive to draw. Several months after the above entry she wrote, on Friday, November 28, 1884, following an enjoyable visit to the National Gallery:

> Swarms of young ladies painting, frightfully for the most part, O dear, if I was a boy and had courage! We did not see a single really good copy.... I always think I do not manage my paint ... but what I have seen today gives me courage, in spite of depression caused by the sight of the wonderful pictures [pp. 120–121].

By the interpolation of her remark "If I was a boy and had courage" she blurts out a deeply rooted feeling about being female and connects this with her feelings of inferiority about her painting ability. It is quite likely that she compared herself to her younger brother who was already showing signs of artistic ability. In any event, however, when she compared her work with the frightful productions of the other "young ladies" it did give her courage to persevere in her art.

Probably the most central theme that pervaded this period of Beatrix Potter's life was her depression and the various ways in which it was manifest.[7]

We may see how prevalent her depression was from the following entries. On December 30, 1882, she wrote: "Old year going fast. It's not been one to forget, it has been the corner—the wicket gate. I'm glad I've been helped past it" (p. 27). This veiled comment of the 16-year-old adolescent girl referred to her great unhappiness the previous year without specifying the cause of it.

Four months later, on April 25, 1883, she wrote:

I am up one day and down another. Have been a long way down today, and now my head feels empty and I am nothing particular. Will things never settle? Is this being grown-up? If I could have seen my mind as it is now, when I left Dalguise I should not have known it [p. 39].

Three months later, on her birthday, Saturday, July 28, 1883, she wrote: "I, seventeen. I have heard it called 'sweet seventeen,' no indeed, what a time we are, have been having, and shall have" (p. 49).

It appears that Beatrix Potter's depression and unhappiness continued undiminished because six months later, on Friday, January 18, 1884, she wrote: "It is a year today since I wrote I had got the dumps. How are my prospects compared with last year. I am not, not in high spirits tonight, something unpleasant having happened, so my opinion should be bended as regards height" (p. 63).

---

[7]A recently published collection of photographs, *A Beatrix Potter Photograph Album* (Beatrix Potter Society, 1993), vividly confirms how depressed she was.

Here again, Beatrix Potter does not record, however, what the "something unpleasant having happened" had to do with. We do learn, however, from the entries in her *Journal* a few months later that she had not been well. On Tuesday, April 29, 1884, she spoke of feeling "like a cow in a drawing room, and [her] head [was] uncertain just now" (p. 83). On Monday, May 5, 1884, she was "still middling and suffering from neuralgia" (*Journal*, p. 83).

On June 14, 1884, she reported that Mr. Gaskell, a Unitarian minister who had been her friend and had influenced her a great deal, had just been buried at Knutsford. As a child, Beatrix Potter had had a great deal of affection for him, and ten years before, when she was 8, she had knitted a comforter for him. Now, in her *Journal*, she describes her remembrance of him at Dalguise and raises the question whether she would "really never see him again." She goes on:

> [B]ut he is gone with almost every other, home is gone for me, the little girl does not bound about now, and live in fairyland, and occasionally wonder in a curious carefree manner, as of something not concerning her nature, what life means, and whether she shall ever feel sorrow. It is all gone, and he [Mr. Gaskell] is resting quietly with our fathers. I have begun the dark journey of life. Will it go on as darkly as it has begun? Oh that I might go through life as blamelessly as he! [p. 94].

Later that year, on Sunday, October 12, 1884, she wrote: "This day last year, how time moves and what it brings! So cold and stormy, and yet such gleams of peace and light making the darkness stranger and more dreary. How will it end for me?" (*Journal*, p. 109).

Two weeks later (Sunday, October 26th), she wrote: "If the next year takes away as many dear faces it will bring death very near home. How strange time is looking back! A great moving, creeping something closing over one object after another like rising water" (p. 109).

Beatrix Potter's depression continued throughout the fall. In mid-December (Saturday, December 13th) she wrote: "I do wish we lived in the country. I have been perfectly well in mind and body these few days. . . . I wish for many things, and yet how much I have to be thankful for, but these odious fits of low spirits would spoil any life" (p. 122).

Then, on Christmas Day of that same year (1884), she wrote: "Christmas Day. Xmas comes but once a year—thank goodness. . . . General depression. I wonder how they all feel underground?" (p. 123).

The basic depression from which Beatrix Potter was suffering was aggravated by episodes of illness. As is true with many individuals, the more serious the illness, the more they are inclined to withdraw into themselves and feel depressed and discouraged.

In an entry with a date line of "London 1885" and "Saturday, March 28" she writes:

> A lamentable falling off. Had my few remaining locks clipped short at Douglas's. Draughty. My hair nearly all came off since I was ill. Now that the sheep is shorn, I may say without pride that I have seldom seen a more beautiful head of hair than mine. Last summer it was very thick and within about four inches of my knees, being more than a yard long [pp. 143–144].

What is of importance is that Beatrix Potter had not recorded anything specifically about having been ill other than the suggestion of not being well in her *Journal* entry of April 29th and the entry of May 5, 1884, when she indicated that she was suffering from neuralgia. Losing some of her hair, a tremendous narcissistic injury, was undoubtedly brought about by some severe systemic illness which may or may not have been diagnosed at the time. In addition, some of her hair may have been "shorn" or "clipped," a common procedure at the time for febrile illness.

The degree of her ongoing depression is evident in her entry of Friday, May 1, 1885, from London: "To Camfield on May Day. Oh the beautiful Spring! If one's spirit was assured to haunt Birds' Place, suicide in the duck pond might be worthy of consideration" (p. 146).

Her entry a few days later (Wednesday, May 6, 1885) suggests that while she may not have been well physically, her depression continued to be connected with her low self-esteem. She recorded that she attended the International Inventions Exhibition at South Kensington which had been opened on May 4th by the Prince and Princess of Wales. Her impression was that the exhibition was:

> Very interesting though unfinished. How is it these high-heeled ladies who dine out, paint and pinch their waists to deformity, can racket about all day long, while I who sleep o'nights, can turn in my stays, and dislike sweets and dinners, am so tired toward the end of the afternoon that I can scarcely keep my feet? It is very hard and strange, I wonder if it will always be so? [p. 146].

By comparing herself to the other ladies in this way, she was suggesting that some of her depression and low self-esteem was linked to her conflicts about femininity.

Less than a month later, on Friday, May 29, 1885, she reiterated her feelings of depression and low self-esteem about her hair loss.

> I always thought I was born to be a discredit to my parents, but it was exhibited in a marked manner today. Since my hair is cut my hats won't stick on, and today being gusty, it must needs blow into the large fountain at the Exhibition [International Inventions Exhibition at South Kensington], and drifted off to the consternation of my father, and the immense amusement of the spectators. We had to wait some time till the gutta-percha man was fetched and waded in to his chin for it.
>
> It was of course too wet to put on, but as it was fine I did not care, for it is one of the peculiarities of my nature that when there *is* anything to be shy about, I don't care in the least, and I caused a good deal of harmless amusement. If only I had not been with papa, he does not often take me out, and I doubt he will do it again for a time [p. 149].

Thus, complicating her feelings about her hair loss as a consequence of her illness was her father's attitude which certainly must have further contributed to her feelings of low self-esteem and the undercurrent of depression.

Six months later, on December 31, 1885, Beatrix Potter wrote:

Oh life, wearisome, disappointing, and yet in many shades so sweet. I wonder why one is so unwilling to let go this old year? not because it has been joyful, but because I fear its successors—I am terribly afraid of the future. Some fears will inevitably be fulfilled, and the rest is dark—Peace to the old year, may the seed sown therein bear no bitter fruit! [*Journal*, p. 168].

Beatrix Potter's depression continued. From the entries in her *Journal*, it appears to have been going on for some four years. On Friday, February 12, 1886, she wrote: "Myself middling, past being low, reached the stage of indifference and morbid curiosity" (p. 182).

Then in December of that year, she wrote that since her last entry in July: "Part of the time I was too ill, and since then the laziness and unsettledness consequent on weakness have so demoralized me, that I have persevered in nothing for more than a week at a time except toothache" (p. 201).

It was not until the end of June, the following year (1887), however, that Beatrix Potter wrote that she had been very ill with "something uncommonly like rheumatic fever" (p. 203).

She wrote that when she was at the Grange-over-Sands on Marecombe Bay in April she felt well initially, and went for a mile and a half walk with her brother, but found that her feet hurt and supposed that it was due to the stones on the shore. The pain spread to the toes of her right foot and continued to hurt her on her journey to Ambleside where she was not able to walk. The pain then spread to the middle of her foot and to her ankle which became swollen.

A Dr. Redmayne was called who believed that she had a sprain and bandaged her ankle. The pain then went to her knee. She developed a fever and spent the next day in bed. She recalls that she was better the following day and that: "Dr. Redmayne thought we might safely go, as papa was so anxious to, it certainly was very awkward. I rather think if I could have stopped in bed and gone on with Dr. Redmayne's medicine, I might have avoided it" (p. 203). She then records on May 5th, 1887, that the pain "went into other knee during journey. Got up stairs with great difficulty and to bed, where I stayed nearly three weeks, if one excepts being moved on to a sofa for two hours every day during last week" (p. 203).

Although Beatrix Potter states that she had "very little fever" she did have a "great deal of rheumatics. Could not be turned in bed without screaming out. Continually moving backwards and forwards, up and down each leg, never in more than one place at a time."

Finally, she was able to dress on May 22nd, was "downstairs [on the] 26th [and] out [on the] 28th."

She writes:

> Amazed to find myself in summer, having last seen the trees in winter. I have had no spring, but no more has anyone for that matter. I have not missed much.
>     We were in a deplorable state all round. Mother at her wits end with me, papa exasperated with the prospect of a Chancery Suit, and the question of what to do with Bertram after his illness [presumably diphtheria] [p. 204].

Of some importance in her detailed entry about her illness is her remark about her mother being at her "wits end" with her. This was an equivocal statement suggesting both her mother's concern and her mother's frustration with her. Moreover, Beatrix Potter blames her father for being so anxious to go on with their trip north despite the fact that she was so ill. She expresses the belief that if she had stayed in bed and had taken Dr. Redmayne's medicine, the severity of her illness may have been avoided.

Taylor (1986) writes that the illness affected her heart and it gave her trouble from then on. From Beatrix Potter's description of her symptoms, we may presume that she had rheumatic fever (she calls it that later in her letters) and developed rheumatic heart disease, a frequent complication of that disease.

## Chapter 3

# *The Journal* (continued)

Beatrix Potter's generalized depression, her low self-esteem, and preoccupation with death were outward manifestations of her internal problems and conflicts. In addition, as she began to develop an interest in the opposite sex, problems with her femininity became more manifest.

On Monday, September 7, 1885, Beatrix Potter wrote an extensive critical discourse about her cousin Mary Catherine's (Kate's) engagement to Captain Fletcher Hayes Grant Cruickshank. Her knowledge of this event was based on a letter that her Aunt Mary (Kate's mother) had written to Rupert Potter, her brother-in-law (Beatrix Potter's father). In the entry in her *Journal*, Beatrix Potter wrote:

> Captain Crookshank (sic),[1] who had been in the Army, is now a Stockbroker "by no means rich," not a word about his religion, friends, or age. One should not judge before one hears all the case, but this sounds a silly business if nothing worse. . . .
>
> Aunt Mary has not a particle of sense, but I can't understand the girl not having more self-pride or ambition. What would your old grandfather [Edmund Potter, 1802–1883, married to Jessy Crompton] have said, he would have been horrified. Father [Rupert Potter] is grieved and exasperated to tears. . . . If he [Rupert Potter] had a beautiful daughter like Kate [i.e., by implication, not like herself] there is no doubt he could marry her

[1]Beatrix Potter frequently made spelling errors.

very well, he is intimate with all the rich and respectable Unitarians' families, or if ambitious, he could easily take her into fashionable society.

Beatrix Potter goes on to say:

> Not that I in the least consider position or wealth as the great objects of life, though I am sure they are more necessary to Kate's happiness than they would be for mine. Too much money is an evil in most hands, but too little is a sore trial to one extravagantly brought up. . . . Love in a cottage is sentimental, but the parties must be very pleasing to each other to make it tolerable.
>
> I can't say that I'm surprised at this business, I thought she would marry someone fast, but this is a poor affair. If he were in the Army even, he might rise. . . . If ghosts are disturbed by after events, grandfather will turn in his grave, he will have little rest, there is a curse on this family. If this is what beauty leads to, I am well content to have a red nose and a shorn head, I may be lonely, but better that than an unhappy marriage [p. 156].

Although Beatrix Potter echoes her father's point of view about the wisdom of her cousin's engagement by stressing the "practical" issues of such an alliance, we do have the impression that she is jealous. By adopting and justifying her father's attitude she defensively adopts a passive role. We may understand her comments as being in the nature of an identification with her aggressor father as a defense against her anxiety: her fear that he would condemn her for her own developing heterosexual interests.

We may see the development of Beatrix Potter's feminine interests in an entry dated June 1894, from Harescombe Grange, Stroud, where she was visiting her cousin, Caroline Hutton:

> It is well in this world to discover there can exist a young woman [Caroline], clever, brilliantly attractive and perfectly well principled, although knowing her own mind, but I cannot help thinking I would sink the whole lump of independence to have anyone so deservedly fond of me as Mr. Hutton is of *Sophy* [his wife]. . . .

Latter day fate ordains that many women shall be unmarried and self-contained, nor should I personally dream to complain, but I hold an old-fashioned notion that a happy marriage is the crown of a woman's life, and that it is unwise on the part of a nice-looking young lady to proclaim a pronounced dislike of babies and all child cousins [pp. 320–321].

Her remarks are extremely contradictory to those she expressed about Mary Catherine's engagement to Captain Cruickshank nine years earlier, on September 7, 1885.

Beatrix Potter had a great deal of respect for the artistic ability of her father's longtime friend, Sir John Millais. Yet, as she confided to her *Journal*, some aspects of his personality were not entirely pleasing to her. One Sunday evening, November 15, 1885, Millais visited the Potters to ask Rupert Potter to photograph a small child for him the next morning. At some point he asked Beatrix Potter how she was "getting on with [her] drawing." She was "rather alarmed" by the question but he immediately changed the subject. She writes:

He addressed some most embarrassingly personal remarks to me, but compliments from him would take longer to turn my head than from any other source. If he sees a tolerably comely girl, he cannot keep his tongue still, and I am perfectly certain that when I was a child he used to tease me in order to see me blush [p. 161].

When Millais died on August 13, 1896, Beatrix Potter wrote a long entry about him in her *Journal* which is both a memoir and a tribute. She writes: "He would have gone long ago if he had been an ordinary poor man. We pity the poor when they are sick, but this was surely the other extreme" (p. 429). She describes him as one of the handsomest men she had ever seen "aside from the defect of his eye, and the odd mark across his forehead" (p. 429).

She recollected that she would always have a most affectionate remembrance of the painter

[T]hough unmercifully afraid of him as a child, on account of what the papers call "his schoolboy manner." I had a brilliant color as a little girl, which he used to provoke on purpose and remark upon at times. If a great portrait painter's criticism is of any interest this is it, delivered with due consideration, turning me round under a window, that I was a little like his daughter Carrie, at that time a fine handsome girl, but my face was spoiled by the length of my nose and upper lip.

He gave me the kindest encouragement with my drawings (to be sure he did to everybody!), . . . but he really paid me a compliment for he said that "plenty of people can *draw*, but you and my son John have observation." Now "my son Johnnie" at that date couldn't draw at all, but I know exactly what he meant [p. 429].

Evidently Millais was both complimentary and critical of Beatrix Potter. While he compared her to his daughter, Carrie, who was a "fine handsome girl" he criticized Beatrix Potter's face as being spoiled by the length of her nose and upper lip. While he praised her for being able to observe, like his son, Johnnie, the compliment was spoiled by her awareness that at this time his son "couldn't draw at all." Considering Beatrix Potter's tendency toward depression and her low self-esteem such comments coming from a man she admired must have been very confusing.

A few months after Millais's death she recorded, on December 3, 1896, that when she was at the Kew station and asked a young woman the location of the ladies' waiting room, the young woman told her that she would not have to pay anything. Beatrix Potter writes that it was "a great shame of railways to charge, but it made [her] wonder if [she] was wanting new clothes" (p. 437). We may wonder in turn about her choice of clothing at this time, a problem that various people were to comment about in her later years.

It seems that any personal reference to her appearance and her dress was in some way threatening to Beatrix Potter. It often happens that when women are insecure in their feelings about themselves as women, they attempt to master this uncertainty by deliberately downplaying their physical appearance and may even dress in a manner that expresses this belittled view of themselves. Despite their wishes to the contrary, such a defensive posture also serves to protect them from any interest which a man may have in them.

By the time Beatrix Potter turned 30, on July 28, 1896, she was able to write that she felt "much younger at thirty than [she] did at twenty; firmer and stronger both in mind and body" (p. 427). Evidently, along with a marked improvement in her general physical health, she was experiencing a growing sense of independence. Her interest in the opposite sex, however, was still attenuated by a good deal of self-criticism and anxiety.

Whatever negative factors burdened Beatrix Potter during the years prior to this, such as residual sequelae of her physical illness, her low self-esteem, and her generalized anxieties, evidently did not daunt her from expressing herself in creative work. She continued to draw, to write, and to photograph.

In May 1890 she recorded an unfinished account in her *Journal* of an incident that brought about a profound change in the course of her life. It all began when she and her brother decided to go into business because they were in need of £6.

It is difficult to ascertain exactly what financial restrictions were placed upon Beatrix Potter and her brother by their parents. Despite the comfortable economic circumstances that the Potters enjoyed, it appears that they were extremely frugal in some matters. We may suppose that while money was available for some purposes, their parents were extremely sparing if not penurious with regard to the amount of spending money they gave Beatrix and Bertram. The young people, deciding that they had to be financially independent, came up with the idea of making Christmas cards and selling them to a commercial printer.

Between February and Easter of that year Beatrix Potter prepared "Six Designs" using her tame rabbit, Benjamin

Bouncer, as a model. Then she and her brother chose five publishers to whom to send the pictures. After the first publisher promptly returned them, they decided to send them to the publishers, Hildescheimer and Faulkner, who accepted them. On May 14th Beatrix Potter received a check for £6.

Some time later her uncle, Sir Henry Roscoe ([1833–1915] married to Lucy Potter [1840–1908] *Journal*, p. 212, fn 9) took Beatrix Potter to visit the publishers where she had an interview with Mr. Faulkner. She writes that he was civil to her "but so dry and circumspect in the way of business that [she could] not think of him without laughing. Not one word did he say in praise of the cards, but he showed a mysterious desire for more. He grinned a little at some of the fresh sketches, but not much" (p. 213).

Some of her new sketches were accepted and published as holiday greeting cards and others were used as illustrations in a book, *A Happy Pair*, containing verses by Frederic E. Weatherly (Taylor, 1986, p. 52). In this very modest way, Beatrix Potter embarked upon a career as an artist and illustrator.

According to the entry in her *Journal* after Beatrix Potter had received the check for £6 and the letter asking for more sketches from Hildescheimer and Faulkner on May 14th:

> [Her] first act was to give "Bounce [the rabbit] (what an investment that rabbit has been in spite of the hutches), a cupful of hemp seeds, the consequence being that when [she] wanted to draw him next morning he was partially intoxicated and wholly unmanageable.
> Then [she] retired to bed, and lay awake chuckling till 2 in the morning, and afterwards had an impression that Bunny came to [her] bedside in a white cotton night cap and tickled [her] with his whiskers [*Journal*, p. 213].

While she describes the rabbit coming to her bedside as "an impression," the likelihood is that this was a dream fragment inspired by the day residue of her receiving the check and the acceptance of her designs which contained drawings of Benjamin Bouncer. He had, in essence, gratified her wish that he, the subject of her drawings, would bring her success. He now appeared in her dream as the bearer of pleasure and delight.

But why was the rabbit wearing a white cotton nightcap and tickling her with his whiskers? The incongruity of a rabbit wearing a nightcap fitted in with her general artistic style of dressing animals in human clothing, thus providing delight to the viewers, a style that persisted in a great many of her subsequent publications.

The other dream element of the rabbit tickling her with his whiskers more than likely referred to some masculine figure who had whiskers, her father, her Uncle, Sir Henry Roscoe, or Mr. Gaskell, the Unitarian minister with whom she had had such an affectionate relationship, or even Mr. Faulkner.

We may speculate that what really "tickled her fancy" in her dream and gave her joyous pleasure was that for the first time her work was appreciated and paid for! The acknowledgment of her work by strangers was a triumph of the greatest possible significance for her.

Beatrix Potter's account of her sale of the "designs" to Hildescheimer and Faulkner, her first real triumph, was, of course, written in code in her *Journal*, and addressed to "My dear Esther." She wrote:

> It is an odd consideration, (absit omen) that one of the first events that I have to write to you about should be a stroke in humble imitation of my heroine, Fanny Burney—perhaps you suspect that it is no coincidence, but I assure you that such was my modesty (or stupidity) that . . . I yet never noticed a likeness until yesterday when my conscience reproached me for not having chronicled my success [pp. 211–212].

> Esther "is believed to be an imaginary person perhaps inspired by Fanny Burney's sister, Esther, whom Fanny Burney addressed in her own diaries" [p. 211, fn 7].

We may understand Beatrix Potter's affinity with Fanny Burney by examining some biographical material about her. Fanny (Frances) Burney (June 13, 1752–January 6, 1840) was an English diarist and novelist. In 1761, when she was 9 years of age, her mother died and six years later her father, Dr. Burney, a fashionable music master, married Elizabeth Allen, a widow. Fanny's sisters, Esther (Hetty), and Susanna were sent to Parisian schools while Fanny was left to educate herself at home.

Dr. Burney entertained many famous musicians, actors, and writers, and other members of the intelligentsia, including Samuel Johnson and David Garrick, and Fanny was exposed to their influence. She read and wrote a good deal but burned many of her early manuscripts because her stepmother did not encourage her writing.

Her first novel, *Evelina, or A Young Lady's Entrance into the World*, published by Thomas Lowndes in January, 1778, was successful. Fanny did not tell her father that she was the author of this book until June of that year, after it had received many favorable reviews and had become very popular. Dr. Samuel Johnson was full of praises about it and remained a staunch admirer of her writing during his lifetime. Her next book, *Cecilia; or Memoirs of an Heiress* was published in 1782.

The following year Fanny Burney met Mrs. Delany who presented her to King George III and Queen Charlotte in 1785. Shortly afterwards the Queen offered her the post of the second keeper of the robes with the salary of £200 a year. Fanny Burney remained in that position for five years, suffering horribly from the lack of intellectual stimulation and the stultifying atmosphere of the court. To make matters worse the constant harassment by her superior, Mrs. Schwellenberg, had an extremely destructive influence upon her. Macauley (1843) devoted an entire essay to Fanny Burney, writing a most glowing and sympathetic description of her work and her personality, describing in detail her unfortunate experience at the court, and crediting it with having had a profoundly detrimental effect on her creativity.

Fanny Burney left the court in 1791 with a pension of £100 a year. Two years later, on July 31, 1793, she married

Alexander d'Arblay, a French exile living in London. He had been an artillery officer and also an adjutant-general to Lafayette. Their son, Alexander, was born on December 18, 1794. She wrote another novel, *Camilla: or A Picture of Youth* (1796), which was a reasonable financial success although its literary value was not considered great.

In 1801 Madam D'Arblay and her husband went to Paris where she remained until her return to England in 1812.

After her husband's death on May 3, 1818, Fanny lived on Bolton Street, Piccadilly. In her later years she edited the memoirs of her father, Dr. Burney, publishing the work in 1832.

Her most notable contribution to literature was her *Diary and Letters* in which she vividly described many of the people she had known during her lifetime (*Encyclopaedia Britannica*, 1954, vol. 7, p. 51).

Beatrix Potter was able to identify with Fanny Burney for several reasons. Burney painted very skillful verbal portraits of people she met, and Beatrix Potter too was able to use language to capture her impressions of people with whom she came in contact. Like her "heroine," Beatrix Potter had the opportunity to meet many important personages of her day through her father's political connections and his friendship with Sir John Millais. In certain respects, Beatrix Potter, like Burney, was self-educated. She read a great deal on her own and also developed her own artistic style and technique.

Beatrix Potter undoubtedly longed to have a relationship with some famous personage such as Fanny Burney had enjoyed with Dr. Samuel Johnson. In addition to this, she wished for the kind of success for her own artistic and literary efforts that Fanny Burney had achieved. Her identification with Burney also must have carried with it the wish that she, like her heroine, would ultimately be married and have a child herself.

Encouraged by her beginning recognition and success in the artistic field, Beatrix Potter's abilities and talents as a careful observer and a meticulous recorder of detail flourished in another direction. Interested as she was in nature, some years before she had begun to draw and record her observations in the field of mycology. The results of her observations were shared with Charles McIntosh, "The Perthshire Naturalist" and postman from Dunkeld, and with her uncle, Sir Henry Roscoe. Her work, executed in incredible detail, is remarkable both from an artistic and from a scientific standpoint (see Taylor, Whalley, Hobbs, and Battrick, 1987; Jay, Noble, and Hobbs, 1992). Nearly all her specimens were gathered between 1887 and 1901 "in the woods of Perthshire and the Lake District but she studied and photographed most intensely from 1893 to 1898" (Taylor et al., 1987, pp. 88–89). In connection with a specimen she had received from Mr. McIntosh, and hidden under a garden footpath to collect after dark, she wrote that her parents were "not devoted to the cause of science" (*Journal*, December 29, 1896, p. 440).

Beatrix Potter's uncle, Sir Henry Roscoe, took her to the Royal Botanic Gardens in Kew where her reception by the director, Sir William Thiselton-Dyer and by George Massee, a principal assistant, was rather cavalier. Encouraged by her uncle, and on the basis of her research, Beatrix Potter prepared a paper entitled: "On the Germination of the Spores of *Agaricineae*" which was supposed to have been presented at the Linnean Society of London on April 1, 1897.

It is recorded that the paper was read there but whether it was read in its entirety or only in summary is not clear. Beatrix Potter, herself, was not allowed to appear at the meeting as women "with one or two exceptions" (*Journal*, p. 443, fn 30) were not allowed to attend society meetings. An editorial footnote in her *Journal* states that: "According to the Minute Book, Mr. George Massee was present, and it is thought that *he* read the Paper" (*Journal*, p. 443, fn 30). What is not stated is that its reception was apparently quite negative with the implication that she should study the subject further, that she didn't really have any specialized training in botany or in the study of fungi.

"She informed Charlie McIntosh, however, that it had been 'well received,' but 'they' say more work is needed on it" (Taylor et al., 1987, p. 91).

In Jay, Noble, and Hobbs (1992), Noble writes:

> We cannot tell whether Beatrix's drawings were ever seen by the members and there is now no trace of the paper in the Linnean. She may even have destroyed it herself, although her journal entry about her Uncle Harry "going over and over it with a pencil" includes the statement, "I shall keep those pencil marks when I am an old woman."

Noble continues:

> The dismissal of her paper by the Linnean Society must have been a considerable disappointment to [Beatrix Potter] in spite of Massee's attempt to soften the blow. But we know her interest in mycology was not quite suppressed, and she continued to study and paint fungi for several years after the publication of *The Tale of Peter Rabbit* had changed her life [Jay et al., 1992, p. 123].

The fact that she was not allowed to attend the meeting and that her paper was not read by her, if it was read at all, must have been terribly disappointing for Beatrix Potter and made her bitterly angry.

While the rejection of her paper, and by implication her work, was a blow to her self-esteem, the triumph that she achieved in the world of children's literature was surely a fortuitous consequence of the spurning of her botanical research. Beatrix Potter's interest in nature did not cease after her paper was rejected. During this period she was also studying fossils and various archaeological artifacts. She collected these assiduously, photographing and drawing what she had found (see Jay et al., 1992, pp. 49–54). Her interest in natural history did not accelerate to the kind of overwhelming dedication that she was capable of achieving, however. Her creativity seemed to propel her in another direction, one that had already proved to be successful, that is, toward creating works that were a combination of art and literature.

## Chapter 4

# The Tale of Peter Rabbit
# (1902) [1893]

*The Tale of Peter Rabbit* is the best known of all of the books written and illustrated by Beatrix Potter. Published by Frederick Warne in 1902, it was an immediate success and served as an incentive for her subsequent books for children. No biographical account of her life omits the sequence of events that led to the publication of this little story.

On September 4, 1893, writing from Eastwood, a dower house near Dunkeld Scotland, Beatrix Potter sent 6-year-old Noel Moore who was suffering from poliomyelitis, son of her former governess, Anne Carter Moore, a picture letter in which she recounted the story of Peter Rabbit. (This letter has been reproduced in many books on Beatrix Potter; see Lane [1946], Linder [1971], Potter [1992].) Seven years later she decided to make a little book out of the story and asked Noel if she could borrow the letter she had written to him. She then rewrote the story, adding some further details and pictures. During the year 1900 she sent it to at least six different publishers, including Frederick Warne, all of whom rejected it. The following year, she decided to have the story published privately and had 250 copies printed by Strangeway and Sons of Tower Street, Cambridge Circus, London (Linder, 1971, p. 94).

In the meantime Canon Hardwicke Rawnsley, a friend of the family, became interested in her idea of making her little story into a book. He contacted the firm of Frederick Warne in September of 1901, offering them *his own* version of her story, written in verse and illustrated with Beatrix Potter's drawings. The publishers turned his book down on September 18, 1901. (It was finally published in 1989 by the Beatrix Potter Society, with an introduction by Irene Whalley, under the title of *Peter Rabbit's Other Tale*.)

On December 16th of that year, Beatrix Potter's first privately printed edition of 250 copies was completed. She gave some of them to her friends and relatives and sold some copies for a small sum (Linder, 1971, p. 96). The book was instantly successful and within a week or two, she decided to have a second impression of 200 copies printed with a few minor changes. This second printing was dated February 1902.

Before the first private edition was completed, however, Frederick Warne reconsidered their initial decision, and as Beatrix Potter was willing to shorten her book, delete a number of illustrations, and provide the others in color, they accepted it for publication. The details of all the arrangements may be found in Linder (1971).

Of particular importance in connection with her early negotiations with Frederick Warne were her very revealing comments about her father. As a postscript to her letter of December 18, 1901, she wrote: "I have not spoken to Mr. Potter, but I think Sir, it would be well to explain the agreement clearly, because he is a little formal having been a barrister" (*Letters*, p. 57).

Several months later (May 22, 1902), she added the following postscript to her letter to the publishers:

> If my father happens to insist on going with me to see the agreement, would you please not mind him very much, if he is very fidgetty [sic] about things. I am afraid it is not a very respectful way of talking & I don't wish to refer to it again, but I think it is better to mention beforehand he is sometimes a little

difficult; I can of course do what I like about the book being 36.

I suppose it is a habit of old gentlemen; but sometimes rather trying [*Letters*, p. 62].

While the general story of *The Tale of Peter Rabbit* is well known, I shall summarize the details of the final version so that we may appreciate the story's underlying significance and pertinence to Beatrix Potter's own dynamics.

Mrs. Rabbit tells her four little rabbits, Flopsy, Mopsy, Cotton-tail, and Peter, that they can go out to pick blackberries but warns them not to go into Mr. McGregor's garden because, she says, their father had an "accident there; he was put in a pie by Mrs. McGregor."

While the other three little rabbits went to gather blackberries, Peter, whom Beatrix Potter describes as being very "naughty," promptly ran to Mr. McGregor's garden. After eating various vegetables, Peter Rabbit became ill and looked for some parsley to make him feel better. Beatrix Potter's illustration shows him holding his paws in the region of his abdomen, thus graphically indicating that he was suffering from indigestion.

Suddenly Peter was confronted by Mr. McGregor who "was on his hands and knees . . . but he jumped up and ran after Peter, waving a rake." Terrified, Peter ran away but lost his shoes, and then got tangled up in a gooseberry net. Mr. McGregor almost trapped him with a sieve but, encouraged by the exhortation of some sparrows, Peter was able to escape. Leaving his jacket behind, he ran into the toolshed where he hid in a watering can. He was almost caught when he revealed his whereabouts by sneezing. This time Mr. McGregor tried to stamp on him but Peter managed to run away in sheer panic. He wandered about trying to find the gate and finally asked a mouse the way, but "she had such a large pea in her mouth that she could not answer." He saw a cat but wisely avoided her and hid under some bushes. After some time, Peter saw that Mr. McGregor's back was turned to him so he was able to find the gate, slip under it, and run home.

Mr. McGregor hung Peter's jacket and shoes on a scarecrow. When Peter got home, he was not well so his mother put him to bed and gave him a table-spoonful of camomile tea while his siblings had bread, milk, and blackberries for supper.

The published version of *Peter Rabbit* is somewhat changed from the original letter to Noel Moore. In that letter, for example, Beatrix Potter said nothing about Peter's father having had "an accident" in Mr. McGregor's garden and that he had been "put in a pie by Mrs. McGregor." Nor is there anything in the letter about Peter hiding in the watering can or almost being crushed by Mr. McGregor's boot.

In the privately printed edition, and in the first few Warne editions, Beatrix Potter had included a picture showing Mrs. McGregor holding a pie, ready to place it on the table in front of her husband. Near the pie is a dog with his forefeet on the table. Only Mr. McGregor's hands holding a knife and a fork are portrayed. The picture of Mrs. McGregor is of a very stern, determined, angry woman. Linder writes that in response to a query sent to her in 1939 Beatrix Potter wrote that this picture was of "Mrs. M (or myself) holding a pie." He describes the appearance of Mrs. McGregor as being that of "a rugged old country woman" (p. 109). In a letter to her Norman Warne wrote: "We still do not like the old woman's face. Will you please have another try at this" (Potter, 1985, p. 98, catalogue number 907). Beatrix Potter substituted another which Linder (1971) writes is "possibly" a caricature of herself, though "not a very flattering one!" (p. 109). Ultimately, after the fourth printing, the illustration showing Mrs. McGregor and the pie was removed altogether.

By writing that the picture was of "Mrs. M (or myself)" Beatrix Potter clearly equates herself with the farmer's wife. At this time in her life, having spent many summers in Scotland

and in the Lake District, she was familiar with the life-style and practices of farmers.

In the context of the story Mrs. McGregor is a dangerous, aggressive woman. In the world of reality she does what any farmer's wife would do. Rabbits were plentiful and were frequently used for food.

Knowing that the story of Peter Rabbit was originally written for a particular child, and later for other children, Beatrix Potter tailored it to allow herself to consider the interests of both the animals and the humans. In this story she was able to empathize with the animals' needs and to invest them with human attributes.

Her ability to transcend the elementary idea that the story was *only* about Peter Rabbit may be seen in that incredible illustration in which he is in bed with only his ears and his front paws showing from under the covers, while his mother is spooning out the dose of camomile tea. Peter's identity is obvious from the context of the story. But the fact that in *this* picture neither his face nor any other part of his body is depicted,[1] allows the reader, especially a child, to put himself (or herself) into that very same situation.

In 1905, Beatrix Potter wrote that "the secret of the success of Peter Rabbit [was] that it was written to a child—not made to order" (Linder, 1971, p. 110). Years later (1940), in a letter to Bertha Mahony Miller, she wrote: "I have been asked to tell again how *Peter Rabbit* came to be written. It seems a long time ago and in another world though after all the world has changed." She went on to say that she: "never quite understood the secret of Peter's perennial charm. Perhaps it is because he and his little friends keep on their way, busily absorbed with their own doings. They were always independent" (*Letters*, p. 422).

Actually, *The Tale of Peter Rabbit* and other Beatrix Potter stories were not just written *for* a child or *for* children but were

---

[1]The only exception was in *Peter Rabbit's Other Tale* with illustrations by Beatrix Potter and verses by her friend, Canon Hardwicke Rawnsley.

also written *about* children and their conflicts. Moreover, as we will see, many of her stories were based on real incidents that she herself observed or participated in, either directly or empathically. Some were based upon or were a direct expression of her own dynamics.

I think that we can go beyond Beatrix Potter's explanation of the secret of the story's "perennial charm." After all, there are many charming stories of people and of animals that lack the appeal we find in *Peter Rabbit*. There is no doubt that Beatrix Potter's skillful amalgamation of precise, descriptive language with her incredibly detailed and beautiful illustrations was a formula that appealed instantly to the reader, both young and old.

But in addition, the problems with which the little story deals in such a highly condensed manner resonate with basic universal problems and conflicts that exist in every individual. This deceptively simple story succeeds in evoking an empathic response to the disobedient rabbit who is almost killed for wanting to gratify his needs, and whose mother finally nurses him to health with great care and kindness, despite his flagrant misbehavior.

When we look at *The Tale of Peter Rabbit* in some depth, we are immediately confronted with a number of other considerations. The original story was, as noted above, written in a letter to 6-year-old Noel Moore. At the very outset Beatrix Potter stated that she did not know what to write to him and therefore would tell him the story of Peter Rabbit. That in itself was an important message: why of all possible stories that she could have told this little boy did she take the trouble to write him *this* particular story of her own invention, clearly a product of her own internal dynamics, one presented in such a fashion as to evoke a virtually universal empathic response?

We may suppose that Noel Moore's poliomyelitis, with its associated leg pains and difficulty in walking, triggered painful memories in Beatrix Potter herself. In her *Journal* in 1887, about two years before her letter to Noel Moore, she recorded that she had been ill with rheumatic fever, had pain and difficulty in walking, and had also been bedridden for a time (chapter 2, pp. 31–32). Thus, through the story of Peter Rabbit she was able to recreate her own anxiety when she had been seriously ill and probably felt that *her* life was threatened.

Beatrix Potter's letter to Noel managed to express a basic fact: that children, and even adults, often feel that their illness is a punishment. Perhaps she felt that this also applied to herself at one time. When a child disobeys a parent, especially a mother or nurse, it is felt that this is punishable by some external force or fate bringing about an illness in the miscreant. Adults confronted by a serious happening, a tragedy, trauma, or illness, will often express their reaction in such words as: "God, what did I do to deserve this."

In her story Beatrix Potter sets forth a list of consequences for Peter's defiance of his mother's rules, all of which contain various allusions to their unconscious significance. The warning which Mrs. Rabbit gives her children is clearly in their best interest: if they go into Mr. McGregor's garden, they will be killed, put in a pie by Mrs. McGregor, and then eaten, just as their father had been. Mrs. Rabbit's wish certainly is to protect them against such a fate by instilling in them an anxiety that if they put themselves into a dangerous situation, they will suffer mortal consequences. Whereas the other rabbit children obey their mother's injunctions, Peter, being "naughty," promptly disobeyed her, and for this he was in danger of suffering capital punishment.

Beatrix Potter attributes Peter Rabbit's behavior of running immediately to Mr. McGregor's garden as being due to his "naughtiness" (i.e., it was because of a basic characterological problem that he deliberately disobeyed his mother). This was a prevalent view about children in the 1890s, and is a view which is still held by many people today. Children who are naughty must have this character trait obliterated from their makeup. They must be punished for their own good—"Spare the rod and spoil the child."

We are given no evidence, however, of Peter's basic naughtiness other than the information that it was the second jacket and pair of shoes that he had lost in two weeks. The sequence of events as Beatrix Potter presents them suggests a further interpretation. Peter's "naughtiness" was an immediate response of a counterphobic nature *after* his mother's injunction. We may suggest that Peter rushed into the very dangerous situation *not* because he was basically defiant and naughty, but rather to master the anxiety that his mother had aroused in him by telling him that he might suffer the same fate as his father if he went into Mr. McGregor's garden. This counterphobic mechanism is very common and may be frequently observed both in children and adults who precipitously rush to do just what they most fear as dangerous in order to prove to themselves, and to those about them, not only that they are not afraid, but also to convince themselves that what they are afraid of, will really not happen. Often, as in Peter's case, the results may be disastrous.

The horror of being killed and devoured is a basic primitive fear. Imagery referable to oral aggression in the story is further elaborated by Mr. McGregor going after Peter with his rake, an implement whose working end contains tines or teeth. Beatrix Potter's picture of Mr. McGregor's hobnailed boot about to descend on the frightened rabbit is another example of the possible fate that he would meet: that he would be crushed.

Further, in his panicky flight through the garden Peter comes across a white cat and is frightened by her because he had heard about cats from his cousin, Benjamin Bunny. The clear implication is that the cat would kill and eat him. Even the scarecrow upon which Mr. McGregor placed Peter's jacket and shoes to frighten the birds is a mute expression of what would happen to anyone who dared to trespass in Mr. McGregor's garden and eat the forbidden vegetables. Nothing would be left of that individual but the clothes he came in, certainly a most frightening thought.

There was still another basis for Peter Rabbit's anxiety. The first and second editions of the story included the account that when Peter ran to hide in the toolshed again, he heard Mr. McGregor making a noise with the rake and someone began to sing, "Three blind mice. Three blind mice." In the first edition Beatrix Potter wrote that "it sounded disagreeable to Peter; it made him feel as though his own tail were going to be cut off: his fur stood on end" (Linder, 1971, p. 96). In the second edition the words "it made him feel as though his own tail were going to be cut off" were omitted. The entire episode was deleted from subsequent editions.

After verbalizing the various possibilities of what can happen to a "naughty" child, one who has bad thoughts or who disobeys his parents, Beatrix Potter reassures Noel in her letter, and the reader in the published story, that Peter does indeed escape from the horrors to which he had deliberately exposed himself. He is able to run home safely where he is taken care of by his mother, who puts him to bed and gives him the tablespoonful of camomile tea to make him feel better.

The final message of her letter to Noel, and to the children who read her little book, by implication is: Even if you have been "naughty" and disobedient, in thought or in deed, and have gotten into trouble or gotten sick because of your greediness (and what 6-year-old child, or even grown-up for that matter, had not) your mother will take care of you and you will be safe and well. This is the ultimate appeal of *The Tale of Peter Rabbit*.

## Chapter 5

# The Tailor of Gloucester
# (1903a) [1901]

Beatrix Potter completed the story of *The Tailor of Gloucester* in December 1901 and gave a handwritten copy with a dedication to Freda Moore,[1] Noel's sister, as a Christmas present. Beatrix Potter then had the book privately printed and this edition was published in December 1902. Frederick Warne published the story in August of the following year. Some years later, in 1910, Beatrix Potter wrote that of all her little books, *The Tailor of Gloucester* was her favorite, and that she liked the privately printed edition better than the ones published by Frederick Warne because it contained more of the "old" rhymes (Linder, 1971, p. 121).

The tailor of Gloucester, a poor, sickly old man with crooked fingers, was making a coat for the mayor just before Christmas. It had turned dark, and snow was falling, so he locked up his shop, leaving the pieces of the coat and the waistcoat out on a table, ready to be sewn together in the morning. Although there was sufficient material for everything, he was short one "single skein of cherry-colored twisted silk."

---

[1] Winifrede Cecily (Freda) Moore was born on January 8, 1891.

He went home where he lived alone with Simpkin, his cat. He gave Simpkin a groat (4 pence) to buy a pennyworth each of bread, milk, sausages, and with the last penny, a pennyworth of cherry-colored silk. The thread, or twist, was most important for he needed it to complete the coat which the mayor was to wear for his wedding at noon on Christmas Day. Simpkin left on his errand. When he returned with the required items, he hid the twist in a teapot, and spit and growled at the tailor because there were no mice for him to eat.

The following day the tailor became severely ill with a fever, mumbling in his delirium, "No more twist." Several days later, on Christmas Eve, the cat left the tailor's house and wandered about the town looking for food.

Beatrix Potter relates that between Christmas Eve and the morning of Christmas Day all the animals can talk and sing, although "very few folks can hear them or know what they say" (Linder, 1971, p. 127). In her story, the animals sang and recited nursery rhymes. The privately printed edition included some twenty songs and rhymes, quoted in their entirety or in part. These have been published by Linder (1971, pp. 124–134). In the edition published by Frederick Warne, however, only six of the rhymes and songs remain while merely the first lines are given of several others.

As Simpkin passed the tailor's shop and peeked into the window, he heard a snipping of scissors and snapping of thread and watched the mice who were singing various songs happily and loudly, punctuated by a chorus of: "No more twist. No more twist." The cat wanted to enter the shop but the mice refused to allow this because they feared he would kill and eat them.

In the privately printed edition Beatrix Potter had drawn a picture in which some rats were having a party. One of the rats is shown drinking ink out of a black bottle. Apparently, the publisher insisted that this picture be deleted because it could be embarrassing to teetotalers and would, therefore, interfere with the sale of the book.

Finally Simpkin returned home where he found that the tailor was no longer feverish and was sleeping peacefully. Ashamed that he had been bad, compared with the good little mice, he put the skein of cherry-colored twisted silk by the tailor's bedside and gave him some tea after he awakened. When the tailor returned to his shop he found that it had been completely cleaned up and that the waistcoat had been finished except for one cherry-colored buttonhole near which was pinned a scrap of paper with the words, "No more twist."

From that time on the tailor's luck improved. He became quite rich and successful. The buttonholes of his clothing especially impressed everyone because the stitches were so small that they looked as if they might have been made by mice.

According to Linder (1971), Beatrix Potter's story was based on a real incident. During one of her visits to Caroline Hutton, a distant cousin, at her home, Harescombe Grange, near Stroud, in Gloucestershire, Beatrix Potter heard the story of the tailor of Gloucester who had cut out a waistcoat one Saturday but had left his shop without sewing it together. Upon his return on Monday, he discovered that the waistcoat had been completed except for one buttonhole. Appended to the garment was a note stating that there was "no more twist" (Linder, 1971, p. 111).

Linder relates the real basis for the story which was told many years later by Mrs. Prichard, the tailor's wife. It was the duty of every new mayor of Gloucester to walk in a procession from the Guildhall of the Root, Fruit and Grain Society to its show at Shire Hall. Mr. Prichard had started the waistcoat for the mayor but it had not been completed due to the pressure of other orders. Although it had been cut out, it had not been sewn together when he left his shop that particular Saturday. His two assistants, anxious to please their employer, returned to the shop secretly and completed the work except for one buttonhole, because they had run out of thread. They pinned a note on the waistcoat indicating that there was "no more twist." The assistants never told their master what they had done. Later Mr. Prichard put the waistcoat in his window with a sign reading: "Come to Prichard where the waistcoats are made at night by the fairies" (Linder, 1971, p. 112).

That Beatrix Potter should have found the true story about the tailor so intriguing is not surprising because all her life she had been fascinated by the thought of fairies. Yet, there may have been another determinant for Beatrix Potter's story in addition to the appeal of the real incident. We know that she was thoroughly familiar with and enjoyed fairy tales (see chapter 1, pp. 12–13). Her story of *The Tailor of Gloucester* has a remarkable similarity to the story of *The Elves* (sometimes referred to as *The Elves and the ᵎmaker*) told in *Grimms' Fairy Tales* (pp. 197–198).

In the Grimms' version, a poor shoemaker had only enough leather for one pair of shoes which he had cut out but did not sew together before he went to bed one night. The next morning the shoes had been neatly completed and very well stitched. They were sold immediately for a good price with which the shoemaker immediately purchased leather for two pairs of shoes. He cut these out but again did not sew them together. The next morning, these shoes were also completed. The procedure was repeated nightly with an increasing number of shoes, all of which he set out in the evening and all of which were completed by morning. The shoes were readily sold so that the shoemaker became wealthy.

Shortly before Christmas the shoemaker and his wife decided to see who had been helping them to make the shoes. They concealed themselves and by candlelight observed two little naked men (elves) appear after midnight and quickly complete the work that had been cut out for them. So grateful were the couple that the shoemaker's wife decided to make clothes for the little elves and the shoemaker himself made them shoes. These they then laid out for the elves instead of the leather cut out for regular shoes. When the elves appeared that night, they were delighted. They dressed in the clothes, sang, and then danced away. They never returned but the shoemaker continued to prosper.

We may immediately see a number of parallels between Beatrix Potter's story of the tailor of Gloucester and the story of the shoemaker and the elves. Both men are poor and conscientious. Both leave wearing apparel unfinished, and in both instances it is completed after the shop is closed. In the Beatrix Potter story the work is accomplished by mice (who replace fairies). In the shoemaker story the work is done by elves. In Beatrix Potter's story Simpkin looks in (spies) on the working mice. In the shoemaker story the couple spy on the naked elves. In both instances the story is set around Christmas time. And, finally, in both instances the tailor and the shoemaker prosper.

There are, to be sure, major differences between the real events about Mr. Prichard, Beatrix Potter's story, and the fairy tale. Mr. Prichard and the shoemaker are married men who presumably are in good health and do not appear to be old. In Beatrix Potter's version, on the other hand, the tailor is very poor, old, and sickly, with old crooked fingers, and his sole companion is Simpkin, a male cat.

Beatrix Potter's description of the tailor being ill with a fever and delirious is particularly interesting because, as far as the story is concerned, there is no objective necessity for this detail to have been included. While she may have felt it was necessary from an artistic or a literary standpoint, there may have been another reason. There seems to be a clue to Beatrix Potter's motive in her dedication of the book to Freda Moore. In it she wrote: "Because you are fond of fairy tales and have been ill, I have made you a story all for yourself" (Linder, 1971, p. 113).

Thus, once again, as she had done for Freda's brother, Noel, with the story of Peter Rabbit, Beatrix Potter wrote a story for a child who was or had been ill and to whom she wanted to offer the reassurance that she would get better. In her own inimitably skillful way Beatrix Potter was able to depersonalize the message by having an old man as the ill person rather than a child or even an animal.

We have seen, in our discussion of *Peter Rabbit*, that Beatrix Potter's empathy for a sick child was enhanced by her own personal experience with rheumatic fever and its complications. Beatrix Potter too may have suffered from bouts of fever and delirium. We may then suppose that the decrepit state of the poor old tailor was actually an expression of a view she had had of herself. Even her description of him having crooked fingers could well refer to her own struggles with rheumatic joint pains which, fortunately, did not continue or interfere with her drawing, any more than having "crooked old fingers" did with the tailor's fine sewing.

Any prolonged and debilitating illness has psychological consequences. The weakness and lassitude are demoralizing (Lane, 1946, p. 53) and are often associated with depression, which at times may be quite profound and lengthy in duration.

In her version of the tailor story, Beatrix Potter was able to express her optimism that like the tailor, she too had begun to come out of the despondency and depression that followed her illness and could look forward to a more successful and productive life.

The initial reaction to *The Tailor of Gloucester* is one of sheer pleasure. We are immediately drawn to its fairy tale quality and are delighted that, like most fairy tales, all ends well. There is more to the story, however, an understanding of which heightens our appreciation for the wealth of material that it contains.

Beatrix Potter makes use of the familiar dramatic literary device in which the playwright or author distributes the characteristics or aspects of the hero's personality or his problems among several figures. While the hero of this story is the tailor, Simpkin serves as a "foil character" for him, expressing another aspect of his personality and his conflicts. The aged tailor is poor, depressed, and lonely. He has pinned his hopes on the success and good fortune that the completion of the waistcoat for the mayor will bring him. But now he is frustrated at not being able to finish his task because there is "no more twist"; and besides this, he is ill. From his request to the cat to purchase such meager amounts of food, we may assume that his diet has also been greatly impoverished, and his failure to complete the waistcoat would greatly add to his miseries. These miseries and his frustrations are expressed in his delirium when he reiterates the words "no more twist" as though all his problems are now concentrated on this solitary fact, and by implication, if only that were resolved, all would be well.

Simpkin, as the tailor's foil or alter ego, is also hungry and frustrated. He blames the tailor for depriving him of food. While the tailor lies ill and delirious, Simpkin wanders about the town unsuccessfully looking for food. Added to his hunger are his depression and loneliness. All the animals are joyously singing but he is totally left out of the fun and conviviality. He, like the tailor, has no one with whom to share his life. The joyful animals may also be considered as foil characters for the tailor as they express what the tailor would wish for most; namely, to complete the mayor's waistcoat that would bring about the tailor's material success. As we have seen, the waistcoat is completed by the mice, and the tailor's fortune is achieved. And yet in the end, the element of frustration is still present because the mice do not have enough thread left to complete the final buttonhole. It is only after Simpkin purchases more thread that the tailor can complete the task.

In fantasies, dreams, and delirium we are often able to see a connection, in a general way, between the events of reality which may be of either a significant or indifferent affective nature, and material derived from earlier times in the individual's life.

A major part of the story deals with Simpkin's wandering about during which he witnesses the pleasures which the other animals are enjoying. Beatrix Potter weaves bits and pieces of popular nursery rhymes into her story at this point. These rhymes are of great interest in themselves but raise the question of why of all possible ones she included these in particular and excluded others. Some of these, such as "Hey Diddle Diddle the Cat and the Fiddle" or "The Three Little Mice Sat Down to Spin" that remain in the final version published by Frederick Warne rather clearly connect with the cat and the mice. Some others, such as "24 Tailors and the Snail," "The London Merchants," "Pipkin and Popkin," have pertinence to tailors. Still others are included because they deal with Christmas Day.

It seems, however, that many of the rhymes are included not so much for their content but for their rhythmical and repetitive qualities. Beatrix Potter emphasizes this by indicating, for example, that the mice "clicked their thimbles to mark the time." The rhythmical quality of many of the rhymes lends itself to the rhythmical work in which the mice were engaged. In addition, the rhythmical repetitive quality and dance rhythms of the nursery rhymes are particularly appealing to children. Among those present in the original version but not in the Warne version are such rhymes as "I Saw Three Ships Come Sailing By, Sailing By, Sailing By" or "Dame Get Up and Bake Your Pies, Bake Your Pies! Bake Your Pies!" Both of these also deal with Christmas Day.

The underlying purpose of such rhythmical poems and dance rhythms is to provide an opportunity for socialized musculoskeletal discharge so essential for the developing body ego. But in addition to this we would note Freud's (1900) observation in *The Interpretation of Dreams*. He writes: "It not uncommonly happens that these games of movement, though innocent in themselves, give rise to sexual feelings" (p. 272).

Keeping this in mind we may ask ourselves to what do these scenes to which Simpkin is exposed refer. We are immediately struck by Beatrix Potter's comment that while the animals and birds sang with words during the night, when daylight returned, they could only sing in their own language. She added that when animals do talk and sing between Christmas Eve and Christmas morning, "very few folks can hear them or know what they say." We may take this as an allusion to some early memories she has repressed: that adults did and said things which she as a child could not understand any more than human beings can understand what animals are saying or doing.

Such a statement would lead directly to our supposition that as a child Beatrix Potter herself could not understand what her parents were talking about, especially when it related to material that alluded to sexuality. This seems to follow from the repetitive, rhythmical quality of the rhythms which she uses as examples. It would appear then that Beatrix Potter had very little in the way of sexual enlightenment except for what she may have picked up here or there.

The incident of Simpkin peering through the window and watching the mice working, singing, and "clicking their thimbles to mark the time," seems to connect with the story of the shoemaker and the elves, as we mentioned earlier. In that story it is a husband and wife who spy upon the two little naked elves, a situation that parallels Simpkin's spying upon the activities of the mice.

The curiosity to which this alludes is an expression of the scopophilic instinct[2] which is a ubiquitous drive. The strength of that drive is based upon variations in constitutional forces. It is the instinctual force which motivates the child to look, to see, to learn, to study, to explore, to be inquisitive in all manner of things. Ultimately it leads to the expansion of the individual's interests along artistic, creative, or scientific lines. Beatrix Potter, through the highly complex pathways of sublimation, evidently had a powerful striving in that direction that led to her recording her observations in great detail, aided, as time went on, by her microscopic observations. Her beautiful and meticulous drawings of the composition of butterfly wings and the external anatomy of insects or spiders clearly bear this out.

In the course of the individual's development, the scopophilic instinct becomes intimately connected with the person's

---

[2]Scopophilic is defined as:
  An inherent drive to look and to derive pleasure from looking. The prefix is derived from the Greek root *scop*, "to look" (also in *telescope, microscope, otoscope*). *Scopophilia* is a translation of the German *Schaulust. Scoptophilia* is sometimes erroneously used instead of scopophilia. *Scopt* is the Greek root for jeering or ridiculing, and *scoptophilia* would refer to pleasure in derision, a meaning never intended [Moore and Fine, 1990, p. 172].

erotic life. The observation of the sexual activity of animals, for instance, or the observation of sexual activity of adults, plays a significant role in determining the vicissitudes of subsequent reactions in many different areas of the individual's adjustment.

Such observations by children are frequently accompanied by a misunderstanding of what is going on. The drama is interpreted as being some kind of fight which may result in severe bodily injury or death to the participants. In the case of the child's observation of adults, it may similarly appear to the child that the couple is involved in wrestling or fighting and also that one or other of the participants will be hurt or even killed. In these instances the child often wishes to interrupt the activity, to destroy one partner, or to become an active participant in the drama itself by identifying with a figure in the act. Children may be both excited and frightened by what they see.

In the story, Beatrix Potter expresses how angry Simpkin is, how he growls with frustration because of the songs and activities of the mice, and wants to enter the tailor shop. Obviously, he does not want to participate in the activity but to interrupt it and to eat the mice. The mice, of course, refuse to allow him to enter the shop.

The similarity between Simpkin observing the mice in their activity and the shoemaker and his wife observing the naked elves in theirs, is very striking. In both instances the mice or elves, representing children, are spied upon. More than likely the situation to which this refers is reversed: it is the children who spy upon the naked parents (or animals) in their nightly activities rather than the parent(s) spying upon the children in their nightly pleasures. There are major differences, however. Whereas the shoemaker and his wife take pleasure in merely observing the elves and the delight with which they receive their gifts, Simpkin wants to interrupt the activity of the mice to kill and eat them. In this instance the aggression of the observer against the joyful participants is clearly expressed.

As part of the final resolution of the story, Simpkin, ashamed of his angry wishes, becomes contrite and gives the tailor the twist and even brings him a cup of tea.

At the time the story was written Beatrix Potter was still unsure whether the publishers would accept her book. She wrote to them on December 19, 1902:

> Thank you for your letter about the mouse book. You have paid it the compliment of taking the plot very seriously; and I perceive that your criticisms are just; because I was quite sure in advance that you would cut out the tailor and all my favourite rhymes! Which was one of the reasons I printed it myself [Linder, 1971, p. 116].

It may also be that apart from their consideration of her book's literary or commercial merits she was concerned that the Warnes might be critical of her and her revelations. She had invested as much care and work in her production as the tailor did in his waistcoat.

It is very likely that Beatrix Potter chose *The Tailor of Gloucester* as the favorite of her stories not only because of her own appreciation of her artistic product but also because it permitted her to reveal in a disguised fashion so much about her own childhood experiences and reactions.

The story about the tailor is important in that it continues the optimistic note that she expressed in *The Tale of Peter Rabbit* and because it goes a step further. Not only would the rabbit find comforting solace and acceptance from his mother, but here there is a glimpse of the hopeful view of what would be in store for Freda Moore as well as for herself. Actually, for her the story was the expression of a wish-fulfillment fantasy—that the fairies, elves, mice (or the publishers) would bring her success and pleasure. Events had already indicated that as Frederick Warne looked favorably on the publication of *Peter Rabbit*, Beatrix Potter could begin to be optimistic about her own future. Subsequently, events proved that this optimism was well founded, for she, like the tailor or the shoemaker, became successful in her own right on the basis of her craft.

While their successful beginnings were achieved by the help of elves or mice, ultimately the humans themselves were able to make their fortunes on the basis of their innate ability to use their own creative talents.

## Chapter 6

# The Tale of Squirrel Nutkin

# (1903b)

On September 25, 1901, Beatrix Potter wrote a letter from Lingholm, Keswick to 8-year-old Norah,[1] a younger sister to Noel and Winifrede Moore. In it she described the squirrels in the woods around the rented house in Derwentwater where she was staying with her parents. She informed Norah that an old lady who lived on St. Herbert Island (later called Owl Island), told her that she believed that the squirrels came over to the island when the nuts were ripe. Speculating about how they got across the water, Beatrix Potter thought that perhaps they made little rafts. We learn that she expressed the basis for this notion in an earlier letter to Noel Moore dated August 26, 1897. In that letter she told him that there was "an American story that squirrels go down the river on little rafts using their tails for sails, but [she thought] the Keswick Squirrels must swim" (Linder, 1971, p. 29; p. 135).

In her letter to Norah, Beatrix Potter wrote that she saw a small squirrel with a tail "only an inch long" who was "impertinent," chattering away and throwing acorns on her head. She named him "Nutkin" and said that he had a brother called

---

[1]Norah Constance Moore (Bardie) was born on July 13, 1893.

67

"Twinkleberry." Then she proceeded to tell Norah how the squirrel lost his tail.

The next year, 1902, Beatrix Potter began working on a story that would become *The Tale of Squirrel Nutkin*, making a number of revisions in the text of the picture letter she had written to Norah. She changed the first sentence of the story to read: "This is a Tale about a tail—a tail that belonged to a little red squirrel." The book was published by Frederick Warne in 1903, the year after *The Tale of Peter Rabbit* appeared in print.

In a hollow oak tree in the middle of Owl Island there lived an owl called "Old Brown." One fall Nutkin, Twinkleberry, and the other squirrels came to the island to gather nuts which they put in little sacks.

Every day for a week the squirrels brought Old Brown gifts, requesting his permission to gather nuts on his island. The first day they brought him three fat mice; the second, a fat mole; the third, seven fat minnows; the fourth, six fat beetles; the fifth, wild honey. In her letter to Norah, Beatrix Potter wrote that on the sixth and last day the squirrels brought Old Brown a pie containing twenty-four blackbirds but changed this in the published version to a gift of a newlaid egg. While the other squirrels were polite and deferential in asking Old Brown's permission to gather nuts on his island, Nutkin was not and impertinently posed a riddle to him each day. Old Brown ignored Nutkin's provocative behavior until the last day when, according to Beatrix Potter's picture-letter, Nutkin made a "whirring" noise and flicked his tail "right in the face of Old Brown's whiskers" (Linder, 1971, p. 67). In the published version, she wrote that Nutkin "took a running jump right onto the head of Old Brown" (Potter, 1903a, p. 70). The owl attacked Nutkin and carried him into his house holding him by the tail, intending to skin him. Nutkin, however, pulled so hard that he broke off his tail and escaped.

We may see a number of parallels between the behavior of Squirrel Nutkin and that of Peter Rabbit. Both animals are described as naughty in contrast to their good siblings. Squirrel Nutkin is provocative while his brother, Twinkleberry, is good; Peter defies his mother's injunctions while his siblings (Flopsy, Mopsy, and Cotton-tail) are obedient. Both animals risk their lives, provoking a situation in which they may be killed and eaten by a powerful male figure. Squirrel Nutkin flicks his tail in the owl's face or, in the published version, "jumps right onto the head of Old Brown." Peter deliberately runs into Mr. McGregor's garden.

Comparing the two stories we see that there is an increase in the severity of the consequences for the animals' provocative behavior. Whereas Peter hears someone singing "Three Blind Mice" which he finds "disagreeable" as there is the possibility that he, like the mice, will have his tail cut off, Nutkin actually loses his tail in his effort to escape from the owl.

In both stories Beatrix Potter describes the principal characters as being fundamentally "naughty." We may suspect that the basis for the naughtiness of Nutkin, as in the case of Peter, was also counterphobic. It was a flagrant defense against Nutkin's anxiety that Old Brown, as a dangerous father figure, would do him some great bodily harm. Nutkin tried to deal with his fear of the owl by baiting him, while the other squirrels dealt with their fear of the owl by bringing him gifts in an effort to appease him.

The anthropomorphic attributes with which Beatrix Potter invests her animals are based on her perception, not only of the animals themselves but also of their similarities to human characteristics, and specifically to traits that were pertinent to her own personal life experiences. Her introduction of Twinkleberry as Squirrel Nutkin's brother is a significant example of this. By bringing him into the story as the good squirrel, Beatrix Potter is able to contrast him with Nutkin, the misbehaving brother. The implied constellation of two siblings, one good, one bad, is highly suggestive of Beatrix Potter's own family: while she was the good child, Bertram was the naughty one. The characterization of Old Brown himself can then be seen as an impressive caricature of their father, Rupert Potter: stern, sullen, and dangerously aggressive, calculated to instill a good deal of anxiety in his children.

That Beatrix Potter as the good sibling probably played (or wanted to play) the role of peacemaker between Bertram and their father, may be seen in a series of miniature letters to children that she wrote between 1907 and 1912, after the publication of this story. These were imaginary letters from characters in her stories, including some from Nutkin and some from Twinkleberry on behalf of his brother.

In these letters Nutkin requests that Mr. Brown return his tail as he missed it. He promises to pay the postage and give him three bags of nuts if the owl would send it back to him. In another letter, Squirrel Nutkin again respectfully asks the "Right Honorable Old Brown Esquire" to return his tail as he is uncomfortable without it, informing him that he heard of a tailor who could sew it back on again. Twinkleberry, writing to Mr. Brown on behalf of his brother, asks him to return Nutkin's tail and apologizes for his brother's rudeness. The pleadings have no effect. An unsigned letter to Squirrel Nutkin informs him that Mr. Brown is unable to return the tail as he ate it some time before and that it nearly choked him.

Of special interest in this connection is that in 1924, in a letter to children who had contributed "pennies" for the Invalid Children's Aid Association (see chapter 34, p. 312), Beatrix Potter wrote that after Nutkin had pleaded with Mr. Brown to "please post [him] back his tail because the cold weather has come," Mr. Brown had written him: "Master Nutkin, you do not deserve it; but as a reward for respect, I enclose tail herewith. OB" (*Children*, p. 207). It took almost twenty years for Beatrix Potter to undo Nutkin's loss of his tail and for her to be able to view Old Brown in a more benevolent way! (Beatrix Potter was then 58 and her father had died eight years earlier.)

The series of riddles which Squirrel Nutkin poses to Old Brown skillfully reflects the curiosity of a small child who does not understand many of the riddles of life and pleads with his parents for enlightenment. One of the main riddles with which children struggle at an early age has to do with the question: where do babies come from? We may be reasonably sure that when her mother was pregnant and Bertram was born, Beatrix Potter, then approximately 6 years old, was eager for information and elucidation. What she was told and by whom, we do not know.

We do know that in this story Old Brown does not provide the inquisitive Nutkin with any answers to his riddles (the riddle of life) nor give him any information, but remains aloof and seemingly indifferent if not wholly contemptuous, content only to satisfy his own needs.

The very first riddle that Nutkin tells Old Brown in the published version is about a "little wee man in a redcoat, a staff in his hand and a stone in his throat"; the solution is a cherry. This first riddle was substituted for another riddle that Beatrix Potter had written in her letter to Norah. In that riddle, quoted here in part, she wrote: "Here we lie, pick'd and pluck'd, and put in a pie." According to the Opies (1951), the solution to *that* riddle is "cur(r)-ants" (p. 207).

We may have additional confirmation of this hypothesis from the fact that in the final version the squirrels bring Old Brown a newly laid egg in a little brush basket on the sixth and last day. In the original version, but omitted from the final version, Beatrix Potter had the squirrels bring Old Brown a pie containing twenty-four blackbirds. The egg in the little brush basket and the pie (from which the birds begin to sing when the pie was opened) both serve as hatching places and are common symbols for gestation. (Opie and Opie [1951, pp. 394–395], provide other interpretations of the latter poem.)

Despite their "innocent" solution, the two riddles taken together seem to have a double-entendre significance implying that they refer to fertilization and gestation.

Meanwhile, on the final day, Nutkin, who has been rude and impertinent to Old Brown and has not asked permission to gather nuts, further provokes him by asking him another riddle. It has to do with Humpty Dumpty.

Humpty Dumpty lies in the beck [stream],
With a white counterpane around his neck,
Forty doctors and forty wrights,
Cannot put Humpty Dumpty to rights!
[Potter, 1903b, p. 63].

The Opies (1951) write that in a different version (1846) "Humpty Dumpty lay in a beck with all his sinews around his neck" (p. 215).

The significance of Humpty Dumpty was described in a paper by Petty (1953). On the basis of clinical material he was able to point out that Humpty Dumpty's fall could be understood as the child's irreparable fall from the lofty position of being the only child, and thus the favorite one, following the birth of a younger sibling. After such a cataclysmic event the former only child is no longer sitting on the high wall in sublime narcissism, and feels that such a position will never exist again. "All the king's horses and all the King's men" can never recapture that supremely lofty feeling again.

Beatrix Potter's story is a masterpiece of autobiographical revelation. In writing the story to Norah Moore, whose next younger sister (Joan Elsie Moore born August 31, 1896) was born when she was 3, she emphatically expressed her own feelings about her mother's pregnancy and her subsequent reactions to Bertram's birth. Her confusion about the "facts of life" and her need for enlightenment are graphically portrayed by Nutkin, the constantly inquisitive and irritatingly impertinent poser of riddles.

In addition to her confusion and resentment at being displaced from her position as an only child when Bertram was born, she was also angry that he was a boy. If we consider

Nutkin's fate at the end of the story, we may suspect that she entertained aggressive feelings toward her brother at the time of his birth.

Of special interest in this connection, and related to her initial statement about how the story was a "Tale about a tail," is her essay published in the May 1929 issue of *The Horn Book*. In this work Beatrix Potter recounts some of her early memories that were associated with her beloved grandmother Jessie Potter who lived at Camfield Place. She writes:

> I only cared for two toys; a dilapidated black wooden doll called Topsy,[2] and a grimy, hard-stuffed, once-white, flannelette pig (which gradually parted with a tail made of tape). The pig did not belong to me. Grandmamma [Jessy Crompton] kept it in the bottom drawer of her *secrétaire*. The drawer had to be solemnly unlocked, and I nursed the precious animal, I being seated on a cross bar underneath the library table . . . and Grandmamma also had very hard gingersnap biscuits in a canister. I remember one of my teeth (milk teeth) came out in consequence (on purpose?) while I was under the table [*Americans*, p. 208].

In all likelihood this flood of reminiscences is associated with Beatrix Potter's mother's pregnancy and her reactions to Bertram's birth. The flannelette pig being kept in a bottom drawer that was locked and then unlocked would seem to connect with the idea of pregnancy. The juxtaposition of Beatrix Potter's recollection of losing one of her teeth and the flannelette pig parting with its tail (i.e., like Nutkin) suggest her reaction to the anatomical differences between herself and her brother who was born when she was about 6 years old, just about the age when children lose their deciduous teeth. Looking again at her miniature letters to children written by Nutkin, we may see that she expresses in them her own childhood plea that her "tail" would be restored, and her regrets for her faults, implying the childhood fantasy that she lost it because she was naughty.

---

[2] We may wonder if it was named after the "Topsy" in *Uncle Tom's Cabin*.

## Chapter 7

# The Tale of Tuppenny

## (1929) [1903]

In 1903, the same year that *The Tale of Squirrel Nutkin* was published, Beatrix Potter wrote *The Tale of Tuppenny*. Twenty-six years later, the story was revised and published for the first time in *The Horn Book* (February 1929), and was used as the first chapter of *The Fairy Caravan*, then called *Over the Hills and Far Away*.

In the original version of *The Tale of Tuppenny*, the scene is laid in the town of Marmalade in the land of Green Ginger, inhabited exclusively by two types of guinea pigs. There were the short-haired ones and the Abyssinian Cavies who were long haired. The barber in the town invented a new hair wash which he called "The quintessence of Abyssinian Artichokes." He advertised that it would make asparagus grow on a door knob. In the town there lived a guinea pig named Tuppenny most of whose hair had been pulled out or lost for some reason. Feeling sorry for him, his friends paid the barber who invented the hair wash eight peppercorns to give Tuppenny three applications with a garden syringe, one each day for three days.

After the third day, Tuppenny's hair began to grow rapidly all over his body. As his hair grew out of control, the little guinea pig boys called him "Old Whiskers." Although he had it cut daily, its growth could not be prevented. Finally, the barber deserted his shop and ran away. Tuppenny sold himself to a traveling showman who exhibited him as "Tuppenny the hairy guinea pig."

The published version in *The Fairy Caravan* follows the same basic plot except that here Messieurs Ratten and Scratch appear with advertisements for a special hair tonic. The price of a small bottle was now ten peppercorns. Mr. Scratch asserted that the nostrum was made of the purest Arabian moonshine and indicated that a certain nobleman, who had eight wives, had been persuaded to buy a large bottle by the first of his wives. He grew a magnificent beard but it was blue.

The short-haired guinea pigs purchased a bottle for Tuppenny. Some hours later Mrs. Tuppenny said that her husband had a fever and was growing a tail. That night Messieurs Ratten and Scratch left town. The next day the guinea pigs saw that hair was growing all over Tuppenny's face and continued to grow as they talked with him. Nobody knew how to stop it from growing. Although Mrs. Tuppenny cut it repeatedly, stuffed pillows and bolsters with it, it continued to grow. When she grew tired of cutting his hair, she started pulling it out. Unable to tolerate the pain, Tuppenny ran away from the town.

Written at the same time, this little story may be viewed as a sequel to *The Tale of Squirrel Nutkin*, in which Nutkin lost his tail. Here Beatrix Potter provides Tuppenny with a nostrum that not only regrows the hair he had lost or that had been pulled out, but also, as she added in the revised version, had him growing a tail. The ability of this hair tonic to restitute the lost hair or tail serves to undo the damage and deficiency with which Tuppenny was afflicted.

It will be noted that in the Nutkin story Old Brown is holding the squirrel by the tail when in a desperate effort to escape, Nutkin pulls away and breaks the tail in two. In the published version of the story of Tuppenny, it is his wife who, by pulling out his hair, symbolically castrates him, and causes him such pain that he runs out of town. Thus, whereas in the Nutkin story it is Old Brown, a powerful male, a father figure, who is responsible for Nutkin's fate, at the end of the Tuppenny story it is a woman, specifically his wife, who is responsible.

There appear to be some very personal reasons behind Beatrix Potter's story of Tuppenny. It will be recalled that she lost her own hair in 1885, an exceedingly traumatic experience for her. We may understand that her story of Tuppenny was the expression of a fantasied restitution of her own hair loss.

The whole subject of loss of a body part through injury or by a deliberate deed comes up many times in Beatrix Potter's *Journal*. She writes, for example, of a dog who had one of his legs crushed by a train (January 15, 1882, pp. 8–9); of another dog who was run over by a carriage (August 19, 1882, p. 22); of lambs' tails being cut off to prevent them from being infested with flea eggs if they got sore from catching on briars (April 2, 1883, p. 37); of a man (Harry Leech) having to have his left hand amputated when his gun exploded and shattered it (December 13, 1884, p. 122); of a servant scrubbing the face of the Gainsborough painting of *Jack Hill in a Wood* with a broom so that the end of his nose was chipped off (January 23, 1885, p. 127); of Charlie MacIntosh, the postman and violinist who had made a study of mosses and fungi and had helped Beatrix Potter with his knowledge of them, having had his left fingers cut off by a circular saw (October 29, 1892, p. 306) and others. On Tuesday, September 13, 1892, she wrote:

> I notice how much the practice of dishorning cattle has come on of late years. There has been some litigation about it. I fancy there is as much to be said for and against, and liable to abuse as many other customs.
>
> From an aesthetic point of view, not obvious to farmers, it is perfectly frightful when applied to anything cross-bred with Ayrshire, as are most of the local cattle.

A natural *hummel* as are all the best bred *Doddies* has an immensely heavy broad head, so much so that a stranger will constantly mistake a *Doddy* cow couchant for a young bull—but the Ayrshire has a high narrow forehead, which in old cows gives a scared wild appearance, even when garnished with long sharp horns. But remove the horns, and the result is an idiotic beast with great flapping ears, and much the same silly type of countenance as that ugliest of animals, the red deer hind [p. 267].

The frequency of the entries in her *Journal* about castration, in addition to the prevalence of material about it in her stories, indicate its importance to Beatrix Potter. We may appreciate its significance from her entry in her *Journal* dated Friday, November 28, 1884. She writes: "The lower classes of Tynemouth have, or had, an extraordinary notion that if they baptized their girls before their boys the latter would have no beards. I wonder if they thought the privilege would be transferred to the ladies" (p. 121).

In describing this "extraordinary notion" of the "lower classes of Tynemouth" she seems to be toying with this idea as it might apply to herself and her brother, that if *she* were baptized before Bertram he would not have developed into a man (i.e., had no beard). When she wonders whether "they thought the privilege would be transferred to the ladies" she expresses the fantasy that girls would then be "like boys" or, specifically, be boys. This fits in with the idea that she expressed in her *Journal*: "If I were a boy and had courage" etc. (Friday, November 28, 1884, p. 120). The implication of her thought, common to many girls, is that her anatomy was determined by some external agency rather than by a genetic fact. Often girls blame their mothers for this.

In the published version of the story of Tuppenny, we may see the emergence of new material that elaborates her view of the aggressive woman who, like Mrs. McGregor, is capable of inflicting great bodily harm. As the injury that Mrs. Tuppenny does is to her husband, Beatrix Potter may be suggesting that in her parents' marriage her mother was the aggressor. Perhaps, too, in that Mr. Tuppenny leaves home because of his wife's aggression, Beatrix Potter may have been concerned that her father, Rupert, might also leave.

## Chapter 8

# The Tale of Benjamin Bunny

## (1904a) [1903]

Whatever feelings of dejection Beatrix Potter had suffered following the repudiation of her work on fungi by the Linnean Society in 1897, seem to have been neutralized by the acceptance and success of *Peter Rabbit*, the scheduled publication of *The Tale of Squirrel Nutkin* in August 1903, and *The Tailor of Gloucester* in October of the same year.

While she was still working on the proofs and final drawings for *Tailor* in the summer of 1903, the publishers asked her about another book. She responded to Norman Warne on July 8th: "I had been a little hoping too that something might be said about another book, but I did not know that I was the right person to make the suggestion!" (*Letters*, p. 77). Evidently, she had a number of possibilities in mind and one already written out. Thinking that "the Tailor and Nutkin [were] rather too ingenious and complicated compared with Peter Rabbit" she asked him whether he thought the next book "ought to be more simple" (*Letters*, p. 78).

Despite her eagerness to continue, and the publisher's willingness to do other books with her, less than a week later she wrote to Harold Warne:

If I had not supposed that the matter would be dealt with through the post, I should not have mentioned the subject of another book at present. I have had such painful unpleasantness at home this winter about the work that I should like a rest, while I am away.

I should be obliged if you will kindly say no more about a new book at present [*Letters*, p. 78].

Nevertheless, she did send them the rough outlines of a number of stories and indicated that the one about Benjamin Bunny was the furthest advanced.

By February 12, 1904, she was able to write that *The Tale of Benjamin Bunny* was nearly finished. Shortly after that, the book was completed and was published in September. The dedication of the book reads: "For the Children of Sawrey from Old Mr. Bunny."

As the story begins, Benjamin Bunny, observing that Mr. and Mrs. McGregor had gone off in a gig for what he presumed to be the whole day, went to visit his widowed aunt, Peter Rabbit's mother. He found Peter, wrapped in a red cotton handkerchief, who said that he had dropped his jacket and shoes when he was being chased by Mr. McGregor. Benjamin encouraged Peter to retrieve his clothes. They found Peter's jacket and shoes on a scarecrow in Mr. McGregor's garden. Benjamin suggested that they fill Peter's handkerchief with onions as a present for Peter's mother. Peter was quite uneasy. He did not eat anything and wanted to go home, eventually dropping half of the onions he had taken.

Suddenly they came upon a cat and both Benjamin and Peter hid underneath a large basket. The cat sat down on top of the basket so that the rabbits could not get out and remained there for five hours (in the original version she had written six hours [Linder, 1971, p. 144]). Late in the afternoon, Benjamin Bunny's father, Mr. Bunny, came by looking for his son. When he saw the cat, he jumped on it, scratched it, kicked it into the greenhouse, and locked the door. Then he took his son out of the basket by his ears and whipped him with a switch. After this he let Peter out and took the handkerchief full of onions. It will be noted that Beatrix Potter's illustration accompanying the text shows old Mr. Bunny holding *Peter* by his ears and beating *him* with a switch!

When Mr. McGregor returned shortly afterward, he was puzzled to see tiny footprints of clogs in the dirt and could not understand how the cat had been locked inside the greenhouse from the outside.

Peter's mother forgave him when he came home because she was glad to see that he had found his shoes and coat.

This little story may be understood as an epilogue to *The Tale of Peter Rabbit*. In it, Beatrix Potter undoes a number of the anxiety elements present in the first story as well as some in the story of *Squirrel Nutkin*. In this way she brings about a satisfactory resolution of the two stories, almost as if she were now finishing them with a fairy tale ending: "And they lived happily ever after."

With the help of Benjamin Bunny, Peter is able to retrieve his coat and shoes, thus undoing his loss and thereby winning his mother's approval. The cat, so dangerous in both the *Peter Rabbit* story and in the story of *Benjamin Bunny*, is locked up and is thus no longer a source of anxiety. Peter's father, who had been killed and eaten, is now replaced by Benjamin Bunny's father, Mr. Bunny, who serves as a revenant for the deceased Mr. Rabbit.

Peter's view of his own father may be understood from the characteristics of Old Mr. Bunny, who not only frees his son from his imprisonment underneath the basket, but also beats up the enemy. Yet, the attribute of a stern father figure is expressed in the characterization of Mr. Bunny as a punitive individual who whips his son for his misbehavior. Beatrix Potter does not specifically state what Benjamin Bunny's misbehavior was, but we may assume that he was being punished for entering Mr. McGregor's garden.

Aggression toward father figures is clearly expressed in this story by having another father figure, Mr. McGregor, unable to understand what was going on. He is perplexed by the small footprints of clogs and cannot figure out how the cat got locked in the greenhouse. Moreover, while Beatrix Potter does not write about it, her illustration of Mr. McGregor with his hand on his chin seems to indicate that he is also puzzled by the disappearance of Peter's coat and shoes from the scarecrow. In these respects, Mr. McGregor is portrayed as being ignorant of the basic facts of animal life. The notion that the father is ignorant of the "facts of life" is also a reversal and a projection of the child's own feelings of ignorance.

There is a curious reference to tails in this story. In the original version, Beatrix Potter had drawn the cat with a tail so large that the publishers had questioned the accuracy of her picture. Actually, she had selected a cat owned by Sir J. Vaughan, a former police magistrate as a model (see Linder, 1971, p. 145). His cat had an extremely long tail, one even larger than the one which Beatrix Potter drew, as she told Norman Warne in her letter of April 6, 1904 (*Letters*, p. 91). When the publishers objected to her picture showing a cat with such a long tail, she offered to shorten it, but she didn't actually do so until a new drawing was needed for a subsequent edition (Linder, 1971, p. 145). The point is that of all possible cats, she selected one with a very long tail as though to undo Nutkin's loss.

Beatrix Potter was not finished with the theme of castration. In one of her letters to Hilda Moore dated September 10, 1904, written just before *Benjamin Bunny* was published, she told her about having two pet mice, "Thingummy-jig" and "Pippin." She writes:

> I do not think Pippin will be able to wag *her* tail about—she has had an inch bitten off the end! I found the piece.
>
> I was very much shocked; but Pippin does not seem to care, she walks about with her short tail straight up in the air.
>
> I do not think that it was the piebald mouse who bit off Pippin's tail; I think it was a brown mouse called Applely [sic] Dapply [*Children*, p. 79].

84

## Chapter 9

# The Tale of Two Bad Mice

## (1904b) [1903]

Beatrix Potter had been working on this book and *The Tale of Benjamin Bunny* contemporaneously in 1903. Both books were published the following year. *The Tale of Two Bad Mice* was dedicated to Norman Warne's niece, Winifred Warne (daughter of his brother, Fruing) with the following words: "For W.M.L.W. [Winifred Mary Langrish Warne] The little girl who had the doll's house" (Linder, 1971, p. 152).

The action of this story is set in a dollhouse, belonging to two dolls called Lucinda and Jane. One day, when they had gone out, two mice, Tom Thumb and his wife, Hunca Munca, went into the dollhouse. When they entered the dining room, they found food spread on the table. Not realizing that the food and the utensils were artificial, Tom Thumb and Hunca Munca attempted to cut the ham without success. The imitation carving knife crumpled so that Tom Thumb hurt himself, and finally, the ham broke off the plate. Then they tried to eat the fish which they found was also artificial and was glued to the dish. Tom Thumb lost his temper and began to smash the ham with the tongs and a plaster shovel. Disappointed and frustrated because none of the food was edible and the canister contained nothing except beads, the two furious mice went on a rampage destroying everything in sight. After they pulled half the feathers out of Lucinda's bolster, Hunca Munca and Tom Thumb managed to squeeze it through the mouse hole. They tried to take a number of other items, including some of Lucinda's clothes, pots and pans, a bookcase, a bird-cage, a chair and a cradle, but were unable to push the bird-cage and the bookcase through the mouse hole. When the little girl to whom the doll house belonged saw what had happened she said that she would get "a doll dressed like a policeman" (p. 53). Her nurse, however, said that she would "set a mouse-trap" (p. 54).

Beatrix Potter writes that the mice were not really terribly naughty because Tom Thumb paid for everything he had broken with a crooked sixpence he found under the hearth rug. On Christmas Eve he and Hunca Munca stuffed it into one of the stockings belonging to Lucinda and Jane. The story ends with Hunca Munca coming every day with her dust pan and broom to sweep the doll house before anyone is awake as if to atone for her destructive behavior.

As background to this story, Lane (1946) noted that during one of Beatrix Potter's visits to Harescombe Grange (see chapter 5, p. 57), two mice were caught in the cage-trap in the kitchen. Beatrix Potter rescued them, brought them home, and tamed them, naming them Tom Thumb and Hunca Munca (pp. 77–78).

While on a week's holiday at Hastings between November 26th and December 3rd, 1903, Beatrix Potter began working on *The Tale of Two Bad Mice* and consulted with Norman Warne about it as the work progressed. Initially their relationship was essentially collaborative but as time went on a close personal relationship between them began to develop. He sent her some "queer little dollies [which were] exactly what [she] wanted" (*Letters*, February 18, 1904, p. 86), and he even arranged to have an artificial ham and other "foods" delivered to her from

Hamley's (a London toystore) that she could use as models for her story. We learn that at her request Norman Warne, now referred to as "Johnny Crow" in letters, made a box with a glass side for Beatrix Potter's pet mice so that she could easily draw them for her new book. At the same time, he also made a dollhouse for his niece, Winifred, to whom the book was subsequently dedicated.

Norman Warne wanted Beatrix Potter to go to his brother's house in Surbiton where she could make drawings of the dollhouse he had built. Mrs. Fruing Warne affirmed her brother-in-law's suggestion by inviting Mrs. Potter to come with Norman and Beatrix to have lunch with the family. Evidently, as her mother objected to going there, Beatrix Potter had to turn down the invitation and wrote to Norman Warne on February 12, 1904:

> I was very much perplexed about the doll's-house, I would have gone gladly to draw it, and I should be so *very* sorry if Mrs. Warne or you thought me uncivil. I did not think I could manage to go to Surbiton without staying [to] lunch; I hardly ever go out, and my mother is so "exacting" I had not enough spirit to say anything about it. I have felt vexed with myself since, but I did not know what to do. It does wear a person out. . . .
> As far as the book is concerned, I think I can do it from the photograph & my box; but it is very hard to have seemed uncivil [*Letters*, p. 85].

Several days later (February 18, 1904), she wrote to Norman Warne again. "I don't think that my mother would be very likely to want to go to Surbiton, you did not understand what I meant by 'exacting.' People who only see her casually do not know how disagreeable she can be when she takes dislikes. I should have been glad enough to go. I did not know what to do" (*Letters*, p. 86).

*The Tale of Two Bad Mice* is rich in content despite Beatrix Potter's initial wish to write a "simple story." It is not just another children's story. It has all the flavor of an autobiographical fragment inspired by her developing relationship to Norman Warne. While they were collaborating on a story, they were, in a sense, playing house. In the postscript to her letter to Norman Warne, April 29, 1904, before she went to Harescombe Grange, Beatrix Potter added, after she had asked him about his plan to go abroad in May: "I will try & think about things while I am away, I mean about the doll's house" (*Letters*, p. 94).

Mrs. Potter was keenly aware of the growing relationship between her daughter and the publisher, a man not of her "station," and she disapproved.

Lane (1978) writes:

> Clearly Mrs. Potter had taken a dislike to the whole Warne family, since publishers in her view were simply tradesmen, and therefore much below what Beatrix herself called "people of our station." (Although, as [Beatrix Potter] wrote privately to Caroline Hutton, "Publishing books is as clean a trade as spinning cotton.") It had not escaped Mrs. Potter's notice that Beatrix and Norman Warne were corresponding almost daily; that her professional visits to the publishing house gave her pleasure, and that she came home from afternoons in Bedford Square in unusually good spirits. This obviously, to Mrs. Potter's way of thinking, simply would not do. . . . She therefore set herself resolutely against any idea of a closer friendship between Beatrix and Norman, and the atmosphere of Bolton Gardens deteriorated accordingly. Mr. Potter undoubtedly supported his wife in this, but it is perhaps worth recording that in disagreeable domestic campaigns of this sort it was Mrs. rather than Mr. Potter who took the lead. . . . Mrs. Potter remained always disapproving, implacable, remote [pp. 125–127].

The growing closeness in her relationship to Norman Warne naturally led Beatrix Potter to develop fantasies about its outcome. Thus she conjured up a dream house, beautiful to look at but not real. The rampage of the mice shows how furious she must have felt about her mother's disapproval.

But again there was more to her fantasies. In the story, the mice took possession of the dolls' belongings—clothes, furniture, and so on. In addition to these objects they took a *cradle*. Not mentioned in the text but clearly illustrated in Beatrix Potter's exquisite picture (p. 48), is Hunca Munca in her own house cuddling one little mouse baby while other baby mice are sleeping in the cradle, their tails protruding from under the pink quilt. Accompanying the text is another picture (p. 52) of Hunca Munca holding up a baby mouse and showing it to the policeman doll as though to plead clemency. In addition (p. 55), after the nurse says that she will set a mouse-trap, the accompanying illustration shows an adult mouse, presumably Tom Thumb (as Hunca Munca is holding a baby mouse in her arms) instructing the little mice about a mouse trap.

If we now put together the three illustrations with the material we have discussed about Beatrix Potter's parents' disapproval of her relationship with Norman Warne, we may appreciate the poignancy of her communication in her pictures. When we see Hunca Munca holding her baby and pleading with the policeman it is as if she, Beatrix Potter, is pleading with her parents (who act like policemen and would keep her in a life threatening trap) to allow her to gratify her wish to be able to show to babies of her own the very tender loving maternal care that Hunca Munca shows to her little baby mice.

The entire "domestic scene" in the story has a number of elements that connect it with Beatrix Potter's own feelings about the household in which she was raised and, specifically, with her feelings about her mother. The second paragraph of her story (p. 10) identifies the doll house as belonging to Lucinda and Jane but Beatrix Potter goes on to say "at least it belonged to Lucinda but she never ordered meals" (p. 10). In the third paragraph Beatrix Potter refers to Jane as the cook who "never did any cooking, because the dinner had been bought ready-made, in a box full of shavings."

Food and love are often equated in the unconscious. Thus, Beatrix Potter indicates in her story that the dolls are negligent in providing food and when they do, it is only pretty in appearance. By describing how frustrated and angry the hungry mice become when they find the food totally inedible because it is not real, she reveals what she really felt about what she received at home. The equation of food and love leads us to the understanding that Beatrix Potter was referring to her feelings about some of the women in her own house: her mother, the nurse, the servants, the cook. As far as she was concerned, these women were all negligent in providing affection and care to her (and to her brother—here in the guise of Tom Thumb). This also fits in with her description of the dolls: pretty but with no genuine feelings. Beatrix Potter was even more explicit about her mother in her letter quoted earlier to Norman Warne where she wrote that: "People who only see her casually do not know how disagreeable she can be when she takes dislikes." All that she and Bertram received was ersatz love and food.

The wholesale destruction of the interior of the dollhouse by the mice not only reveals Beatrix Potter's angry feelings about her mother's disapproval of her relationship with Norman Warne, but also expresses how very frustrated and "vexed" she felt during the developmental years of her childhood. Small wonder that near the end of her life she wrote (May 1942) that her home at 2 Bolton Gardens was her "unloved birthplace" and stated that she was "rather pleased to hear it [was] no more" (*Americans*, p. 213). The pleasure that she verbalized had to do with the final realization of the wish that she had expressed years earlier when she wrote about the destruction of the dollhouse by the two bad mice. At the time this story was written (1904), she was beginning to see a way out. She recognized that her books were providing her with a growing sense of independence. She wrote (April 19, 1904) to Norman: "It is pleasant to feel I could earn my own living. The country is getting quite green" (*Letters*, p. 92). Her comment meant that Spring, a time for growth, rejuvenation and reproduction, had arrived.

Beatrix Potter had an incredible ability to express her own problems in such a way that the reader can enjoy the final product for its own merits as literature and art and not connect it with the personal problems that concerned her at the time. This in itself was a remarkable achievement. Our ability to see the total picture can only enhance our appreciation of her talent.

## Chapter 10

# The Tale of Mrs. Tiggy-Winkle
# (1905a) [1902, 1886]

In a letter to Norman Warne, dated July 2, 1905, Beatrix Potter wrote that she had begun *The Tale of Mrs. Tiggy-Winkle* in August of 1886 (*Letters*, p. 121). Linder (1971) states that she had carefully planned it in 1901 although it was not actually written down until the following year (p. 155). On the title page of the manuscript Beatrix Potter had written: "Made at Lingholm, Sept. 01 told to cousin Stephanie [Hyde Parker] at Melford, Nov. 01—written down Nov. 02. There are no pictures, it is a good one to tell" (Linder, 1971, p. 155). The book was finally published in 1905 and dedicated "For the real little Lucie [Lucie Carr] of Newlands."

*The Tale of Mrs. Tiggy-Winkle* is about a little girl named Lucie who lived on a farm. Although she was a good little girl, she was always losing her handkerchiefs. On this particular occasion she had lost three of them and her pinafore as well. She asked a number of animals (a kitten, a chicken, and a robin) whether they had seen them, but they did not reply. Seeing some white objects spread on the grass on a hill, she climbed up there, but these were not her handkerchiefs.

Then Lucy found a small door in the hill and heard some-one singing. When she entered the doorway she found herself in a tiny room where a short person was ironing clothes. This person was wearing a white cap from which protruded prickles. The "person" was actually a hedgehog who introduced herself as Mrs. Tiggy-winkle, "an excellent clear-starcher." After iron-ing a damask tablecloth belonging to Jenny Wren, which was stained with currant wine ("difficult to wash out"), she pro-ceeded to press many articles of clothing belonging to different animals, a number of whom figure in Beatrix Potter's other stories. Among these were Peter Rabbit's blue jacket, Squirrel Nutkin's red tailcoat (with no tail), as well as Lucie's pinafore and her three handkerchiefs.

Eventually, Mrs. Tiggy-winkle made tea for the two of them. They sat before the fire but Lucie did not sit too close to Mrs. Tiggy-winkle because she was concerned that the latter's prickles (hairpins sticking wrong end out) would injure her. After this they packed the clothes in bundles. Lucie's pocket handkerchiefs were folded inside her pinafore and fastened with a silver safety pin. As they trotted down the path, the animals came out to meet them and Mrs. Tiggy-winkle gave them their clean clothes. When all the clothes were duly distrib-uted, Lucie turned to thank the washerwoman and to say good night to her, but she saw Mrs. Tiggy-winkle running away with-out the clothes she had been wearing. She had become very small and was entirely covered with prickles, assuming her nor-mal hedgehog appearance.

Beatrix Potter then ends the story with a kind of epilogue, set in small type, in which she says that although some people believe that Lucie had been asleep, it did not explain how she could have found her handkerchiefs and pinafore, pinned with a silver safety pin. And then Beatrix Potter adds that she herself had seen the door in the back of the hill called Catbells and she was well acquainted with Mrs. Tiggy-winkle.

This statement immediately alerts us to recognize that there were some elements of reality in the story. This is further substantiated by the fact that the heroine of the story is a real girl, Lucie Carr, and Mrs. Tiggy-winkle herself is based on Kitty MacDonald, the Potters' washerwoman when they first rented the Dalguise House in Scotland in 1871. Beatrix Potter was 5 years old then, and they continued to spend summers there until she was 16.

In an entry in her *Journal*, dated Monday, August 1, 1892, Beatrix Potter wrote that she visited Kitty MacDonald, who was 83 at the time. She described her as "delightfully merry" but went on to say that:

[H]er neighbors teased her for a witch . . . about the immense fires which she kept up day and night for the last few weeks. She had got the attics quite full of sticks. . . . She is a comical, round little old woman, as brown as a berry and wears a multitude of petticoats and a white mutch. Her memory goes back for seventy years and I really believe she is prepared to enumerate the articles of her first wash in the year '71 [p. 250].

Five years later, Wednesday, August 31, 1897, Beatrix Potter described another visit to Kitty MacDonald in her *Journal*. She wrote:

Perhaps the Kincraigie folk had some ground for saying she was a witch, for, when we came up to her little cottage, there was a little toad sitting in the middle of the little flat, grey stone inside the doorsill. When we knocked it hopped away under the closet door, and the little old body came out in her light slippers, winking and blinking [p. 260].

A fanciful thought perhaps, but Beatrix Potter seems to imply that she viewed the toad as a "familiar," somehow connected with Kitty MacDonald.

We find ourselves in a recognizable position because here again Beatrix Potter has used material from the world around her as models for the characters in her story. Many of the scenes that she painted for her stories have been identified and people have derived a great deal of pleasure from putting together the real objects or locations with her pictures. Linder (1971) identifies the door at the back of the hill as having its origin "in some paintings made of a hillside path at Kelbarrow, Grasmere, in August 1899" (p. 156). Moreover, Beatrix Potter's own notes on the side of the original manuscript, dated 1902, state that some of Mrs. Tiggy-winkle's possessions had evidently come from the mines in the area. The silver safety pin, for example, with which Lucie's handkerchiefs and pinafore were pinned, actually was a silver brooch that belonged to Kitty Mac-Donald (*Journal*, Tuesday, October 18, 1892, p. 294). Linder (1971) states that a year before she died Beatrix Potter wrote some memories of the old washerwoman on the back of a newspaper wrapper: "She wore a small plaid crossed over shawl pinned with a silver brooch" (p. 159).

In the 1902 manuscript of the story, Beatrix Potter included a conversation between Mrs. Tiggy-winkle and Lucie about the mines in the area. In that version, and left out of the final version, Lucie persistently asks Mrs. Tiggy-winkle what kind of mine it was (i.e., gold, silver, copper, lead, etc). Mrs. Tiggy-winkle answers her questions by agreeing with her in each case and showing her objects made of the particular metal. One of these, the Goldscope mine, had not been worked since the English Civil Wars in the seventeenth century. Other mines in the area contained a variety of metals, some precious, but in insufficient quantity to be of working value (Linder, 1971, p. 162). The fact that Beatrix Potter took the trouble to specify the metals that were present in the mines seems to indicate she was again alluding to some realities in the story.

In the margin of the manuscript Beatrix Potter had written notes to herself to help her edit it. Lucie asks Mrs. Tiggy-winkle, who is taking the damp clothes out of the basket and preparing to iron them, what each particular item is and to whom they belonged. In her marginalia, Beatrix Potter writes: "These clothes would amuse children [as the story was meant to be read to them], the chief difficulty would be to get enough variation in the *pictures* of the washerwoman" (Linder, 1971, p. 162). Then Beatrix Potter writes with respect to the many questions that Lucie asks: " 'as many articles as the audience has patience for, there were several others I have forgotten' " (Linder, 1971, p. 163). Again, Lucie keeps asking "What's this? What's that?" and Mrs. Tiggy-winkle patiently tells her what the different objects are, most of which belong to the various animals in her stories.

From our standpoint, the characterization of Lucie as a real child who asks an adult, "What's this? What's that?" is very typical. Such curiosity is a common characteristic, present in the course of the development of the child's ego, because the child wants to understand the complexities of the real world in which he or she is living. Lucie has no difficulty in recognizing her handkerchiefs or her pinafore because these things are a part of her world. Her repeated refrain, however, has a familiar ring to it and is somewhat similar to Squirrel Nutkin's asking Old Brown riddles. Lucie's questions are simpler than the riddles which Squirrel Nutkin poses. Moreover, they are addressed to a woman and not to a man as Squirrel Nutkin's were.

From our knowledge of children's development, the purpose of such questions frequently has a much deeper meaning than the simple identification of objects, as we have seen with Nutkin's riddles. Behind such questions is a child's wishing to know and to be enlightened about the facts of life. In this instance Lucie asks the knowledgeable adult, Mrs. Tiggy-winkle, to supply her with such information. We may suppose that in this story there is the memory of another autobiographical childhood fragment when Beatrix Potter asked adults, including Kitty MacDonald, many questions in an effort to obtain enlightenment.

One reaction to a child's not being enlightened is that the child feels lost and confused and may act this out by losing objects. Early in the story, Lucie, after losing her handkerchiefs, asks various animals (a kitten, a chicken, and a robin) if they had seen them, but they do not provide her with any satisfactory answers. She wanders about looking for them. Evidently there was anxiety connected with these losses because in the original manuscript Beatrix Potter has Lucie say, after she has lost her pocket "handkersniff": "I don't like to go home!" (Linder, 1971, p. 160) and begin to cry. Lucie expected that she would be considered naughty and reprimanded for losing her handker-chiefs just as in Beatrix Potter's story about Peter Rabbit, he may have expected that he would be reprimanded for losing his coat and shoes again.

Lucie's anxiety is expressed in another way in this story. As we have learned, Mrs. Tiggy-winkle was modeled after Kitty MacDonald. We may well imagine that when Beatrix Potter was a child herself, Kitty MacDonald regaled her with stories and memories that must have amused and fascinated as well as frightened the little girl. We would wonder to what extent the psychopathology that was expressed by Kitty MacDonald in her later years—her eccentric ideas about her neighbors teasing her as being a witch, her strange behavior, as her making "immense fires" and her collecting sticks—may have already been present when Beatrix Potter was a child and added an additional basis for her anxiety. To complicate matters it will be recalled (chapter 1, p. 11) that as a child Beatrix Potter was taken care of by a Miss McKenzie who imbued her with "a firm belief in witches and fairies" which managed to persist in some way and probably gave rise to her later belief in magic and in animistic ideas, together with a degree of anxiety.

The story about Mrs. Tiggy-winkle gives us a further indi-cation of Lucie's (and Beatrix Potter's) anxiety. Beatrix Potter writes in the 1902 version of the story that "all over [Mrs. Tiggy-winkle's] clothes and through her shawl there were hair-pins sticking wrong end out; so that Lucie did not like to sit too near her" (Linder, 1971, p. 163). When they have tea together, Lucie sits on the same bench with her but at some distance away so that she will not be injured by the hedgehog's prickles.

There is another determinant to Lucie's anxiety. Beatrix Potter relates that as Lucie approached the door in the hill, she heard someone singing: "Lily white and clean, oh!/ With little frills between, oh!/ Smooth and hot—red rusty spot/ Never here be seen, oh!" (Potter, 1905a, p. 22). This was in reference to the damask tablecloth belonging to Jenny Wren that is stained with currant wine which Mrs. Tiggy-winkle said was "very bad to wash."

In her letter of June 8, 1905, to Norman Warne Beatrix Potter provides a specific association to the stain. She wrote:

> She is supposed to be exorcising spots and iron stains, same as Lady Macbeth (!), the verb is imperative, and apparently it is not reasonable to use "no" with a vocative noun. It is a contradiction to address "no spot!" I am afraid this is rather muddled; I used to know my Latin grammar but it has faded. . . [*Letters*, p. 120].

The reference is to Lady Macbeth's speech in Act V, Scene 1, following the gentlewoman's remark to the physician that she had seen Lady Macbeth rubbing her hands and continuing this for a quarter of an hour. The quotation is as follows:

> Out, damned spot! Out, I say! One, two
> —why, then 'tis time to do 't. Hell is murky. . . .
> What need we fear who knows it,
> when none can call our power to account?
> Yet who would have thought the old man
> to have had so much blood in him?
>
> [38–45]

And later:

> What, will these hands ne'er be clean?
>
> [48]

And further:

> Here's the smell of blood still. All the
> perfumes of Arabia will not sweeten this little
> hand. Oh, oh, oh!
>
> [56–58]

By identifying Mrs. Tiggy-winkle with Lady Macbeth, Beatrix Potter further emphasizes the aggressive and dangerous qualities of Mrs. Tiggy-winkle. Such an identification is particularly impressive when we recall Lady Macbeth's earlier speech in Act I, Scene 7 where she urges her husband to kill Duncan.

> I have given suck, and know
> How tender 'tis to love the babe that milks me.
> I would, while it was smiling in my face,
> Have plucked my nipple from his boneless gums
> And dashed the brains out, had I so sworn as you
> Have done to this.
>
> [54–59]

What is important to note is that in the 1902 manuscript of the story Beatrix Potter's sole reference to the stained tablecloth belonging to Jenny Wren is that: "It's very ill to wash" (Linder, 1971, p. 162). Nothing whatsoever is said about Lady Macbeth, and Beatrix Potter's reference to her is to be found only much later in her letter to Norman Warne on June 8, 1905, while she was working on the manuscript with him.

Beatrix Potter expresses her anxieties to Norman Warne by calling his attention to the connection between Mrs. Tiggy-winkle and Lady Macbeth. *Tiggy-Winkle* was originally planned and written before Beatrix Potter and Norman Warne had developed a close personal relationship. The content of the story suggests that at this time she had begun to fall in love with him and had the fantasy of being married and having a family of her own, as we saw in our discussion of *The Tale of Two Bad Mice*, written at the end of 1903 and published the following year. She may have hoped that Norman Warne would propose to her and her fantasy would become a reality. Such thoughts engendered tremendous anxiety in her about her mother's disapproval and antagonistic attitude, as we can see from her characterization of Mrs. Tiggy-winkle being potentially dangerous because of her prickles. As her friendship with Norman Warne developed, and as it gradually took the form of a love relationship, her mother's openly antagonistic attitude about it served to mobilize Beatrix Potter's anxieties further. Yet, she bravely persevered and continued her relationship with him.

## Chapter 11

# The Tale of the Pie and the Patty-pan
## (1905b) [1903]

At the same time that Beatrix Potter was working on *The Tale of Mrs. Tiggy-Winkle*, she was also working on *The Pie and the Patty-pan*.[1] She had originally planned this story in 1903 but, according to Linder (1971), she felt that that version was "too thin" so she altered the plot and rewrote the whole story (p. 169). Completed in 1905, the work in its final form bears the fruits of her collaboration with Norman Warne.

Before the book was finally printed, Beatrix Potter wrote to Norman Warne that "If the book prints well it will be my next favourite to the 'Tailor' " (Linder, 1971, p. 171). The book was dedicated to Noel, Freda, and Norah's younger siblings, Joan and Beatrix Moore. She wrote: "For Joan, to read to Baby."[2]

In the published version of the story Ribby, a cat, sends a letter to Duchess, a dog, inviting her to tea and promising her something nice that she is baking in a pie dish. She informs

---

[1] In 1930 the title was changed to *The Tale of the Pie and the Patty-pan* (Linder, 1971, p. 172). In the first version, Beatrix Potter had titled it: *The Story of Duchess and Ribby* (Linder, 1971, p. 173).

[2] Joan Elsie was born August 31, 1896; Beatrix (Baby) on November 3, 1903.

Duchess that she will be able to eat it all herself, while she, Ribby, would eat muffins. Duchess promptly answers the invitation, agreeing to come, adding, however, that she hoped that it wasn't mouse. Realizing, however, that this was not polite, she changed her sentence to read that she hoped it would be "fine."

Duchess, however, was obsessed with the idea that Ribby would feed her mouse pie, which she could not eat. She therefore decided to substitute her own pie, made of veal and ham, for Ribby's pie. Her pie was in a pink and white pie dish similar to one she knew Ribby had. Duchess put in a little tin patty-pan to hold up the crust of her pie.

In the meantime, just before going to purchase some items for the tea party, Ribby put *her* pie into her lower oven, choosing that one because the upper oven baked too quickly. On her way to the village shop she passed Duchess. They bowed to one another but did not otherwise greet each other because they were going to have a party.

Duchess quickly ran to Ribby's house where she put her pie in the upper oven, because she had been unable to turn the handles of the lower oven. Thus she did not find Ribby's pie. When she heard Ribby coming home, she ran out the back door. Ribby heard a noise but was reassured because her spoons were locked up.

Duchess appeared at Ribby's house at the appointed time, having picked some flowers for her. The conversation between them was quite formal and extremely polite. When Duchess commented about the delicious smell of pie, Ribby said that it was mouse and bacon. While they waited for the pie to finish cooking, Ribby poured tea for the two of them and Duchess allowed her to put a lump of sugar on her nose. When she dropped it and began searching for it, she did not see which oven Ribby had opened to get out the pie.

As they were eating Duchess said that she was feeling for the patty-pan with her spoon. Ribby told her that it was not necessary in pies made of mouse and stated emphatically that there was no patty-pan in the pie. Despite her reassurances, however, Duchess insisted that there was one and they argued about it in a very polite manner.

Suddenly Duchess began to howl, exclaiming that she would die for she had swallowed the patty-pan. Ribby's continued efforts at reassurance were of no avail and Duchess's symptoms got worse. Finally Ribby insisted on running to get Dr. Maggotty, a magpie. She found him putting rusty nails into a bottle of ink, exclaiming: "Gammon? ha! HA!" and then "Spinach? ha! HA!"

While she was gone, Duchess, convinced that she had swallowed the patty-pan, suddenly realized that something was baking in the upper oven and that this was her own veal and ham pie. Through a hole in the pie crust she could see the little tin patty-pan. Duchess, who had ignored Ribby's repeated statements, now realized that she must have been eating mouse pie and this was why she felt ill. Because it was such an awkward situation she decided to put her own pie in the backyard.

When Ribby and Dr. Maggotty arrived, he again asked if it was "Gammon." Duchess said that she was feeling better and that she would be well if the doctor only felt her pulse. The magpie gave her a bread pill and some milk.

After this Duchess said that she thought she should go home before it got dark. When she left Ribby's house, she ran to the backyard and found three jackdaws eating pie-crust and Dr. Maggotty was drinking gravy out of the patty-pan. She went home feeling silly. Later, when Ribby came out and saw the patty-pan, she could not understand it as all her patty-pans were locked up in the kitchen cupboard. She determined that the next time she gave a party she would invite her cousin Tabitha Twitchit.

Beatrix Potter's little story is a masterpiece of caricature, a parody of a social scene that she must have witnessed many times in her home. The conversation between the dog and the cat, who are traditional enemies, while brimming with superficial politeness, has undertones of deceit and condemnation. The description of their behavior constitutes an incredible mockery of women who participate in silly discussions of trivia and express extremely prejudicial attitudes, while observing the highly artificial Victorian rules of etiquette for an English tea. What, after all, could be a more vivid parody of their conversation and their prejudices than the gossip that Ribby engaged in with her cousin Tabitha Twitchit. Learning that Ribby had invited Duchess for tea, Tabitha disdainfully remarks: "A little *dog* indeed! Just as if there were no CATS in Sawrey! And a *pie* for afternoon tea! The very idea!" (Potter, 1905b, p. 28). Beatrix Potter recorded a number of similar snobbish conversations in her Journal.

Prior to this time it is very doubtful whether Beatrix Potter could have allowed herself to articulate any criticism of her mother and her circle of friends, especially in a story meant for publication. At this point in her life, however, while she had been working intently with Norman Warne on the preparation of this little story, the relationship between them had intensified to such a point that she allowed herself to reveal a small measure of her aggression against her mother and the superficial values of some of her mother's friends. She was bitter about the hypocrisy in her mother's attitude about Norman's social status particularly because *her* mother's family (Leech) had made its money in the textile business.

Beatrix Potter's clever mockery and caricature are further expressed in her choice of the magpie, Dr. Maggotty, for the role of the doctor in the story. She puns that because he is a *pie* himself, he would therefore understand. Dr. Maggotty frequently used the word "Gammon." In dialect this means a leg or a foot, and is defined by Webster as "a ham or flitch of bacon, salted and smoked or dried" as well as "the lower end of a side of bacon." The word is also used colloquially, however, to mean "talk that is intended to deceive. Humbug." Thus Dr.

Maggotty recognizes that Duchess is really feigning illness and can be cured by a pill made of bread alone.

The absurdity and derogation of the physician is perpetrated in Beatrix Potter's account of the doctor's professional activities and ministrations. When Ribby finds him, Dr. Maggotty is busily putting rusty nails into a bottle of ink that he had acquired from a post office. When Duchess states that she would feel quite well if he only felt her pulse, he gives her a bread pill which she is to take with some milk. The entire description of Dr. Maggotty is clearly a caricature of physicians in general and perhaps specifically those who took care of her when she was ill with rheumatic heart disease, or recommended a change of scene for her father when he was having urinary problems.

If we compare the final version of *The Tale of the Pie and the Patty-pan* with the original version of *The Story of Duchess and Ribby* written at "Hastings, Nov. 26–Dec. 3, 03," with the subtitle, "Something very, very NICE," we see significant changes. These were not made only because the story "was too thin."

In the first version of the story Duchess graciously accepts Ribby's invitation to tea and pie but expresses the hope that she will not serve her fish. Beatrix Potter then gives a detailed account of Ribby's preparations for the tea, including removing her silver spoons from the locked cupboard and polishing them. Duchess carefully brushes her beautiful hair, picks some flowers for Ribby, and also takes along something to eat in a basket. When she arrives promptly for the tea, they gossip about the news that three of James's hens had been killed. Duchess says that she believes that the wicked fox had killed them. Ribby says that it was a rat because four white eggs were stolen. Duchess, however, corrects her saying there were only three brown eggs and insists that it must have been a fox. She then adds that the fox also took a black chicken and two white hens. Ribby corrects her insisting that it was the hen who was black and the two chickens who were white.

When the pie is ready, it turns out to be chicken pie indicating that the culprit was not the fox at all but was Ribby herself. When Duchess asks her if there are any pieces of hard-boiled egg in the pie, Ribby replies that she couldn't find any eggs because there were none in the henhouse, accusing "the rat—or the fox" of having stolen them. With this Duchess reveals the contents of her basket: three brown eggs.

From the content of the early version of *The Pie and the Patty-pan*, we may readily see why Beatrix Potter wanted to rewrite the story. The initial version not only reveals her feelings about her mother and her associates: that they were superficial, opinionated, and bigoted, but it is also extremely outspoken. In the initial version, by revealing that Ribby is a murderer (of chickens) and a thief, and that Duchess is also a thief (of eggs), Beatrix Potter is able to indict her mother and her friends in a most powerful way. While she described and pictured Duchess as beautiful, she also regarded her as extremely dangerous. The wicked behavior of Ribby and Duchess allowed Beatrix Potter to state her view that her mother's wealthy family and her friends were as reprehensible as the two animals. Coming at this time in her life it was a reaction to her strong feelings about her mother's criticism of Norman Warne's family. Yet as Beatrix Potter evidently felt guilty about entertaining such intensely aggressive feelings about her mother, she had to attenuate them by expressing her criticism in a more subtle and genteel manner.

Norman Warne was beginning to show some signs of ill health in 1905, and Beatrix Potter must have been worried about him. Her mother's disdainful attitude toward him must only have intensified Beatrix Potter's anger with her. Her guilt about these feelings led her to view her original story as thin, and forced her to compose a toned down version that would be more acceptable and marketable than the original story. There is another point. It would hardly have endeared either Ribby or Duchess to children if they had been presented as having destructive and dishonest tendencies.

## Chapter 12

# Norman Dalziel Warne

The year 1905 began pleasantly for Beatrix Potter. Her creativity was flourishing and she was happily working on several projects. She was busily involved in the preparation of *The Tale of Mrs. Tiggy-Winkle*, which was to be her next book, while also working on *The Tale of the Pie and the Patty-pan* and *Appley Dapply's Nursery Rhymes*. In addition, she had begun to design some wallpaper. In both the literary and artistic projects she worked closely with Norman Warne. In February she had sent him drafts of *The Tale of Mr. Jeremy Fisher* and *The Pie and the Patty-pan*, but stated that she did not intend to finish "the hedgehog book straight off" because she might have a chance of drawing a child later in the spring (*Letters*, p. 112).

Norman Warne was away from time to time during the early period of this year, and her letters disclose that she was looking forward to his return to discuss what she had achieved in the meantime.

Beatrix Potter's feelings toward him continued to be complicated because of her parents' attitude. While she bravely determined to continue the relationship, she felt guilty because it was in direct defiance of them.

In contrast, Margaret Lane (1946) writes that Fruing Warne's young daughters were told that:

[T]hey must now call Miss Potter, "Auntie Bee" and that she and Uncle Norman were going to be married. The children accepted her joyously, though she was not, to them, without her intimidating aspect. Winifred Warne "the little girl who had the doll's house" . . . remembers her at this time as "someone to be reckoned with, someone who would demand a great deal of one in the way of character, and be unsatisfied with less than the best. We have kind aunts, and charming aunts, and silly aunts, but she was someone to look up to and live up to." Winifred's mother, Fruing's wife, was inclined to laugh a little over "Miss Potter's utter lack of vanity—her plainly done hair, and sensible boots and umbrella"; and Winifred's nurse was scornful of Miss Potter's inexperience when one day she helped to dress the little girls in the nursery—("My nurse's remarks showed what she thought of literary people. *Peter Rabbit* did not weigh in the balance against drawers put on back to front"); but her acceptance at Bedford Square was kindly and complete, and it was there, during the troubled summer of 1905, that she had her first experience of what happy family life could be [pp. 84–85].

What was Norman Warne like as a person? Lane (1978) says that Norman Warne was "shy, self-contained and unobtrusive" and "spent much of his leisure in devising treats and pastimes for his nephews and nieces" (p. 123). From Taylor, Whalley, Hobbs, and Battrick (1987) we learn that Norman Warne was a "gentle, good looking" man who was undoubtedly his mother's favorite. The youngest of three brothers, he was also the youngest in a family of six children. Besides these comments about him, some of his letters to Beatrix Potter which deal strictly with their business relationship have been published in Linder (1971), including the letters dated May 25 and May 26, 1905. These two letters, entirely in Norman Warne's handwriting, are in the Beatrix Potter Collection at the Victoria and Albert Museum in London. Photocopies of the originals were referred for a graphological analysis with the expectation that a study of Norman Warne's handwriting might reveal some aspects of his personality.

The graphologists were initially told only the age and occupation of Norman Warne and that he had died in August 1905 after having proposed marriage to Beatrix Potter a month before. They knew nothing else about him. I found that the graphological report, prepared by Patricia Siegel[1] made some interesting observations about Norman Warne.

In the introduction to her graphological report on Norman Warne, Siegel wrote:

> Not having an original handwriting for examination puts certain limitations on the handwriting analyst. Deductions are made about pen pressure and stroke quality as suggested from a photocopy, but such deductions entail some risk of error. In this case, the analyst's task is further complicated by illness. Although Norman Warne was not acutely ill at the time of writing, his nervous system may have been affected to a degree, nevertheless. Acknowledging this, personality characteristics are still evident and are clearly indicated by letter forms and spacial elements which confirm assumptions made about stroke quality. . . .
>
> Norman Dalziel Warne was a gentleman, formal, courteous and circumspect. He was proud and dignified in his bearing. A man of culture and breeding, he projected an overriding sense of propriety and obligation to the high expectations of his peers. He was a responsible man, with a committed sense of values.
>
> He was not without vanity, however. Self-conscious, he was cautious and inhibited in his presentation, careful to give the correct image of grace and sophistication. He had a reserved but sociable nature and cared strongly about how others viewed him.
>
> Intellectually astute, his mind was sharp and versatile. Intuitive, artistic sensibility coexisted with an analytical propensity. He was disciplined and diligent with exacting standards and a penchant for precision. As a high achiever, he strived to be exceptional. His thinking was clear, systematic, and objective. He thought conceptually and had an aptitude for associating

---

[1]Patricia Siegel is a faculty member of The New School for Social Research, New York City, where she codirects the psychology of handwriting progam. She is a professional handwriting consultant, both as a graphologist and a handwriting identification expert. Ms. Siegel has a B.S. degree from Cornell University and studied in the handwriting program under Daniel and Florence Anthony at The New School. She is also a consulting reader for the journal *Perceptual and Motor Skills*. Her publications include articles in the *Journal of the American Society of Professional Graphologists* and *The Psychiatric Clinics of North America* and a chapter in *Experiencing Graphology*. In addition to lecturing at conferences and seminars, her analyses and views on handwriting analysis have been presented in major magazines and on television and radio. She is currently Vice President of The American Society of Professional Graphologists.

and integrating ideas. Despite his focus on originality, his reason ruled his imagination. But still, he was an idealist and a romantic, an emotionally sensitive man who was seeking fulfillment. He was susceptible to stress and did not have a tough, pragmatic nature. He needed positive feedback and support for his efforts.

Norman Warne concealed his vulnerabilities. Beneath the civility and refinement, were strong feelings he could not express freely. His outer behavior was restrained by his desired image, by high expectations of perfection and by a self-surveillance which prevented full involvement in life. Natural instincts were curbed. His uneasiness was masked behind a polite facade. Yet, he could express himself creatively.

Socially introverted, Mr. Warne felt most comfortable in creative and scholarly pursuits in which he could enjoy his own company. He was remote and shared his interests with a select few. He felt intellectually superior and could exhibit arrogance or impatience with those less astute. A moderate degree of pretension was mixed with an appropriate degree of humility.

There were also idiosyncratic elements to his personality and a prickly pedantic quality covered by formal correctness. He could be irritable and stubborn when his guard was down. But it is more likely that he directed his irritability inwardly with self-criticism.

His stamina and resilience were not strong. Intellectual expression contrasted with emotional suppression. He was moody and temperamental. Although he functioned well and was productive, there were depressive tendencies in his personality. Disciplined habits of a lifetime, a deep sense of responsibility, well-intended civility, and a willfulness allowed him to maintain a well-ordered life. But he was agitated and anxious under the surface. Apprehensions made him tentative in unfamiliar settings. There are indications of fatigue, that he was being worn down while making an effort to maintain himself.

Norman D. Warne followed the conventions of his time and the expectations of his educational [social] class. While taking his social responsibilities seriously, he also tended to withdraw into his own intellectual world.

Sometime in the middle of May of 1905, Norman Warne who "had never been robust" (Lane, 1946, p. 85) became ill. Beatrix Potter's letters around that time do not disclose if initially she was greatly concerned about his condition. On June 6th she wrote to him: "I am not going away until after Whitsuntide, but probably you are?" (*Letters*, p. 118). In the postscript of her letter two days later (June 8th), however, she wrote: "I wish another book could be planned out before the summer, if we are going on with them, I always feel very much lost when they are finished" (*Letters*, p. 120). While the statement clearly had to do with her literary productivity and the publisher's acceptance of her books, we may wonder whether her wording "if we are going on with them" and "I always feel very much lost when they are finished" alluded to some of her concerns about him and about the fate of their relationship. This supposition seems to be confirmed in her postscript to her letter to Norman Warne two weeks later (June 26th) in which she wrote: "I do so *hate* finishing books, I would like to go on with them for years" (*Letters*, p. 121). Her postscript was metaphoric. It seemed to imply that not only was she afraid of the books being completed and that she would have nothing else creative to do, but also that by completing them, she might lose her relationship with Norman Warne.

In the body of her letter of June 26th she wrote to him: "It is Hunca Munca's travelling box [that Norman Warne had made for her (see chapter 9)] that is shaky, it seems a shame to ask for joinering when it is such fine evenings, but perhaps it would not take so long to mend, I had so very much pleasure from her other little house" (*Letters*, p. 121).

While Beatrix Potter's concern was about Hunca Munca's traveling box and spending Norman Warne's time in "joinering" rather than in other pleasureful activities, we may suspect that it was also a metaphor for her concern about *his* "shaky condition."

In her letter to him on July 2, 1905, she writes: "I enclose the remainder of Tiggy, regretfully; I began that story in Aug. 86 [1886], & I am just beginning to be able to do it—and without undue 'slaving!' What saith the proverb; 'a spaniel, a woman, and a walnut tree—the more you beat them—the better they be?' " (*Letters*, p. 121).

We do not know how Norman Warne responded to her letter but two days later, in a postscript to her letter, she wrote:

"I fancy your reading of the proverb is right!" (*Letters*, p. 122). We must consider that Beatrix Potter's statement, written to the man who she hoped would become her husband, was somewhat masochistic. After all she was brought up in an era when children, even as adults, had to ask their parents' permission to marry. Any steps leading to such a decision were subject to considerable soul searching and conflict, especially as she knew of her parents' disapproval of her relationship to him. Beatrix Potter was a dutiful daughter so that any thought or intention of opposing her parents' wishes was bound to evoke tremendous guilt feelings. It would not be difficult to suppose that despite her loving Norman Warne and wishing to marry him, the continual badgering from her parents had the effect of increasing her guilt feelings for wanting to go against their wishes. By citing the proverb to Norman Warne she clearly expressed the intensity of her own guilt feelings about their relationship and her unconscious need to be punished and beaten for her feelings toward him.

It can be seen from Norman Warne's medical record that he was already ill when Beatrix Potter wrote to him on July 21st: "I am sorry you have had toothache & the dentist, it is horrid in hot weather" (*Letters*, p. 122). Her remark may have referred to more than a concern about his toothache as by now she certainly must have realized that Norman Warne's physical condition was becoming serious. That she suspected how grave it was may be seen from her comments in the next paragraph of her letter to him:

> I have made a little doll of poor Hunca Munca, I cannot forgive myself for letting her tumble. I do so miss her. She fell off the chandelier, she managed to stagger up the staircase into your little house, but she died in my hand about 10 minutes after. I think if I had broken my own neck it would have saved a deal of trouble. I should like to get some new work fixed before going away to Wales. I am feeling all right for work, but *very worried* [*Letters*, p. 122; emphasis added].

114

Four days later, on July 25th, Beatrix Potter received a letter from Norman Warne asking her to marry him, and she accepted. Her parents were openly opposed. Taylor writes:

> The Potters were horrified, in particular Beatrix's mother, for after all Norman was "in trade," and even though Beatrix was now thirty-nine, it was not usual for a young lady to go against her parents' wishes. Beatrix, however, was determined to marry Norman and she agreed to a compromise. She would wear his ring but there would be no announcement and the engagement would be kept a secret from all but the immediate families [*Letters*, p. 123].

This was a sharp contrast to the attitude of Norman Warne's family. His widowed mother and his sister, Millie, with whom Norman lived, accepted her warmly. Her delight at Norman Warne's proposal was tempered not only by her parents' disapproval but also by her worry about his condition.

Less than a week later (July 30th) Beatrix Potter wrote to Harold Warne: "I will call on Monday morning at the office; I shall bring Miss Florrie Hammond with me. You will not think me very cross if I say I would rather *not* talk much *yet* about that business? though I am *very glad* you have been told" (*Letters*, p. 124). The reference to Florrie Hammond was to her governess who remained a faithful employee of the family. Evidently Beatrix Potter did not want her to know about her engagement to Norman. In the same letter she wrote:

> I do trust that your brother is not going to be very ill, I got scared before he went to Manchester, wondering if he had been drinking bad water.
> I shall be able to ask you after his health, as Miss Florrie is not quite "all there" & stone-deaf!
> It is a very awkward way of happening; I think he [Norman] is going a little too fast now that he has started; but I trust it may come right in the end [*Letters*, p. 124].

Taylor (1986) writes that three weeks after Norman Warne's letter of proposal he was so ill that his mother, on her eightieth birthday, wrote to one of her grandchildren of the family's concern: "I wish dear Norman was getting better, but it is very slow work. He is so weak and cannot take anything but milk. He keeps very cheerful for all that but he can hardly stand" (p. 102).

We are able to learn a great deal about Beatrix Potter's reaction to Norman Warne's proposal from a letter she wrote some six months later (February 1, 1906) from Bath, to Millie, Norman Warne's unmarried sister Amelia, whom Norman affectionately called "Old Mill." In that letter she wrote about the names of the streets in Bath and said:

> I find the names of the streets rather melancholy here, do you remember Miss Austin's [sic] "Persuasion" with all the scenes & streets in Bath? It was always my favourite and I read the end part of it again last July, on the 26th the day after I got Norman's letter, I thought my story had come right with patience & waiting like Anne Eliott's [sic] did [*Letters*, p. 139].

To understand Beatrix Potter's reference let us digress at this point to summarize Jane Austen's *Persuasion*, written between 1815 and 1816 and published posthumously in 1818.

The book begins by describing Sir Walter Elliot, a baronet, who was born on March 1, 1760. At the age of 24 he married Elizabeth Stevenson. They had three daughters and one stillborn son. His eldest daughter, Elizabeth, was two years older than Anne, the heroine of the story. Mary, the youngest daughter, was born when Anne was 4 years of age. The children's mother died in 1800 when Anne was 13.

Sir Walter is portrayed as a silly, narrow-minded, pretentious man who boasted of his lineage and took great pains to try to impress everyone with the importance of his social position. He lived at Kellynch Hall with Elizabeth and Anne, both of whom were unmarried. To a great extent, Elizabeth was identified with her father's personality and shared his sense of values. Totally conceited and highly narcissistic, she lorded it over Anne.

As the story opens, Sir Walter, ever impressed by material considerations, finds himself in rather impoverished circumstances. To avoid embarrassment he finally decides to rent Kellynch Hall to Admiral Croft and his wife and move to Bath.

One of Mrs. Croft's brothers was Captain Frederick Wentworth who, at the time the story begins, was in the Navy. He was very successful and wealthy. This had not been so eight years earlier when he and Anne, then 19, had fallen in love. Sir Walter withheld his consent for their marriage, viewing the relationship between Anne and Captain Wentworth as "a very degrading alliance" (p. 55). He felt that Frederick Wentworth, who was not wealthy, had no prospects of becoming successful, even though the young man himself was confident that he would be rich and successful. To make matters worse, Lady Russell, a very wealthy widow and a friend of the family, who was fond of Anne, also opposed the union. While Lady Russell viewed Captain Wentworth as brilliant, she felt he was headstrong and believed that any permanent relationship with Anne was potentially unstable. As a result, she used all her power to persuade Anne to give up her lover. Anne finally agreed to do so and Wentworth left the area.

Now, Anne was 27. While she did not blame Lady Russell for having persuaded her to give up Captain Wentworth, she felt that she would have been a happier woman if she had maintained her engagement to him.

Despite Anne's objections, her father and Elizabeth decided to move to Bath. Before their residence was available, they moved for a time to Uppercross Cottage, some three miles away from Kellynch Hall.

Anne's sister, Mary, was an infantile, hysterical woman, given to hypochondriacal complaints and a marked tendency to exaggerate her physical indispositions or disabilities. On the other hand, her husband, Charles Musgrove, who had at one time been attentive to Anne, was described as superior to his wife in sense and temper. Unfortunately, he "did nothing with much zeal, but sport; and his time was otherwise trifled away" (p. 70).

Initially, when Captain Wentworth appeared upon the scene, Anne wanted to see him after the years of separation, yet she found many reasons to put off the meeting. When she finally did meet him, she found him more manly and open, and viewed him as the same young man that she had fallen in love with some eight years before. Captain Wentworth on the other hand:

> [T]hought her wretchedly altered, and. . . . He had not forgiven Anne Elliot. She had used him ill; deserted and disappointed him; and worse, she had shewn a feebleness of character in doing so, which his own decided, confident temper could not endure. She had given him up to oblige others. It had been the effect of over-persuasion. It had been weakness and timidity. . . . he had no desire of meeting her again. Her power with him was gone for ever [p. 86].

Now it was his desire to marry and he was interested in one of Charles Musgrove's sisters. As time went on, Captain Wentworth and Anne Elliot were often in each other's company, but they did not really talk to one another other than what the "commonest civility required" (p. 88). Anne was not sure what his feelings were toward her but felt that he was indifferent. He seemed to be interested in Louisa Musgrove, Mary's sister-in-law. Jane Austen implies that Captain Wentworth's attentiveness toward Louisa was a reaction to his feelings of depression and anger resulting from Anne's rejection of him.

One day the young people went to Lyme Regis and were at the Cobb (a pier or breakwater). Louisa was jumping off some stairs and despite Captain's Wentworth's cautioning her not to jump any more, she did so, fell, and hit her head. She was unconscious and it appeared that she suffered a concussion. The party was panicky and indecisive but Anne Elliot took over and directed their activities, insisting that they call for professional help.

It took some weeks for Louisa to recover fully from the effects of her injury. During this time the relationship between the Captain and Louisa evidently deteriorated and she became interested in another man. Anne felt that Captain Wentworth's relationship to her now had an opportunity to develop again.

In the meantime a Mr. William Elliot, a distant cousin who was heir to Sir Walter's title and estate, began to show attention to Anne. Although she found his interest in her somewhat agreeable, she clearly did not like him and refused his overtures. Later she discovered from a friend of hers that his character was rather disreputable. Captain Wentworth, however, not realizing that Anne had absolutely no interest in Mr. Elliot, was jealous of their relationship. Once again he felt that he had no chance with her, that matters were just as they had been when she had rejected him eight years before.

Jane Austen wrote two versions of the ending. One version was initially censored; the other version was published. As it is more than likely that Beatrix Potter was familiar with the published version and read this on July 26th, "the day after [she] got Norman's letter," we will relate that ending here.

Anne's sister, Elizabeth, invited Captain Wentworth to attend a party at Bath. He was not certain if he wanted to go to the party, however, because he was afraid that Anne was interested in Mr. Elliot. Finally, as he was very disturbed by this, he wrote a letter to Anne.

I can listen no longer in silence. I must speak to you by such means as are within my reach. You pierce my soul. I am half agony, half hope. Tell me not that I am too late, that such precious feelings are gone for ever. I offer myself to you again with a heart even more your own, than when you almost broke it eight years and a half ago. Dare not say that man forgets sooner than woman, that his love has an earlier death. I have loved none but you. Unjust I may have been, weak and resentful I have been, but never inconstant. You alone have brought me to Bath. For you alone I think and plan.—Have you not seen this? Can you fail to have understood my wishes?—I had not waited even these ten days, could I have read your feelings as I

think you must have penetrated mine. I can hardly write. I am
every instant hearing something which overpowers me. You sink
your voice, but I can distinguish the tones of that voice, when
they would be lost on others.—Too good, too excellent creature!
You do us justice indeed. You do believe that there is true attachment and constancy among men. Believe it to be most fervent,
most undeviating in

F.W.
    I must go, uncertain of my fate; but I shall return hither,
or follow your party, as soon as possible. A word, a look will be
enough to decide whether I enter your father's house this evening or never [p. 240].

Anne was ecstatic when she read Wentworth's letter. They were
now able to talk to each other. She realized that the captain's
jealousy of Mr. Elliot had prevented him from approaching
her, evidently fearing that she would reject him once more.

    It was a happy reunion of two lovers. At one point, Anne
Elliot says:

You should not have suspected me now; the case so different,
and my age so different. If I was wrong in yielding to persuasion
once, remember that it was to persuasion exerted on the side of
safety, not of risk. When I yielded, I thought it was to duty; but
no duty could be called in aid here [p. 246].

Captain Wentworth blamed himself, saying: "I could think of
you only as one who had yielded, who had given me up, who
had been influenced by any one rather than by me. I saw you
with the very person who had guided you in that year of misery.
I had no reason to believe her [Lady Russell] of less authority
now" (pp. 246–247).

    Later on in a conversation between them Anne remarked:

I have been thinking over the past, and trying impartially to
judge of the right and wrong, I mean with regard to myself;
and I must believe that I was right, much as I suffered from it,
that I was perfectly right in being guided by the friend [Lady
Russell]. . . . To me, she was in the place of a parent. Do not
mistake me, however, I am not saying that she did not err in
her advice. It was, perhaps, one of those cases in which advice

is good or bad only as the event decides; and for myself, I certainly never should, in any circumstance of tolerable similarity, give such advice. But I mean that I was right in submitting to her, and that if I had done otherwise, I should have suffered more in continuing the engagement than I did even in giving it up, because I should have suffered in my conscience. . . . and if I mistake not, a strong sense of duty is no bad part of a woman's portion [p. 248].

Captain Wentworth asked Anne if she would have answered his letter if he had written to her when he returned to England a few years back with a thousand pounds. She replied that she certainly would have.

After this the couple is reunited and Sir Walter Elliot and Lady Russell give their approval for the marriage to take place.

In the initial censored version of the ending, now also published, Captain Wentworth's letter is completely omitted. The denouement of the understanding between Anne Elliot and Captain Wentworth is accomplished through a question. Admiral Croft asks him to ask Anne whether she plans to marry Mr. William Elliot. When she tells the Captain in no uncertain terms that she has no interest in Mr. Elliot, he then declares his love for her and the couple is reunited.

There are a number of striking points in *Persuasion* that must have influenced Beatrix Potter to reread the last part of the book, with which she was thoroughly familiar, after receiving Norman's letter proposing marriage. She must have felt a deep sense of kinship with Anne Elliot, a well-read, highly sublimated, sensitive, artistic woman, who was deeply in love with Captain Wentworth.

Anne Elliot, the heroine of the novel, and Beatrix Potter both received a proposal of marriage in a letter from the men they loved. In the story Anne Elliot had been discouraged from marrying Captain Wentworth by her conceited father and by her well-meaning mother-substitute, Lady Russell. In the real-life situation, as we know, Beatrix Potter was also discouraged by her patents who were condemnatory of her involvement with Norman Warne.

In the story Sir Walter's values are sham, and Jane Austen skillfully documents his materialistic values showing them to be representative of those in the society in which they lived. It was Anne Elliot who rebelled against their superficiality. In the case of Beatrix Potter's parents, their materialistic and shallow values, as exemplified by their contempt toward Norman Warne and his family for being "in trade," were similar to the shallow values of the Elliots. Beatrix Potter thoroughly disagreed with them and rebelled against them, ultimately wanting to free herself completely from their life-style.

In the story, Captain Wentworth, though brave and ambitious, fears that if he allowed himself to express an interest in Anne Elliot, he would be rejected again as he had been before. Perhaps Beatrix Potter felt that like Captain Wentworth, Norman Warne was uncertain whether she reciprocated his affection for her and feared that, like Anne Elliot, she would reject him because of her parents' disapproval.

Anne Elliot's story "came right with patience and waiting" and had a happy ending. In addition, Anne reconciles with Lady Russell, forgiving her for her original disapproval of the relationship. Whereas Anne Elliot admits that she "was wrong in yielding to persuasion once," she believes "it was to persuasion exerted on the side of safety, not of risk." She goes on to say: "I was right in submitting to [Lady Russell] and that if I had done otherwise, I should have suffered more in continuing the engagement than I did even in giving it up, because I should have suffered in my conscience." These lines must have clearly expressed the storm in Beatrix Potter's mind when she received Norman's letter of proposal.

It is indeed a sad irony of fate that Jane Austen herself lost a prospective husband through death in the summer of 1802.

On Friday, August 25, 1905, a month after his letter of proposal to Beatrix Potter, Norman Dalziel Warne died at the age of 37 at his home in London. Linder (1971) writes: "Thus ended four happy years of close co-operation, during which period they had planned and produced the first seven of Beatrix Potter's books. Although Norman Warne did not live to see the published book [*The Pie and the Patty-pan*], he had seen it in its final stages" (p. 172). On his death certificate, Arthur Ricketts, M.D. stated that the cause of his death was lymphatic leucocythaemia of two and a half months duration. His brother, Fruing Warne, was present at his death. Beatrix Potter was in Wales visiting an uncle at the time Norman Warne died.

In the provisions of his will Norman Warne appointed his brothers, Harold Edmund and William Fruing to be the executors and trustees of his estate, giving all his property interest in Frederick Warne to them. He instructed them to distribute the monies derived from this investment as follows: one fourth to his sister, Amelia Louisa Warne; one fourth to Harold Edmund Warne; one fourth to William Fruing Warne; one fourth to be held in trust for his nephew Frederick Warne Stephens but this part was to be paid to his mother during her lifetime. He also willed £1000 to be held in trust for his niece, Jane Fruing Stephens, and £250 for his godson, Norman Dane Dumaresq. Beatrix Potter was not mentioned in his will.

Norman's Warne's death was a terrible shock to Beatrix Potter. We can only infer the depth and degree of her love for this man who, as far as we know, was her first adult love and the passport by which she could leave home forever and be a free woman in her own right. As may be expected, she received little sympathy from her parents when Norman Warne died. Millie Warne, Norman's unmarried sister, was a great source of consolation however. The friendship between the two women continued throughout Beatrix Potter's lifetime. Norman Warne's mother was entirely supportive, as was Fruing, his wife, and children, and the other members of the Warne family who had accepted her completely.

It is of great credit to Beatrix Potter's indomitable spirit that she was able to return to her creative work. On September

5th, ten days after Norman Warne's death, she wrote to his brother, Harold, from Gwaynynog, Denbigh, in north Wales that the proof sheets of *Tiggy-Winkle* had arrived and then stated: "It will be a trying thing to come for the first time to the office, but there is no help for it. I have begun sketching again; I am badly behind with my stock of summer work but I shall be able to make it up if there is a fine autumn" (*Letters*, p. 125). The difficult and painful work of mourning Norman Warne's death lay ahead.

## Chapter 13

# The Tale of Mr. Jeremy Fisher
## (1906a) [1893, 1905]

On July 30, 1892, Beatrix Potter wrote in her *Journal* from Heath Park, Birnam, near Dunkeld that she had been busy that morning completing a drawing of a jackdaw for Nister, adding "for which, by the way, they have not paid" (p. 249). She had sold a few drawings to this company which, two years later, purchased nine of her drawings entitled, "A Frog he would a-fishing go" and published them in a children's annual during the 1890s[1] (Linder, 1971, p. 178).

We learn that on September 5, 1893, the day after she had written her now famous Peter Rabbit letter to Noel Moore, she wrote a six-page picture letter to his brother, Eric, telling him some things about Mr. Jeremy Fisher.[2] Then on October 11, 1895, Beatrix Potter wrote to Margery (Molly) Gaddum telling her the story briefly but without mentioning the name Jeremy Fisher. She enclosed seven drawings (*Children*, pp. 98–99).

---

[1]Linder notes that the imprint was "London: Ernest Nister and New York: E. P. Dutton & Co. The book was printed in Bavaria and was called *Comical Customers*" (p. 178).

[2]Taylor writes that "the last time that letter was seen in public was in 1947 when it was sold in the same auction with so many of Noel's letters" (*Children*, p. 17). The whereabouts of this letter are still unknown.

Nothing further seems to have been done about Beatrix Potter's frog story until November 6, 1902, when she wrote to Norman Warne that she would like to do Mr. Jeremy Fisher some day: "I think I could make something of him" (Linder, 1971, p. 178). As time went on, there was the matter of the copyright on the drawings which Beatrix Potter finally bought back from Nister for six pounds "directly after Peter Rabbit was printed" (Linder, 1971, p. 178). On February 3, 1905, when she sent Norman Warne a draft of *Jeremy Fisher* together with *The Pie and the Patty-pan* she wrote that he did not need to "bother to read them before hand if [he was] busy" (*Letters*, p. 112).

Some ten days after Norman Warne's death, on September 5, 1905, Beatrix Potter wrote to his brother Harold that she and Norman had thought of doing a book about the frog. She writes: "I know some people don't like frogs! But I think I had convinced Norman that I could make it a really pretty book with a good many flowers and water plants for backgrounds. The book would be easy and plain sailing" (*Letters*, p. 125).

While Beatrix Potter may have had practical reasons for suggesting to Harold Warne that they consider publishing the story of *Jeremy Fisher* at this time, there was more to it. It had been a promise to Norman and as such, it was imperative that it be kept. Perhaps she felt she owed it to him. Promises made to someone who dies are often experienced as sacred vows.

Later that year (December 18, 1905) she informed Winifred Warne that she had been drawing "a frog with a fishing rod" and thought that it was going to be a funny book (*Letters*, pp. 137–138).

Beatrix Potter continued to work on the book which was published in early 1906 and dedicated to Stephanie Hyde-Parker from "Cousin B."

The story deals with Mr. Jeremy Fisher, a frog, who decides to go fishing when it begins to rain. He wants to catch some minnows for his dinner thinking that if he caught more than five, he would invite his friends, Sir Isaac Newton and Mr. Alderman Ptolemy Tortoise, even though Mr. Alderman only ate salad.

Putting on his mackintosh and a pair of galoshes, and carrying his rod and basket, Mr. Jeremy Fisher went to his boat (actually a water lily leaf). After about an hour he became bored and ate a butterfly sandwich for lunch. First, a water beetle "tweaked the toe of one of his goloshes" and then a stickleback bit at the bait but escaped after injuring Jeremy Fisher's fingers. Some small fishes laughed at Mr. Jeremy Fisher.

Suddenly a large trout grabbed Mr. Jeremy Fisher and dived down to the bottom of the pond with him in his mouth. Not liking the taste of the mackintosh, the trout spat him out and only swallowed his galoshes. Jeremy Fisher managed to swim to shore, still wearing his torn raincoat, scrambled out of the pond, and hopped across the meadow, relieved that he had not been caught by the pike. Even though he had lost his rod, he consoled himself that it didn't matter because he was certain that he would never dare to go fishing again.

His friends did come to dinner, the Alderman Ptolemy Tortoise bringing a salad in a bag. Instead of minnows, they had roasted grasshopper with lady-bird sauce, which Beatrix Potter thinks "must have been nasty" even though frogs "consider [it] a beautiful treat" (Potter, 1906a, p. 59).

Beatrix Potter freely admitted that she was influenced by the work of Randolph Caldecott who had drawn a series of illustrations for a book entitled *A Frog He Would A-Wooing Go* (1883). She said that she had tried to copy his work unsuccessfully (*Letters*, pp. 454–455; *Children*, p. 140).

In this connection Taylor (Potter, 1992) points out the significance of Beatrix Potter's letters to Andrew (Drew) Fayle.[3] She writes:

---

[3]According to Taylor (Potter, 1992), "All that is known about Andrew Fayle is that in 1909 he wrote to Beatrix Potter from a house called 'Kylemore' in Rathgar, which was at the time a fashionable Dublin suburb" (p. 140).

One of the Fayle letters is unique among the miniature letters so far discovered in that it is signed by an animal character that does not come from one of the Potter books. Anthony Rowley first appeared in the early nineteenth-century version of the popular song "The Love-sick Frog," but Beatrix was familiar with him through Randolph Caldecott's picture book, *A Frog He Would A-Wooing Go*, published in 1883. . . . Beatrix's own first drawings for *The Tale of Mr. Jeremy Fisher* had been used in 1896 by the publisher Ernest Nister to illustrate yet another version of the song called "A Frog he would a-fishing go," although Anthony Rowley was not present on that occasion [*Children*, pp. 140–141].

In Beatrix Potter's letter to "Master Drew," she wrote the following, over the signature of Sir Isaac Newton:

Dear Master Drew,

I hear that you think that there ought to be a "Mrs. J. Fisher." Our friend is at present taking mud baths at the bottom of the pond, which may be the reason why your letter has not been answered quick by return. I will do my best to advise him, but I fear he remembers the sad fate of his elder brother ['Froggy' in *A Frog He Would A-Wooing Go*] who disobeyed his mother, and he was gobbled up by a lily white duck! [*Children*, p. 142].

Caldecott's version generally follows the traditional poem as given in Opie and Opie (1951, pp. 177–181). The poem begins:

> A frog he would a-wooing go,
>   Heigh ho! says Rowley,
> A frog he would a-wooing go,
> Whether his mother would let him or no.
>   With a rowley, powley, gammon and spinach,
>   Heigh ho! says Anthony Rowley [p. 177].

The frog then goes off wearing an opera hat. He meets a rat and the two go off to see Mrs. Mousey. (In the Caldecott version it is *Miss* Mousey.) The mouse lets them in. She is going to spin.

They ask her for some beer. The mouse then asks the frog for a song but tells him it should not be very long. When he replies that he has a cold that has made him as hoarse as a dog, she decides to sing a song that she has made up. While they are thus merrymaking a cat and her kittens come in. The cat seizes the rat by the crown and the kittens hold the little mouse down. Taking his hat and wishing them goodnight, the frog escapes but, as he was crossing the brook, a lily white duck gobbles him up.

> So there was an end of one, two, three,
>    Heigh ho! says Rowley,
> The rat, the mouse, and the little frogg-ee.
>    With a rowley, powley, gammon and spinach,
>    Heigh ho! says Anthony Rowley [p. 179].

In Caldecott's version of the poem the initial picture shows the frog, carrying a bunch of flowers, and asking his mother's permission to go wooing. Her expression is singularly prohibitive and angry. There is no reference to the frog going fishing.

In contrast to the Caldecott picture book, Beatrix Potter's story completely omits the frog's romantic interests. Whereas in the original story the frog is punished for disobeying his mother, as she noted in her letter to Master Drew, and pursuing his instinctual urges of a heterosexual nature, Beatrix Potter's story deals solely with his fishing and with his almost fatal encounter with the trout. The consequences of the frog's wishes in the original story are his own death, the death of the rat, and of the mouse. In Beatrix Potter's version the frog's life is spared at the price of sacrificing his rod, basket, and galoshes. In Beatrix Potter's original illustrations for Nister, the frog gives up his wish to go fishing (he decides that he "has had enough of fishing") after his fingers have been nipped by a fish (Linder, 1971, p. 181). In Beatrix Potter's published version, the frog's decision is final: "I am sure I should never have dared to go fishing again." The basic idea expressed in Beatrix Potter's story is that the pursuit of any instinctual tendency, whether sexual or aggressive, will be punished. The familiar theme of sacrificing a body equivalent, such as we have seen with Peter Rabbit who "loses" his coat and shoes to save himself, is expressed here. And, if we add the reference to Caldecott to this formulation, the punishment is to be meted out by the angry and forbidding mother. In this way the theme of the dangerous mother figure that we have seen in the reference to Lady Macbeth in *The Tale of Mrs. Tiggy-Winkle* is continued. Because of her parents' (largely her mother's) criticism of her relationship to Norman Warne, it is almost as though she took literally the Biblical injunction that: "The wages of sin is death" (Romans, VI, 23).

The two stories, *The Pie and the Patty-pan* and *The Tale of Mr. Jeremy Fisher*, may be considered complementary. The former deals with her mother and her social circle of ladies, whom Beatrix Potter regarded as prejudiced and silly, engaging in idle, catty small talk and not listening to each other. The latter story deals with her father, and perhaps *his* friends, whom she may have viewed as being unempathic and having narrow-minded attitudes. In this respect she views her father as Sir Walter Elliot in *Persuasion*. We may see, therefore, that through her creative efforts Beatrix Potter was able to take another step toward independence from her parents. By her satirization of them in these two stories, she was able to distance herself from their hurtful attitudes.

## Chapter 14

# Three Brief Stories

*The Story of a Fierce Bad Rabbit* (1906b)
*The Story of Miss Moppet* (1906c)
*The Sly Old Cat* (1971) [1906]

Any loss of a love object to which an individual is exposed results in a disturbance of psychic equilibrium that must then be restored by the process of mourning. This involves a gradual loosening or cutting of the ties that have bound the person to that object and the investing of his or her energies in some other object or some other interest or activity. The process itself is a silent and lengthy one, differentiated from the initial reaction of grief following the death of a loved one. It is accompanied by pain and a degree of regression to earlier attachments, or to memories or experiences with other objects with which the lost object may have been associated in the mourner's mind. Regressions that occur under those circumstances often bring about a return to and a reconsideration of childhood problems and conflicts. As the process involves detachment or severing of ties from the object, the process itself mobilizes aggression. This only adds to the pain because it leads to feelings of remorse and guilt for the ambivalent feelings toward the lost love object which are a natural part of any love relationship. When the relationship is ended by death, there is also the further problem of dealing with the anger and aggressive feelings toward the dead person for dying and leaving one to mourn. It is understandable that a great many factors influence the duration and success of the mourning process. Such was the case with Beatrix Potter after the death of Norman Warne. What followed was for her an extremely difficult and confused period of transition to a new life.

Sometime in the early summer of 1905, before Beatrix Potter accepted Norman Warne's proposal of marriage in July of that year, she had purchased Hill Top Farm in the village of Near Sawrey (*Letters*, p. 132). Following his death she became increasingly more focused toward the goal of moving away from London and establishing a residence in the Lake District. To accomplish this she began the serious work of having the property renovated. She engaged Mr. and Mrs. John Cannon, who were farming the land, to work for her, allowing them to stay in her house. Beatrix Potter did not live in the Lake District until 1913. She stayed at Hill Top occasionally but according to Taylor (1986) she "was not able to spend more than a month out of the year" because of her close ties to her parents. She would go to Sawrey "for a few days whenever she could get away" (p. 108). During this time her books were becoming popular and this provided her with a good source of income and financial independence. Now she plunged into a flurry of creative activity. While she was working on *The Tale of Mr. Jeremy Fisher* she did a considerable amount of drawing and sketching for her other projects. Early in 1906 she prepared three short stories for children (*The Story of the Fierce Bad Rabbit, The Story of Miss Moppet,* and *The Sly Old Cat*). Only the first two of the stories were published. The third, *The Sly Old Cat*, was not published until 1971. Linder (1971) included the text and original illustrations in the first edition of *A History of the Writings of Beatrix Potter*.

*Three Brief Stories*

## The Story of the Fierce Bad Rabbit

Harold Warne's daughter, Louie, had told Beatrix Potter that Peter was too good a rabbit, and she wanted a story about a "really naughty" one. This little story was written especially for her. The manuscript is dated February 23, 1906.

The "bad" rabbit who had "savage whiskers" and a "turned up tail" aggressively took a carrot away from the "good" rabbit, scratched him, and chased him into a hole. As the "bad" rabbit sat munching this appropriated carrot, a man shot at him. The rabbit ran away, leaving his partially eaten carrot behind him. Beatrix Potter's pictures show that the "bad" rabbit lost his tail and his whiskers.

We may understand that this little story describes the punishment for the "bad" rabbit's aggression. The specific mention of the rabbit who has "a turned up tail" which the hunter blasts off, symbolically indicates castration, a theme we have seen in *Peter Rabbit* and *Squirrel Nutkin*. In this instance the punishing figure is a man who combines the punitive and aggressive attributes of Mr. McGregor and Old Brown.

While the stimulus for this story was Louie Warne's request, Beatrix Potter's agreement to write it, and its specific content, were based on her own dynamics evidenced by the fact that she had repeatedly dealt with similar material before. In this case, the life of the rabbit is spared in accordance with the well-known formula of "part for the whole." Beatrix Potter has the rabbit's whiskers and tail shot off but the rabbit himself in otherwise unhurt. From any reality standpoint it is, of course, highly unlikely that anyone could succeed in shooting a rabbit in such a fashion that he does not kill him but only blasts away his whiskers and tail. We may understand that the emergence of such a story at this particular time may have to do with Beatrix Potter's confused feelings about aggression, punishment for it, and guilt in connection with her reaction to Norman Warne's death.

## The Story of Miss Moppet

This short story tells of a mouse who peeped out from behind a cupboard to make fun of a kitten named Miss Moppet. When the kitten jumped to catch the mouse, she missed him and bumped her head in the process. In an effort to catch the mouse, Miss Moppet tried to trick him by tying up her head in a duster and pretending that her head hurt, presumably from bumping it. Through a hole in the duster, however, the kitten carefully watched the mouse. As the mouse approached her, she suddenly pounced on him, caught him by his tail, and then tied him up in the duster. As Miss Moppet intended to tease the mouse just as the mouse had teased her, she tossed the mouse up in the air like a ball. The mouse, however, managed to escape through the hole in the duster and danced a jig on the cupboard.

This little story expresses a kind of play indulged in by children in which there are elements of teasing and controlled aggression. In her story Beatrix Potter attempts to rationalize Miss Moppet's aggression against the mouse on the basis of the mouse's having teased her. On a draft of one of her illustrations, which shows Miss Moppet's left front paw on the mouse's tail, she wrote: "She should catch him by the tail—less unpleasant" (Taylor, Whalley, Hobbs, and Battrick, 1987, p. 129). Beatrix Potter then comments critically that it "is not at all nice of Miss Moppet" to tease the mouse by tossing it in the duster as one would a ball. We may conjecture that Beatrix Potter probably saw instances of such aggressive play among children and may even have played such games as ball, hide and seek, and even peek-a-boo (games alluded to here) with her brother, Bertram. Her rivalry with her brother was readily understandable not only because he was her younger sibling but also because he was a boy. Beatrix Potter's critical remarks seem to echo a parent's or guardian's critical view of the aggressive aspects of such behavior.

*Three Brief Stories*

## The Sly Old Cat

The plot of *The Sly Old Cat* is also quite simple. A cat invited a rat to a tea party. She greeted him with consummate politeness but then set forth a number of "rules" for the tea party. She would eat her bread and butter first and then the rat could have the crumbs that were left. She would drink her tea next and the rat would lick up the drops that were left in the milk jug. After that, the cat would have her dessert. The rat felt that the cat was very rude to him and that she intended to eat him for her dessert.

As the cat tipped the milk jug to drink out of it, the rat pushed the jug over the cat's head. While she was banging about trying to get free of the jug, the rat drank the rest of the tea, put the muffin in a paper bag, and went home where he ate it in one sitting. In the meantime, the cat finally got free of the jug by breaking it against the leg of a table.

Basically, the story of *The Sly Old Cat* expresses the familiar complaint heard among siblings that one sibling gets all of the food or rewards and the other feels that he or she is left with nothing but the crumbs. In *The Sly Old Cat*, the relationship between the cat and the rat is somewhat ambivalent. The rat believes that the cat will eat him for dessert, because of the very nature of cat and rat relationships. If he really was convinced of that, however, then why would he have accepted the invitation to go to the cat's house for dinner in the first place? At a crucial point, however, the rat's aggression is unleashed. He shoves the jug over the cat's head, appropriates the muffin, and leaves triumphantly.

Furthermore, we may ask, what kind of host is he who sets such impossible, rude rules of social conduct? This type of behavior can be frequently found among children when the dominant child sets forth rules and the other child seems to agree for a time but ultimately finds that the rules are intolerable.

There seems to be more to it in this example, however. In the title of the story Beatrix Potter indicates that the cat is old as well as sly. We may readily suspect then that the emphasis in this story is not so much on sibling rivalry but rather on the situation in which it is the parents or guardians that set the rules which the child must obey. After a certain point the child has had enough and the accumulated aggression against the authorities finally emerges.

It is significant that the first of these stories was written about six months (February 23, 1906) after Norman Warne's sudden death, a loss that was terribly traumatic for Beatrix Potter. Her flurry of creative activity served as a way to help her deal with her reactions to his death. It enabled her actively to bring about a controlled regression in the service of the mourning process. As we indicated earlier, regressions that occur under those circumstances often bring about a return to and a reconsideration of childhood problems and conflicts. We may suppose then that Beatrix Potter utilized material from her own childhood, reviving in various ways important and highly emotionally charged conflicts with which she had been confronted as she was growing up. It was a safe way for her to express her feelings about the repressed aggressions that she felt not only toward Norman Warne but also those feelings she had experienced throughout her developmental years.

## Chapter 15

# The Tale of Tom Kitten
## (1907) [1906]

*The Tale of Tom Kitten*, begun in the summer of 1906, continued Beatrix Potter's work of mourning Norman Warne's death. The story was published the following year and was dedicated to: "ALL PICKLES[1],—especially to those that get upon my garden wall" (Potter, 1907, p. 7). The garden wall was located on Beatrix Potter's Hill Top farm at Sawrey.

This story is about Mrs. Tabitha Twitchit and her three kittens whose names are Mittens, Tom Kitten, and Moppet. Tabitha Twitchit was expecting her friends for tea on this particular occasion, so she washed and dressed the kittens. Tom had grown so much that his clothes did not fit properly and he was uncomfortable wearing them. Tabitha Twitchit let the kittens go out into the garden, setting limits where they could go. She instructed them to keep their clothes clean and to walk on their hind legs. As may be expected, the kittens got their clothes dirty and even lost some of them while playing and jumping about. Tom Kitten lost his hat and some of the buttons on his tight-fitting clothing.

---

[1]"Pickles" is an English term meaning, affectionately, pests—as children can be—troublesome or mischievious kids.

Three ducks came along and two of them put on Tom's hat and Moppet's tucker. The kittens, watching the ducks and amused at their antics, fell off the garden wall on which they were sitting. In the process, Tom's clothes all came off and the drake put them on.

Pretty soon Tabitha Twitchit came out into the garden and found the kittens sitting on the wall again but none of them had any clothes on. "She pulled them off the wall, smacked them, and took them back to the house" (p. 49). Very angry with the kittens she sent them upstairs because her friends would be arriving shortly. When they arrived, Tabitha Twitchit told them a lie: that the kittens were in bed with the measles. The kittens, however, went on a rampage in the bedroom, creating a good deal of commotion and noise, which "disturbed the dignity and repose of the tea party" (p. 53).

It is of interest to note that during the preparation of the manuscript for publication, Harold Warne apparently criticized Beatrix Potter for writing that "all the rest of Tom's clothes came off" and wanted her to insert the word "nearly" before the word "all" [i.e., nearly all]. She objected and wrote to him on February 9, 1907: " '*Nearly* all' won't do! because I have drawn Thomas already with *nothing*!—That would not signify; I could gum something over but there are not many garments for Mr. Drake to dress himself in; and it would give the story a new & criminal aspect if he forcibly took off & *stole* Tom's trousers!" (*Letters*, p. 150). Parenthetically, we may wonder at Beatrix Potter's choice of the words *criminal* and *stole* in her letter. Her strong letter suggests that she had begun to suspect something about Harold Warne's character. (We may see further reference to this in chapter 29.)

In the penultimate paragraph of her letter to Harold Warne she wrote: "Tell Louie [Harold Warne's daughter to whom *The Fierce Bad Rabbit* was dedicated] I shall have to teach her kitten manners. I was scratched fearfully by the original manx Tom. I had to whip him" (*Letters*, p. 150).

The stories which Beatrix Potter wrote in 1906 deal thematically with children's behavior. In addition, however, the stories implicate a woman's, and specifically, a mother's, aggression against her offspring. In *The Story of Miss Moppet* the kitten is playfully aggressive as she seizes the mouse by the tail. By the time Beatrix Potter wrote *The Sly Old Cat* later that year, it is the older cat who sets rules of conduct that are basically unfair to the rat, who is convinced that he will be devoured.

In *The Tale of Tom Kitten*, the final story in 1906, Tabitha Twitchit, the mother cat, is imbued with attributes that are clearly human. Despite her reasonable wish to have the children neat and clean for the anticipated company, Tabitha Twitchit's demands are entirely unreasonable. It is too much to expect the kittens to keep their clothes clean, to walk on their hind legs, and not to play when they are allowed to go outside. She puts them into a tempting situation but deprives them of pleasure at the same time. Moreover, Beatrix Potter criticizes Tabitha Twitchit for stuffing Tom into clothes that are much too small for him—implying that she should have known that the buttons were bound to fall off.

Tabitha Twitchit's sending the kittens upstairs to their rooms is, to be sure, reasonably acceptable punishment under the circumstances that she had created. Lying to her guests by telling them that her children were in bed with measles, however, is a totally different matter and Beatrix Potter clearly disapproves of it. The story portrays the mother cat not only as being harsh and unempathic, but also as a liar. We have seen similar faulty behavior demonstrated by Duchess and Ribby in the original version of the *Pie and the Patty-pan*. There Ribby initially lies about having killed James's hens and Duchess lies about stealing the eggs.

Unlike the directly expressed aggression in the story of *The Fierce Bad Rabbit* where the hunter shoots and symbolically castrates the rabbit by blasting off his tail and whiskers, the aggression embodied in *The Tale of Tom Kitten* is much more subtle. It provides a clearer picture of what Beatrix Potter must have experienced either from her mother or from the harsh nurse who took care of her as a child. Any such deceptive behavior by a nurse or caretaker, or even by her mother, would have rankled within her for many years.

In the previous chapter we indicated that by her ability to plunge into creative work, Beatrix Potter was able to deal with some of the underpinnings of the depression that made the work of mourning so difficult. But in addition to working these matters out through her creative work, she had ongoing emotional support from Norman Warne's mother and from Millie Warne. Beatrix Potter and Millie Warne maintained a correspondence which, while it could in no way deal with Beatrix Potter's underlying feelings, was very personal and kept her in close touch with a very sympathetic person who was genuinely fond of her. Beatrix Potter also continued in a whirl of activity as she refurbished and improved her new acquisition, Hill Top, and displayed a genuine interest in cultivating her garden. Altogether, these external factors worked wonders in restoring a personality that was basically incredibly strong. While the scars of the traumatic loss remained, Beatrix Potter continued to function in a very healthy way.

## Chapter 16

# The Tale of the Faithful Dove

# (1956) [1907]

"Founded upon fact, but the incident occurred at another seaside town. I think Folkestone," wrote Beatrix Potter many years later on the first manuscript of this story she had written in early February 1907. On the second manuscript she noted that she "used Winchelsea and Rye as background" and that the story "was written for the Warne Children" (Linder, 1971, p. 338). On November 18, 1908, she sent it to Harold Warne describing it as being "more like the Tailor—older and sentimental" (*Letters*, p. 164) and indicating that "It was made before Roly Poly and Jemima." "The story," she went on to say, "has been lying about a long time, & so have several others. I should like to get rid of some one of them. When a thing is once printed I dismiss it from my dreams! & don't care what becomes of the reviewers. But an accumulation of half finished ideas is bothersome" (*Letters*, pp. 164–165).

Nothing more came of it until December 1918 when Fruing Warne wrote to her about this story describing it as "charming" and "brilliant." By this time, however, her eyesight was a problem and besides, she wrote: "I could not possibly 'dress' up the pigeons; no birds look well in clothes."

Again nothing was done about the book until 1956 when it was published by Frederick Warne with illustrations by Marie Angel. It was reissued in 1970.

*The Tale of the Faithful Dove* concerns a dove named Mr. Thomas Tidler and his wife, Amabella. Although they were a devoted couple, they did argue at times. On this particular occasion Amabella had laid an egg in a nest high up in the Ypres Tower but then left it to sun herself. Thomas Tidler scolded her saying that: "When a person has laid an egg, a person should *not* leave the fortifications" (Linder, 1971, p. 341).

Suddenly, a peregrine falcon swooped down on Mrs. Tidler. The falcon's mate followed behind while Mr. Tidler, "with pathetic senseless courage flew behind his wife, to keep between her and the danger" (Linder, 1971, p. 341). To escape from the falcon, Mrs. Tidler had "half by accident—half of purpose—dived down the mouth of a tall red chimney pot" (Linder, 1971, p. 342). Mr. Tidler flew back to the Ypres Tower hoping to find his wife there. As he could not, "he ate nothing and moped" (Linder, 1971, p. 342). He wished that the falcon had taken him instead of his wife.

Amabella had fallen down the chimney of an empty house where the fireplace had been stuffed with a sack. Although she could stand up, she could not fly out of the chimney so she was trapped. The next morning, she laid another egg, commenting that she would have to sit there for sixteen days (seventeen days in the 1970 edition). She was hungry. At night she heard the pattering and dancing of mice as well as a mouse playing a fiddle.

The following day, an old female mouse found her, and after listening compassionately to her tale, offered to get help. She conveyed the information of the dove's whereabouts to some starlings who in turn managed to inform Mr. Tidler. Mrs. Tidler told him she had laid an egg and asked him to bring her some corn. For more than two weeks her diligent mate with great devotion and perseverance brought her large quantities of corn. Her egg hatched and she had a son whom she wanted to call Tobias but Mr. Tidler wanted him called Toby.

One day the sexton of the church called a plumber and his helper to work on the leaking roof. Their attention was called to the dove on top of the roof. When the apprentice climbed up on the chimney stack, Mr. Tidler knocked his hat off as he tried to look into the chimney. The boy then climbed into the garret and pulled out the sack that had been stuffed into the chimney. When he did this, Mrs. Tidler and Toby fell out of the chimney into the fireplace. The boy wanted to take the pigeon which the plumber said would make a pigeon pie. Once again Tidler knocked the boy's cap off and as he went to grab it, Toby slipped through his fingers into a spout on the roof. It was too dangerous to get the dove from that location, so the boy gave up trying to catch it.

Mr. Tidler taught Toby to fly. Father, son, and Amabella roosted in the Ypres Tower that night.

While the basis of this story was an actual touching story that Beatrix Potter had heard, her decision to tell it in her own way at this time had a great deal of personal significance. Since it was written a year and a half after Norman Warne's death, we may view this story as a continuation of the work of mourning in which Beatrix Potter was still involved. It expressed a fantasy that she must have entertained—that she and Norman would have married and been as devoted a couple as Mr. and Mrs. Tidler were, and that she would have become pregnant, and they would have had a child, possibly a son, whom her husband would have taught. She had said that her books were written for children and had dedicated this story to the Warne children. By dedicating the story in this way, she expressed the gratification of a fantasy that if she had been married to Norman and had a child or children, they would have been Warne children and the book would have been written for them.

In this story Mr. Tidler wanted to protect his wife from the peregrine falcon, acting with what Beatrix Potter described as "pathetic senseless courage." Was this, we may wonder, a wish that Norman Warne had been able to have done the same for her? Or, it may have been an expression of her own wish that she, in some way, could have protected him.

## Chapter 17

# The Tale of Jemima Puddle-Duck
# (1908a)

*The Tale of Jemima Puddle-Duck* was dedicated to Ralph and Betsy Cannon, the children of Beatrix Potter's manager and caretaker at Hill Top Farm.

Jemima Puddle-duck wished to hatch her own eggs by herself. Although she tried to hide them, they were always found and taken away. Deciding to make her nest away from the farm, she set off in search of a safe dry place. On her way, she met a handsome, polite gentleman, a fox, to whom she told the purpose of her journey. The fox showed her his wood shed, graciously informing her that she could sit there as long as she wished. She made her nest there and the fox promised to take care of it until she returned. In the following days, she laid nine eggs in the nest. Then she told the fox that she intended to begin sitting the following day and would bring a bag of corn with her so that she would not need to leave her nest until the eggs hatched.

Telling her he would provide her with oats, the fox persuaded her to have a dinner party with him the next day and asked her to bring herbs and onions for an omelette (compare with *The Sly Old Cat*, chapter 14). As Jemima Puddle-duck was a "simpleton," she was not suspicious of the obvious motives of the fox. Kep, a collie on the farm, however, asked her what she was doing and where she was going, so Jemima told him the story. Kep then rounded up two foxhound puppies.

When Jemima Puddle-duck returned to the fox's shed the next day, he was rather abrupt with her. Suddenly, the dogs appeared and after much ferocious growling, barking, and other noises, the fox disappeared. The puppies, however, "gobbled up all the eggs." Although Kep and the puppies were somewhat injured in the fray, they accompanied Jemima Puddle-duck back to the farm.

Jemima Puddle-duck laid some more eggs later on and was allowed to keep them herself but only four of them hatched. She lamented that it was due to her nerves but Beatrix Potter explains that "she had always been a bad sitter."

The main theme of this story is wished-for motherhood, a theme which was present in *The Tale of the Faithful Dove*. It expresses Beatrix Potter's own wish that she had been a mother. Of interest in this connection is that in the opening paragraph of the second version of the story, not used in the final version, Beatrix Potter poignantly wrote: "What a gratifying thing it is in these days to meet with a female devoted to family life." Instead, in the final version she wrote:

> What a funny sight it is to see a brood of ducklings with a hen!
> —Listen to the story of Jemima Puddle-duck, who was annoyed because the farmer's wife would not let her hatch her own eggs [Potter, 1908a, p. 9].

Originally Beatrix Potter had written that Jemima Puddle-duck "was aggrieved," but then changed it to "was provoked" because although "aggrieved [was] a better word," she wondered if children would understand it (Linder, 1971, p. 189).

Beatrix Potter's remarks about the farmer's wife had direct bearing on her own response to her mother's attitude toward her and her feeling "annoyed" that in some way her mother had been responsible for her not having been able to fulfill her instinctual wishes. She tried to find the right word for her feelings, projecting upon the possibility of children not understanding the word *aggrieved* her own view that her mother would not understand how she felt. In addition to this, the words "a female devoted to family life" probably had a very personal connection to her view of *her* mother's lack of devotion to herself and her brother.

The whole matter of childbearing was connected with Norman Warne's death three years before. Beatrix Potter was, of course, well aware that at her age, 42, the likelihood of her becoming a mother was not great. The poignant note at the end of the story referring to Jemima Puddle-duck always being a "bad sitter" had further reference to her view of her own reproductive capacity.

Apart from these matters, however, this story expresses a fantasy that a female may be so desperate to have a family that she may become attracted to, or may be readily seduced by, some clever, dishonest, but polite "gentleman" who has his own selfish interests at heart and whose consideration for her would be a sham.

We do not know, of course, whether Beatrix Potter had thoughts or fantasies along these lines, or whether they were stimulated by a comment or proposition by some man whom she had met (see chapter 25, p. 190). Having led a very sheltered and restricted life, it is entirely likely that at times she viewed herself as being "a simpleton," quite naive in the ways of the world, and had wished she could have been rescued by someone who was more worldly. Thus, when she describes the collie, Kep, as listening wisely to Jemima Puddle-duck's tale, she makes it clear that he completely understood what the fox was after. We may raise the question whether Kep, Beatrix Potter's collie, was, in some respects, imbued with the attributes of her superego. In this way, as the heir to her father or some other experienced or knowledgeable person, he could function as her mentor and savior—who would protect her from her own impulses. Of importance too is that Beatrix Potter dismisses Jemima Puddle-duck's claim of anxiety ("her nerves") and provides the explanation that her problem was somehow constitutionally based. In so doing Beatrix Potter is able to defend herself from recognizing her own anxieties.

## Chapter 18

# The Tale of Samuel Whiskers or
# The Roly-Poly Pudding

## (1908b) [1906]

The original version of this story, entitled *The Roly-Poly Pudding*, was written by Beatrix Potter in 1906 at the time she was making frequent visits to Sawrey and lodging there while she was overseeing the renovation of Hill Top. During this period she learned that a tremendous number of rats lived in the walls and passages of her house. Dedicating her book to her tame albino rat named Sammy, she wrote: "In remembrance of Sammy, the intelligent pink-eyed representative of a persecuted (but irrepressible) race. An affectionate little friend, and most accomplished thief" (Potter, 1908b, p. 2). Her pet rat, however, was not the subject of this story. The title was changed to *The Tale of Samuel Whiskers* in 1926.

Mrs. Tabitha Twitchit, mother of Moppet, Mittens, and Tom Kitten, was preparing to do some baking so she put Moppet and Mittens in a cupboard to keep them out of mischief. She could not find Tom Kitten, however. While she was searching the house for him, Moppet and Mittens escaped from the cupboard.

On hearing Mrs. Ribby knock at the front door, Moppet jumped into the flour barrel while Mittens hid in an empty jar. Tabitha Twitchit tearfully told her cousin Ribby that she had lost her son, Thomas, and was afraid that the rats had got him. The two cats then went about thoroughly searching the house. When they returned to the kitchen they found Moppet in the flour barrel and dragged her out. She told them that she had seen a rat stealing some dough. Mittens, discovered in the empty jar, told them that she had seen a large male rat stealing some butter and a rolling pin. Hearing a "roly-poly" sound in the attic Tabitha and Ribby feared that Thomas was in grave danger so they sent for John Joiner, a dog who had a saw.

We learn that while their mother was putting Moppet and Mittens in the cupboard, Tom hid in the chimney and then climbed up inside it, hoping to reach the top of the house where he might catch sparrows. As there were many flues in the chimney, he got lost and fell through a hole. He suddenly found himself confronted by Samuel Whiskers, an enormous rat. The rat called his wife, Anna Maria, who immediately pulled off Tom's coat and trussed him up with a string. Samuel Whiskers watched the proceedings while taking snuff and then asked his wife to make him "a kitten dumpling roly-poly pudding" for his dinner (Potter, 1908b, p. 46). To do this, Anna Maria said that they had to have butter, dough, and a rolling pin. It was to secure the necessary supplies for the dinner that the rats descended to the rooms below and were seen by Moppet and Mittens.

When the rats returned to their place under the attic floor, they smeared Tom with butter, rolled him in dough, and then used the rolling pin to smooth it out while he mewed loudly and struggled desperately. Suddenly they heard a dog scratching and the sound of a saw. Realizing that they would be discovered, Samuel Whiskers and Anna Maria ran off, taking whatever possessions they could in a wheelbarrow belonging to Miss Potter. Tom was rescued.

The story ends with Beatrix Potter saying that the rats moved to Farmer Potatoes' barn where they multiplied prolifically. Moppet and Mittens grew up to be good rat catchers and hung rat tails on the barn door to indicate how many they had caught. Tom Kitten, however, remained afraid of rats and never faced "anything that [was] bigger than a mouse" (p. 75).

While the reader, or the child listening to the story, knows all will turn out well in the end, an aura of anxiety anticipating some terrible catastrophe pervades the entire story. The distraught Tabitha Twitchit, unable to find her son Tom, believes that he is lost and that he either was or would be devoured by rats. She tells her cousin Ribby that she once saw a huge old father rat and when she was going to jump on him "he showed his yellow teeth at her." Tom's helpless horror is evident in Beatrix Potter's description of his being trussed up, smeared with butter, and encased in dough which is rolled smooth by the two rats. He cries pitifully in fear. He bites, spits, mews, and wriggles to avoid his fate. The entire sequence of the story, fraught with repeated references to oral aggression, alerts the reader to the most frightening of terrors: to be killed and devoured, a theme manifest in a number of the Beatrix Potter stories we have discussed.

Beatrix Potter's view of a mother figure is highly ambivalent. In this story, the theme of aggression is intimately connected with Tom's complicated relationship to mother figures. The initial description of Tabitha Twitchit's reaction to her son's disappearance was that she became "distracted and mewed dreadfully." She wept and wrung her paws. These are the reactions of a loving, caring mother. But then another aspect of a mother's (or her substitute's) personality becomes manifest in the characterization of Anna Maria who, on seeing Tom, immediately ("before he knew what was happening") pulled off his coat, rolled him in a bundle, tied him up with string, and designated what ingredients were necessary for the roly-poly pudding.

In contrast to her active and aggressive role, Samuel Whiskers is quite passive. He calmly sits and takes snuff while watching Anna Marie truss up Tom Kitten. Later, he follows her instructions to steal the butter and the rolling pin. At the end of the story, when Mr. and Mrs. Whiskers have moved to Farmer Potatoes' barn, Beatrix Potter describes the farmer as a man who is seemingly impotent, incapable of coping with the rising number of rats descended from Mr. and Mrs. Whiskers.

We have already seen that Beatrix Potter used her stories as vehicles to communicate some elements of her own inner dynamics. As we look at *The Tale of Samuel Whiskers*, we may see that it has to do with some recollections of her own experience, real or fantasied, with her own mother, her mother substitute, or some other person in her acquaintance. While the ambivalence or split may have been between two mother figures (i.e., her own mother and her governess, or her mother and her grandmother Potter of whom she was so fond) it is equally possible that what Beatrix Potter was trying to express was that her view of her mother was similarly divided (i.e., "good" mother, "bad" mother)—a state of affairs by no means uncommon in children. It may be seen in stories or fairy tales that deal with the fairy godmother and the wicked stepmother or witch.

In the opposition to Beatrix Potter's involvement with Norman Warne, Mrs. Potter, like Anna Maria in the story, was the main protagonist, and Rupert Potter, like Samuel Whiskers, passively followed her lead. Beatrix Potter's ambivalence toward her father is particularly manifest in her characterization of Samuel Whiskers. Although she depicts the rats as totally malevolent creatures in her story, she named Samuel Whiskers after her pet rat, Sammy, her "affectionate little friend."

On April 20, 1933, Beatrix Potter wrote a letter to Elizabeth Willink[1] in which she sheds further light on her little story.

---

[1] In a private communication Lady Elizabeth Willink stated that her grandmother, Margaret (Hamer) Andrewes, who wrote juvenile literature under the pseudonym of Maggie Browne, was acquainted with Beatrix Potter. She had written to her when she

## The Tale of Samuel Whiskers or The Roly-Poly Pudding

Castle Cottage
Sawrey
Ambleside

Ap. 20. 33

My dear Elizabeth,

I have seen Tabitha Twitchit at last! She was always "not at home" when I called at her house. The door was locked. I thought I could hear a noise inside, like rushing about and up-setting chairs; but nobody came to open the door when I knocked.

Today I found Tabitha at home. She says she has been at Cousin Ribby's house, helping her to do spring cleaning. They have shaken the carpets, and washed the blankets and sheets. She says she locked up her kittens indoors while she was out. I asked about her son Thomas. She is very sorry to tell you, Tom is as naughty as ever. She is quite worried about him; but she hopes he will improve before the end of the book.

She says—what is the good of spring cleaning if he gets into the fireplace and shakes down clouds of soot? And leaves smuts and black footmarks all over the table cloth? She has boxed his ears again with her claws out. But instead of saying he is sorry and he will be a good kitten—he begins to spit at her! oh shocking!

I think he will learn better manners as he grows older. But Tabitha is worried; she says his badness will fill a big book—(which seems to be out of print, but we have found a copy)

So Tabitha and I send the book to Elizabeth with love from all the kittens and from Beatrix Potter.[2]

Clearly the description is of a naughty animal (or child) and a distraught mother. Clinically, we are often able to see that the "naughty" behavior in some children and adolescents is a *consequence* of the parents' unempathic attitude or aggressive behavior toward them. The child then defies the parents and

---

was unable to get a copy of *Peter Rabbit* for her granddaughter, Elizabeth Willink (née Andrewes). This letter was Beatrix Potter's reply.

[2]I am grateful to Lady Elizabeth Willink who kindly allowed me to quote this unpublished letter.

provokes or engineers a situation in which he is the recipient of further aggression. Tom Kitten's "naughtiness" may be understood from this standpoint.

From the entries in her *Journal* in which she writes about her brother, Bertram, we may well infer that Beatrix Potter's characterization of the naughty, misbehaving, defiant male child portrayed as an animal in her stories may frequently refer to her brother.

## Chapter 19

# The Tale of the Flopsy Bunnies
# (1909a)

In 1909, buoyed up by the interest of her publishers who wished to produce more Peter Rabbit books, Beatrix Potter wrote *The Tale of the Flopsy Bunnies*, another sequel to *The Tale of Peter Rabbit*, and *The Tale of Benjamin Bunny*. She dedicated the book: "For all little friends of Mr. McGregor and Peter and Benjamin" (Linder, 1971, p. 195).

Linder (1971) writes that: "Benjamin was now grown up and married to Peter's sister Flopsy, and they had a family of six—which according to some of the miniature letters, consisted of two boy-rabbits, followed by three girl-rabbits, and finally another boy-rabbit!" (p. 195).

Beatrix Potter begins her story with the comment that the effect of eating too much lettuce is soporific to rabbits but that she herself had never felt sleepy after eating lettuce. When there was not enough food for the little rabbits, Benjamin Bunny would borrow cabbages from Peter Rabbit who kept a nursery garden. When he had no cabbages to spare, however, the Flopsy Bunnies went to the rubbish heap in the ditch outside of Mr. McGregor's garden.

One day, the rabbits found a great number of overgrown lettuces which they devoured and then fell asleep. Benjamin Bunny also went to sleep but had covered his head with a paper bag to keep off the flies. Suddenly, Mr. McGregor, who had been mowing his lawn, dumped a bagful of clippings on the sleeping bunnies. The rabbits did not awaken but "dreamt that their mother Flopsy was tucking them up in a hay bed." When the farmer noticed that there were bunnies under the grass clippings, he picked them up and dropped them into a sack. The bunnies still did not awaken but "dreamt that their mother was turning them over in bed."

While Mr. McGregor went to put away his mowing machine, he left the sack on a wall. Mrs. Flopsy Bunny came by, wondering where her children were. Mrs. Tomasina Tittlemouse had observed what had happened and told Benjamin Bunny and Flopsy, then she nibbled a hole in the sack. The Flopsy Bunnies were pulled out and the rabbits stuffed rotten vegetable marrows, turnips, and an old blacking brush into the bag.

When Mr. McGregor returned, he retrieved the bag and started home while the rabbits followed at a respectable distance to see what would happen. Mrs. McGregor, described as a rather stern woman, was not particularly impressed by her husband's announcement that he had "six lettle fat rabbits" (Potter, 1909a, p. 46). After feeling the hard shapes of the vegetables in the sack, she said that the rabbits were not fit to eat but that after she skinned them and cut off their heads, their skins would do to line her old coat. Mr. McGregor, however, objected saying that he would sell the skins to buy himself some tobacco. When Mrs. McGregor untied the sack and saw the vegetables she became very angry and felt that her husband had "done it a purpose" (p. 53).

He was very angry too. A rotten vegetable marrow was thrown out of the window and hit the youngest Flopsy Bunny. The rabbits then all went home. Both Mr. and Mrs. McGregor were disappointed not to get what they had wanted: he, the tobacco; and she, the rabbit skins.

What is striking about this story is that in the second sentence Beatrix Potter writes: "*I* have never felt sleepy after eating lettuces; but then *I* am not a rabbit" (p. 9). Thus, while this story has to do with rabbits, the disclaimer that she is not a rabbit clearly indicates a denial that the story has any personal significance.

The Flopsy Bunnies had two dreams—collectively. In the first one, under the stimulus of Mr. McGregor dumping the grass clippings over them, they dreamt that their mother was tucking them in a hay bed. The second dream, which occurred when Mr. McGregor dropped them into his sack, was that their mother was turning them over in bed.

Through her invented dreams, Beatrix Potter demonstrated a mechanism which the dream work uses to turn a potentially disturbing stimulus into something pleasant. The dreams were clearly a fulfillment of a wish. The dreams (or the dream work) processed the dangerous stimulus into something that was affectionate and pleasant and permitted the dreamers to continue sleeping. The rabbits, said the dreams, were not in mortal peril: their mother was tucking them into a nice soft bed, and, later, she was turning them over. They were perfectly safe; their mother was taking good care of them.

By having the six rabbits dream the same dream Beatrix Potter was expressing a phenomenon that occurs when the members of a particular group share a common fantasy in response to a common wish or threat. Considered from the standpoint of her own dynamics, these dreams provide a clue that in their story, which is like a day dream or fantasy, Beatrix Potter was able to process the unpleasant realities of her own life into circumstances that were pleasant and had a happy ending. In the fantasy she was able to regress to an early period of her life in which she viewed her mother as the loving protector.

The dangerous situation for which these dreams were created was the threat of annihilation. The little rabbits had been captured. They were to be killed, skinned, have their heads cut off, and eaten. In this story, however, unlike the original Peter Rabbit story, the eating is omitted because Mrs. McGregor declares that the Flopsy Bunnies are "not fit to eat." Nevertheless, there are anticipated gains to Mr. and Mrs. McGregor because the rabbit pelts are to be converted into something for their pleasure. They are to be sold to purchase tobacco or to be used to line an old coat.

In the story the young rabbits are able to observe a scene of the McGregors' family life. In the course of the observation, however, the youngest Flopsy Bunny is struck and hurt by a rotten vegetable marrow that is thrown out of the window. Mrs. McGregor, a rather shrewish woman, calls her husband a silly old man, is angry with him, and accuses him of having tricked her on purpose while he, in turn, shouts at her.

Bringing this scene of domestic discord into the story is significant, especially since the vegetable marrow thrown out of the window hurts the youngest bunny. Children often think that it is their fault that their parents argue and are angry with each other. Frightened by the intensity of their parents' anger, they fear it will be directed against them for many reasons, and that they will be hurt as a consequence. There was no real reason from the standpoint of the story for Beatrix Potter to have included the detail that the thrown vegetable marrow hurts the youngest bunny rabbit. Thus, we may suppose that the wrangling between the McGregors in this story is an expression of Beatrix Potter's actual memory or an interpretation of the conflicts between her parents. We have some confirmation from Beatrix Potter's *Journal*, that there were quarrels in the Potter household. On April 24, 1884, writing from Minehead, she commented on an earthquake that had taken place. "[O]ld mother earth gives us an explosion. I wish I had been in London to feel it *slightly*. One does not often get a chance of feeling an earthquake fortunately, in nature that is to say, for domestic ones are only too frequent" (p. 83). The quarrels of Rupert and Helen Potter, however petty or intense, must have been very distressing, if not frightening, to Beatrix Potter and her brother, Bertram.

Once more, in the story of the *Flopsy Bunnies*, we are able to see two opposing views of a mother figure. In contrast to the aggressive Mrs. McGregor, Beatrix Potter presents the image of a kind, concerned, maternal figure in the form of the mother of the Flopsy Bunnies, and in Mrs. Tittlemouse. It is she who ultimately brings about the rabbits' rescue by gnawing a hole in the bottom of the sack into which the rabbits had been dropped. Her act permits their worried mother, Flopsy Bunny, and their father, Benjamin Bunny, to free the baby bunnies and to put the vegetables into the sack in order to trick Mr. McGregor. In a subtle way, however, she characterizes the father as being passive and not attendant to the dangers to which his offspring are exposed.

As we have seen in her story of *The Tailor of Gloucester*, Beatrix Potter was able to combine her own literary creations with material with which she was familiar. *The Tale of the Flopsy Bunnies* seems to have been adapted from a classical fairy tale, probably Grimms' *The Wolf and the Seven Little Kids*, a story with which we know she was familiar.

In the Grimms' story, as she leaves to get some food, a concerned mother goat warns her kids not to let the wily wolf into the house because he would devour them. (Compare this version with the wily fox in the story of *Jemima Puddle-duck*.) The wolf, however, disguises his voice by eating a lump of chalk and conceals his black paws by rubbing dough and white meal on them. He succeeds in entering the house and swallows six of the seven kids. When the mother goat returns and learns what has happened from the youngest kid, who had hidden in the clock-case, they go out in search of the wolf and find him sleeping under a tree. The mother goat cuts open the wolf's stomach allowing the kids to escape, fills his stomach with stones, and sews him up again. When the wolf awakens he is thirsty so he goes to a well to drink but falls in and is drowned (*Grimms' Fairy Tales*, pp. 39–42).

The similarities between Beatrix Potter's story and the Grimms' story are striking. The basic idea of both stories is that the good mother or mother figure rescues her babies from being destroyed and all rejoice at the punishment or frustration of the aggressor. In addition, both stories express a typical pregnancy and childbirth fantasy. In both instances the babies (rabbits or kids) are placed in a sack or stomach whole, from which they are liberated very much alive by some action on the part of the benevolent mother figure. Beatrix Potter's need to present this kind of material seems to point to her preoccupation with ideas derived from early childhood fantasies and continue her wish to have had a child of her own that she could have taken care of.

The ending of Beatrix Potter's story suggests a resolution that she and her brother must have hoped and wished for many times in their lives: that the relationship between their parents would have been more harmonious, and that she and her brother, like the Flopsy Bunnies, would be able to live in an atmosphere of peace and tranquility. Behind that was another wish, expressed in the dreams of the Flopsy Bunnies—that their own mother would have lovingly taken care of them and would have cuddled them when they were frightened and in danger.

## Chapter 20

# The Tale of Ginger and Pickles
# (1909b)

In addition to *The Tale of the Flopsy Bunnies*, Beatrix Potter also wrote *The Tale of Ginger and Pickles* in 1909. The book is dedicated: "with very kind regards to old Mr. John Taylor, who 'thinks he might pass as a Dormouse' (Three years in bed and never a grumble!)" (Linder, 1971, p. 199).

This tale is about a tiny village shop, named "Ginger and Pickles," that sold all matter of sundries to rabbits and other animals. It was run by Ginger, a yellow tomcat, and Pickles, a male terrier. The mice were afraid of Ginger, and the rabbits, of Pickles. Ginger asked Pickles to serve the mice because they made his mouth water. Pickles, in turn, admitted that he had similar feelings about rats but felt it would never "do to eat [their] own customers" as they would go to their competitor, Tabitha Twitchit's store. To this Ginger replied that they would go nowhere.

Ginger and Pickles sold their products on unlimited credit. The "cost of the purchase" was recorded in a book. While they did a good business, they obviously had no income. As a result, Ginger and Pickles were forced to eat their own products after closing their shop each night.

On the first of the year, Pickles, unable to purchase a dog license, was afraid of the police. When Ginger and Pickles began to do their accounts, they found that their "customers" had run up tremendous bills. While they were working on them, they heard a noise in the shop. There, a policeman, who was "only a German doll" (Potter, 1909b, p. 42), had suddenly appeared, and was writing in a notebook. After he disappeared they found that he had left an envelope containing a listing of their rates[1] and taxes. Unable to pay the amount owed, Ginger and Pickles decided to close their shop permanently and promptly left.

They did not leave the neighborhood, however, although some people wished they had. Beatrix Potter indicates that Ginger was living in a warren and looked "stout and comfortable." While she wrote that she did not know what his occupation was, the picture that accompanies the story, reveals the cat holding a trap with another trap on the ground and three rabbits are seen in the background. Pickles became a gamekeeper. The accompanying picture shows the dog carrying a gun and there are rabbits in the background. After Ginger and Pickles left, Tabitha Twitchit raised the price of everything a half-penny and still refused to give credit.

Beatrix Potter ended the first version of the story with a short paragraph stating that the shop of Ginger and Pickles was reopened by Sally Henny Penny, a chicken who got very flustered when she counted out change but insisted on being paid in "ready money." In the second version, Beatrix Potter expanded this conclusion somewhat and inserted a small section before it in which she wrote that a Mr. John Dormouse and his daughter had started to sell peppermints and candles. The candles were too heavy for the mice and besides they drooped in warm weather. Moreover, Miss Dormouse refused to take back "the ends" when they were brought in with complaints. When John Dormouse was complained to, however, he lay in bed and would say nothing but "very snug."

---

[1]A property tax.

Following this, Beatrix Potter continues to the conclusion of the second version by writing that Sally Henny Penny sent out notices stating that she was going to reopen the shop.

Linder (1971) comments that Beatrix Potter's addition of the part about John Dormouse seemed to have thrown the story "slightly off" and stated, moreover, that her original version was thought to be the better of the two.

Much has been made of the fact that the drawings in the story were based on actual scenes from the little shop in Sawrey kept by John Taylor's wife. Beatrix Potter wanted to put him in the story, possibly because she had put his son in *The Tale of Roly Poly* as the dog, John Joiner. In a letter to Mrs. Miller (November 24, 1941) Beatrix Potter wrote: "Old John was a sweet, gentle old man, failed in his legs, so he kept [to] his bed. . . . When I saw old John, who was very humourous and jokey, I asked him how I could put him—old John—in a book if he insisted on living in bed? So a week afterwards, enclosed with an account, there came a scrap of paper, 'John Taylor's compliments and thinks he might pass for a dormouse' " (*Americans*, p. 159).

At first sight the book seems to be a caricature of some of the activities at the small village shop in Sawrey using many of Beatrix Potter's story animals. A close inspection, however, reveals that there is more to it. The partners and proprietors of the shop, a dog and a cat, both males, seem to have an idealistic, cooperative, and collaborative business. They are portrayed as the very epitome of generosity. Thoroughly altruistic, they are able to control their aggressive impulses and to give "credit" to all who come to "buy" their purchases. Their altruism, however, does not pay, and eventually their shop must be closed. Ultimately neither animal is able to control his instinctual aggression but reverts to capturing and killing other animals for food.

We may wonder what prompted Beatrix Potter to write such a story at this particular time.

There is a certain surrealistic or dreamlike quality to it, a combination of elements from reality and from fantasy. The shop is real and is run by animals that are also real, even though their attributes are human. They practice a totally unreal type of business policy, however, certainly not one that is encountered in Sawrey or elsewhere. The policeman, who is "only a German doll," suddenly appears, writes in his notebook, and then suddenly disappears leaving an envelope containing a statement for taxes.

We are familiar with Beatrix Potter's juxtaposition of reality and fantasy from some of her other stories (e.g., *The Tale of Mrs. Tiggy-Winkle*). By the use of this technical device she is able to express her thoughts and fantasies which are based on some reality. We may have some clues about what these had to do with at this time from some of her correspondence.

Beatrix Potter was involved with her publishers in making arrangements for the production of china, dolls, and wallpaper based on her characters. In a letter dated January 18, 1908, to Harold Warne, for example, she wrote, concerning a proposed agreement to produce china depicting some of her animal characters: "I think the words 'all earthenware' would prevent me from offering the statuettes to other firms, and I should not care to offer them to the German people. I hope you will be able to get rid of them" (*Letters*, p. 157).

Her feelings of disapproval about trade with Germany continued for some time as we see from her letters. By January of 1910, for example, Beatrix Potter was busy on posters for a Unionist campaign for tariff reform. Taylor writes:

Beatrix felt passionately against Free Trade, having failed to find a British manufacturer for her *Peter Rabbit* doll and then seeing the shops filled with a cheap (and unauthorized) German version. She prepared a number of posters, some featuring a doll made in Camberwell, leaning against a gravestone marking the death of the South London Toy Trade "killed by Free Trade with Germany," posters which Beatrix called her "Camberwell beauties" [*Letters*, pp. 173–174].

Beatrix Potter's displeasure about the financial arrangements for dolls and her dissatisfaction with a Mr. Hughes for his management of her projects continued to be topics in her correspondence with Harold Warne. On April 23, 1910, she wrote:

> I am of opinion that the matter has in a sense 'gone by default,' having been slipped over so long; & the shops being full of imitation rabbit dolls—which it is now very late to object to. I certainly should *not* myself choose to employ him [Mr. Hughes] again over another doll; he is strongly pro German & has *no desire* to save English patents [*Letters*, p. 180].

From the material in her correspondence we may see that the element "German doll" in *The Story of Ginger and Pickles* had to do with the troublesome negotiations about the rabbit dolls which were going on with the German manufacturer through Mr. Hughes.

For some time Beatrix Potter had also been concerned with the matter of translations of her books into other languages. For example, in a letter dated July 29, 1908, she told Harold Warne about a Dr. Erick Pistor from Vienna who wished to translate *The Tale of Peter Rabbit* into German and to find a publisher for the translation. Beatrix Potter wrote to him that she was: "perfectly sick and tired of waiting for a German publisher." She goes on to say: "I said [to Dr. Pistor that] nothing could be done at present, because you were trying to arrange with a publisher at Berlin. If that comes to nothing, could we try whether anything can be done through this gentleman? Would the Berlin man include Vienna?" (*Letters*, p. 159).

Thus we may see that Beatrix Potter was occupied with a variety of complex business matters at this time. She actively opposed the Free Trade Laws, wanting to protect English patents while struggling to improve the shoddy quality of the German rabbit dolls. Furthermore, she was frustrated by Harold Warne's inability to acquire French and German publishers for *Peter Rabbit*. Unquestionably, she wanted to earn money through her publications to use in pursuing her other interests.

The German police doll who appears and disappears leaving an envelope dealing with taxes also can be connected with Beatrix Potter's concerns about her own business as well as her careful adherence to details. The pertinence of this element to her own business is apparent in a letter she wrote to Harold Warne on August 16, 1909: "My rates and taxes don't come in one envelope, does it matter?"

There were other reasons for Beatrix Potter's monetary concerns, however. We learn from Taylor's editorial comment that during this time (1909) Beatrix Potter was "buying another farm in Sawrey, Castle Farm. In all her property dealings she took the advice of William Heelis, a partner in the local firm of solicitors, W. H. Heelis & Son, Hawkshead" (*Letters*, p. 170). She needed money and the Warnes were not reliable about paying the royalties that were due to her at the agreed upon time.

On August 17, 1908, she wrote to Harold Warne:

> Could I depend on having £50 end of this month, £50 in October and some more by Christmas?
> Perhaps the question is not necessary; but I had understood there would be some sent in July—which didn't come, & I got rather anxious. . . .
> I do not in the least mind waiting for money, *if* I know beforehand. I should like to know what I have, to spend this autumn, without being rash [*Letters*, p. 161].

Three months later, on November 17, 1908, she informed Harold Warne that she had been talking to a bank about money for buying a field in Sawrey and again asked him to send her a "cheque" (*Letters*, p. 164).

About a month later, on December 15th, she wrote again, asking Harold Warne to send her "another bit of money presently" (*Letters*, p. 166).

On January 5, 1909, she repeated her request for money with some obvious irritation: "I wonder whether part of the cheque can be sent here? . . . I am not short; but it will seem rather a large cheque to be paid all at once, and it has gone on a longer time *than usual*" (FW).

Although the correspondence around the time that this story was written does not clearly disclose the extent of the problems with the financial arrangements, from the content of the story, and from the available correspondence *afterwards*, we may clearly discern an undercurrent of resentment about Harold Warne's method of dealing with her royalty payments.

We may well wonder whether in the story of *Ginger and Pickles* Beatrix Potter was caricaturing the partnership of Harold and Fruing Warne and their business practices. The sales of her books were enormous, yet there did not seem to be any likelihood that she, who had been extending them credit, would ever be paid. She may have viewed herself as having been unrealistic in supplying them, as *her* creditors, with merchandise which they did not appear to be paying for. Perhaps Beatrix Potter entertained the notion that she would eventually have to close *her* shutters and leave, that is, take her business elsewhere. Or, that she would be like Sally Henny Penny, the chicken who got very flustered when she counted out change but insisted on being paid in "ready money."

It would have been difficult for her to consider such a decision because she was grateful to the firm for having published her books successfully. She was able to derive financial rewards from the royalties that had been paid on her publications as well as other copyrighted objects, such as dolls, china, and wallpaper. Besides, there were the ties to the Warne family that were not easily disregarded. Still she had a lurking feeling that something was very much amiss, that *their* true colors would come out and that *they* would eventually profit as Ginger and Pickles did after *their* shop was closed. It was because of this confusing picture that Beatrix Potter's relationship with them was so conflicted.

In *The Story of Ginger and Pickles* we are able to see both aspects of Beatrix Potter's personality in handling business matters. She could be kindly and generous in extending credit, yet after a certain point her patience came to an end and her justified aggression came out. Her correspondence reveals this ambivalent attitude toward her publishers. She had been gracious, but as time went on she became quite indignant at having to ask repeatedly or beg them for an allowance, monies that rightfully should have been coming to her.

## Chapter 21

# Wag-by-Wall [*The Little Black Kettle*]
# (1944) [1909]

In November of 1909, the same year she wrote *The Tale of the Flopsy Bunnies* and *Ginger and Pickles*, Beatrix Potter worked on a story she called *The Little Black Kettle*, but did not complete it. She put it aside until 1929 when she rewrote it as part of *The Fairy Caravan* with the title *Wag-by-Wall*. But then she omitted it from the published version of that book. About a decade later, after Mrs. Miller asked her if she might publish the story in *The Horn Book* magazine, Beatrix Potter rewrote it again. In a letter to Mrs. Miller in November 1941 she commented: "I cannot judge my own work. . . . I thought of it years ago as a pendant to *The Tailor of Gloucester*—the lonely old man and the lonely old woman; but I never could finish it all" (*Letters*, p. 434).

Beatrix Potter thought it was a "pretty" story and worked on it again, making a number of changes and deleting a number of verses. She agreed with Mrs. Miller's suggestion that it would be a good Christmas story and changed the setting to Christmas Eve. Mrs. Miller, however, then decided to hold back the story until the twentieth anniversary issue of *The Horn Book*. Beatrix Potter agreed to this on November 5, 1943, but indicated: "I like to think some of your storytellers may read the story turn about with the old Tailor of Gloucester at Christmas gatherings in the children's libraries" (*Letters*, p. 462). The original, unfinished story of *The Little Black Kettle* is reprinted in Linder (1971).

That version of the story, which was dated November 25, 1909, deals with a poor old woman named Sally Scales who had an old, carved chest, a pendulum clock, and an old kettle that used to belong to her grandmother. Because it sang, she had the old kettle patched repeatedly even though the blacksmith told her that there was more patch than bottom and that it would cost more to patch it than to buy a new one.

One evening a white owl sitting on Sally's roof peered down the chimney and fell onto the hearth in a shower of soot, stones, and mortar. Sally opened the door to let the owl fly away.

The next morning Sally found that the spout of her little black kettle was broken off and was lying in the soot, but near it were five golden guineas. She then discovered many more gold coins in an old woolen stocking in the chimney. The money had fallen out from a hole in the toe. Beatrix Potter concluded her story by writing: "And Sally Scales bought blankets, and a pig, and more tea, and peat, and she had the spout mended but she would not buy a new one, she lived to the end of her days with the little black kettle" (Linder, 1971, p. 331).

Beatrix Potter made a number of changes from the original story for the final version, published posthumously in 1944, including changing the name of Sally Scales to Sally Benson. Sally's husband, Tom, had died after a prolonged illness that had created many debts. She lived alone in a simple cottage that had belonged to her grandfather, a cattle dealer. He had made a good deal of money but no one knew what he had done with it. He had never spent very much and had never given any of it away. While the old furniture was rather poor, there was a handsome clock that had belonged to him. It was a "Wag-by-the-wall" clock, "a pendulum clock" whose sound was "Tic: toc: gold: toes: tic: toc: gold: toes: " (Potter, 1944, p. 14). Sally

Benson loved her old clock and her old kettle. Patched many times, the kettle still sang and she refused to buy a new one.

A pair of white owls lived in the shed of the house and the hen owl laid four eggs from which little owlets hatched.

As time went on, Sally's economic circumstances worsened drastically. Her cow died. Rain spoiled the harvest. There was a famine and other misfortunes occurred. The situation finally became so desperate that, since she had no one to turn to, she knew that she had to sell the cottage and end her days in the poorhouse.

Sally and Tom "had lost their only child—a daughter" (Potter, 1944, p. 46) because she ran away and married a wastrel. The couple had a baby girl whom they named Goldie-locks. Sally sent her daughter and son-in-law money for her granddaughter when they requested it. When she no longer had any money to send them, however, they "faded out of sight" (Potter, 1944, p. 46).

On this particular Christmas Eve, Sally had received a letter from a stranger informing her that her daughter and her son-in-law had died and that the writer, a neighbor, had taken Goldie-locks, an 8-year-old little girl, into her home. The neighbor asked Sally to send her money to pay her fare so she could send the child to her. She could not keep Goldie-locks because she had five mouths of her own to feed.

Sally was sitting by the fire weeping for her grandchild when one of the white owls who sat on the chimney stack fell asleep and fell into the chimney. Down the chimney toppled the owl bringing soot, small stones, mortar and heavy stones before it. Sally picked up the owl and found that one of its wings had been scorched but otherwise he was all right. She fed him some milk with a spoon. Among the stones on the hearth was an old stocking with a hole in the toe from which protruded a gold coin.

Then the wag-by-wall clock began to whirr and struck fourteen instead of twelve and the words it had always said: "Tic: toc: gold: toes: tic: toc: gold: toes: changed to: Tick er: tocks:

Goldie-locks" (Potter, 1944, p. 62) and it continued to say this from then on.

Sally Benson arranged to have her granddaughter live with her, bought another cow and a pig, grew potatoes and other things in her garden. She enjoyed old age. Little Goldie-locks grew up and married a young farmer. They lived happily ever after and always kept the singing kettle and the wag-by-wall clock.

Beatrix Potter sets a scene of sadness and despair at the very beginning of the story by describing Sally's multiple economic and personal losses. Sally has lost not only her husband, Tom, but also her daughter who ran off and married a wastrel and had died. To make matters worse, she would now lose her only granddaughter, Goldi-locks, because she had no money to pay the child's fare so she could come to live with her grandmother.

Then, by inventing a deus ex machina in the form of an owl, Beatrix Potter provides a solution to the old woman's difficulties. Only after the owl falls into the chimney and loosens the mortar, the stones, and the stocking full of gold pieces does the clock change its "words."

In this story we are able to see the full expression of wishes that Beatrix Potter was only able to allude to in her animal stories. She must have recognized that she had to go beyond Sally's rescue from dire poverty in order to complete the original story she had begun in 1909. By now, in 1943, Beatrix Potter was able to come to a solution of the painful problem referred to in the story. Sally Benson had lost her only child, a daughter who had left her and then died, and her daughter could only be replaced by a granddaughter who had to be rescued. Evidently, Beatrix Potter could not express this before because it would have been too frank an admission of her feelings about losing Norman Warne, and not being able to have a child of her own.

## Chapter 22

# The Tale of Mrs. Tittlemouse
# (1910) [1909]

The original manuscript of *The Tale of Mrs. Tittlemouse* must have been written toward the end of 1909 as its dedication was: "For Nellie [Warne] with love and best wishes for A Happy New Year. Jan. 1st, 1910" (Linder, 1971, p. 206). The book itself was published in July of that year (*Letters*, p. 182).

The story deals with a woodmouse named Mrs. Thomasina Tittlemouse who lived in a bank under a hedge. Beatrix Potter describes her as a very tidy mouse who was always sweeping and dusting.

She had many uninvited visitors. One of them was a beetle[1] who had lost its way. Mrs. Tittlemouse sent it away because it had dirty feet. Another was a ladybird that she also banished, telling her that her house was on fire and that she must "fly away home to [her] children!" (Potter, 1910, p. 17). She evicted a fat spider, telling it that this was not Miss Muffet's house and complaining that it left cobwebs all over her nice clean house. A surprise visitor was Babbitty Bumble, a bumblebee who went

---

[1]In the original text, it was an "*earwig*" but because the publishers objected, Beatrix Potter changed it to a beetle.

into a storeroom where other bees were hiding in a large pile of dry moss.

Suddenly, she was visited by Mr. Jackson, a large toad who lived in a very dirty, wet ditch below the hedge. He sat down to dry himself but as his coattails dripped water; Mrs. Tittlemouse had to mop up the floor. After a while she offered him some cherrystones for dinner but he could not eat them because he had no teeth. When she offered him some thistle-down seed, he blew it all over the room. Finally, Mr. Jackson asked Mrs. Tittlemouse for some honey, telling her that he could smell it and that was why he had come. Although she said she had none, the toad began looking into the cupboards and in various passages. While he was doing this, he saw some "creepy-crawly people"[2] and caught one of them. Eventually the toad found the bees and the honey.

In the meantime Mrs. Tittlemouse shut herself up in her nut cellar. After a while she came out of hiding. All her "visitors" were gone but the place was a mess, with "smears of honey; and moss, and thistle-down—and marks of big and little dirty feet—all over [her] nice clean house!" (Potter, 1910, p. 49). She gathered some twigs to partially close the front door so that it would be too small for Mr. Jackson to get through. The next morning she began a thorough cleaning of her quarters, a task that took her two weeks. When it was finally accomplished, she gave a party for five other little mice. Mr. Jackson was not invited, however. He smelled the party, but because he could not squeeze in through the doorway, the mice handed him acorn cupfuls of honeydew[3] through the window.

In this story Beatrix Potter seems to have returned to the point where she ended *The Tale of Two Bad Mice* (chapter 9).

---

[2]Originally these were woodlice but Beatrix Potter changed the text to read "creepy-crawly people" because the Warnes objected to having such creatures in a children's book.

[3]Honeydew is the exudate of ergot fungus (Taylor, Whalley, Hobbs, Battrick, and 1987, p. 91).

After the rampage during which the mice demolished the doll-house, Hunca Munca returned daily with her dust pan and broom to sweep out the place. The "good housekeeping," almost excessive in degree, served to atone for her having been so destructive. In *The Tale of Mrs. Tittlemouse,* the woodmouse is described as fastidious, and her cleanliness, while necessary to undo the mess that her visitors left, seems excessive, the thorough cleaning of her quarters taking two weeks.

In this story Beatrix Potter seems to satirize a domestic scene that she must have witnessed countless times when she was living with her parents. In all likelihood the woodmouse is probably a caricature of some figure out of her past whose function it was to keep the house spotlessly clean and who fretted about the mess left by children or guests. It seems that here Beatrix Potter quite subtly also alludes to her mother's attitude about cleanliness and order.

There is a quality of bitterness expressed by Beatrix Potter in this little story. While she uses Mrs. Tittlemouse to condemn the thoughtlessness of her uninvited guests, she skillfully expresses her own perceptions of their characteristics. In the case of the ladybird, for example, Mrs. Tittlemouse's remark to the insect is of paramount importance. Calling her "mother" Mrs. Tittlemouse sends her home to her children because the insect's house is on fire. There are many versions of this rhyme (see Opie and Opie, 1951, pp. 263–264). One version reads:

> Ladybird, ladybird,
>   Fly away home.
> Your home is on fire
>   And your children all gone;
> [Opie and Opie, 1951, p. 263].

In some of the rhymes the children are burned or even dead. By referring to this rhyme Beatrix Potter implies that a mother is neglectful of her children's safety.

In her characterization of Mr. Jackson, Beatrix Potter condemns him as uncouth and so offensive that she has Mrs. Tittlemouse erect a barricade around her doorway to keep him out. We may wonder whether this was in some way a subtle allusion to what Beatrix Potter felt was the situation in her own home.

Once again Beatrix Potter's anger at her mother comes out in a story. It was a veiled but courageous indictment.

## Chapter 23

# The Tale of Timmy Tiptoes

# (1911)

Linder (1971) states that *The Tale of Timmy Tiptoes*, the only book that Beatrix Potter completed in 1911, is believed to have been written primarily for American children "because they would be familiar with both chipmunks and bears" (p. 208).

The dedication of the book is: "For many unknown little friends, including Monica." Later, she wrote: "I do not know the child. She is the school friend of a little cousin, who asked for it as a favour, and the name took my fancy" (Linder, 1971, p. 209).

Timmy Tiptoes, a fat little gray squirrel, persuaded his wife, Goody, that it was time to gather nuts and store them for the winter and spring. He convinced her to do this by telling her that when they awakened from their hibernation in the springtime, they would be thinner and there would be nothing to eat. Every day they stored nuts in a hole high up in a tree, and in several hollow stumps near the tree where they had built their nest.

Beatrix Potter commented that squirrels who buried their nuts in the ground lost more than half of them because they could not remember where the nuts were buried. The most forgetful squirrel was one named Silvertail who found some nuts that did not belong to him. A fight ensued with other squirrels who were also gathering nuts.

At this time, a flock of birds flew by and one sang: "Who's bin digging-up *my* nuts?" (Potter, 1911, p. 21). The bird then flew to where Timmy and Goody were collecting their nuts and repeated the same song, which, Beatrix Potter says, "meant nothing at all" (p. 22). The other squirrels, however, on hearing the song, attacked Timmy Tiptoes. Meanwhile, the little bird that had caused the trouble flew away. Although Timmy fled toward his nest, the other squirrels followed him, repeating the words of the bird's song. They caught him and dragged him to a tree where there was a small hole, and pushed him into it, squeezing him so "dreadfully, it was a wonder they did not break his ribs" (p. 26). Silvertail said that they would leave Timmy in the hole until he confessed to digging up the nuts of the other squirrels. In the meantime Goody Tiptoes had gone home not knowing what had happened to her husband.

Timmy Tiptoes had fallen down a hollow tree. When he finally revived, he found himself tucked in a small moss bed and very sore. A small chipmunk loaned him its nightcap and offered him food. Although Timmy was concerned that he would not be able to get out of the hole unless he lost weight, the chipmunk persuaded him to eat more and more nuts until he grew fatter.

When Goody Tiptoes hid some nuts under a tree root, they fell upon a small chipmunk who told her that her husband, Chippy Hackee, had run away and left her. Mrs. Goody Tiptoes told her that Timmy Tiptoes had also run away. Mrs. Chippy Hackee, having been told of her husband's whereabouts by a little bird, led Goody Tiptoes to the tree with the hole in it. There they heard the voices of a fat squirrel and a chipmunk singing, and the sounds of cracking nuts and nibbling. When Goody Tiptoes suggested that Mrs. Chippy Hackee squeeze into the hole, she replied that although she could, she wouldn't do it because her husband bit.

Goody Tiptoes called down to her husband and, recognizing her voice, he came up and kissed her, but he was so fat, he could not get out of the hole in the tree. Chippy Hackee, on the other hand, did not come out but stayed down below.

Two weeks later a wind blew off the top of the tree thus opening the hole so that Timmy Tiptoes could get out. He went home with Goody, who had brought an umbrella to shield them from the rain. Despite the rain, Chippy Hackee continued to stay in the tree trunk for another week.

When a large bear came walking through the woods, sniffing and looking for nuts, however, Chippy Hackee ran home. By then he had developed a cold. Beatrix Potter's picture shows him soaking his feet in a tub of hot water and mustard. Mrs. Hackee herself is in the background looking rather stern.

In the final picture of the story, Timmy Tiptoes is making certain their nut store is padlocked and Mrs. Goody Tiptoes is caring for their baby squirrels inside the tree.

In this story Beatrix Potter continues to utilize the metaphor of the animal world to portray very human problems, specifically those in marriage. The main protagonists of the story are Mr. and Mrs. Tiptoes whose relationship to each other is one of love, caring, and mutual collaboration. Eventually they live together and have a family. The final picture of the story shows Timmy Tiptoes locking up their storehouse of nuts and protecting his wife and baby squirrels.

The relationship between Chippy Hackee and his wife, on the other hand, is one marked by marital discord. Mrs. Chippy Hackee confides to Goody Tiptoes that her husband had run away and later refuses to go down the hole in the tree to see him because she says that he bites. After a wind has blown off the top of the tree, making it possible for Chippy Hackee to leave his confinement and go home with his wife, he remains in the hole for a week even though it is raining. He only leaves it when he sees a black bear sniffing around. The final picture of Chippy Hackee is one in which his wife looks sternly at him while he is soaking his feet in the mustard bath. We may suspect that this picture of marital disharmony must have had its inspiration from scenes Beatrix Potter had probably witnessed when she was growing up.

Beatrix Potter's negative view of her father, Rupert, which she often mentions in her *Journal* (see chapter 2), may well be typified in her picture of the glum, sullen chipmunk that sits by himself for a whole week in the rain and does not go home. The picture of the stern Mrs. Hackee most probably refers to Helen Potter as photographs of her show her as being rather stern, and references to her in Beatrix Potter's letters over the years seem to bear this out. By contrasting the Hackee's marriage with that of the Tiptoes, Beatrix Potter expresses her wish that her parents' home life had been different from what it was and that they had had the kind of loving relationship that existed between Timmy and Goody Tiptoes.

## Chapter 24

# Stories of Country Life

## (1913) [1911]

In addition to writing *The Tale of Timmy Tiptoes* in 1911, Beatrix Potter began to experiment with other literary productions. She wrote four short stories in the North Country dialect and submitted them to *Country Life* magazine.

### Carrier's Bob (August 1911)

Bob was a terrier dog who faithfully preceded the horses and the wagon of his master, a poor carrier named Isaac Simpson.[1] One winter day Isaac Simpson died and his widow hired Jock Sowerby to drive her deceased husband's carts. Bob, however, never went out with the carts again. He became depressed and remained pretty much by himself, wandering about the countryside.

A year after Isaac Simpson's death, a package was stolen from the cart and Jock Sowerby bought a new cur dog who

---

[1]According to Linder (1971) the story was based on an actual situation. He quotes Beatrix Potter: "The dog was a portrait of old Isaac Brockbank's terrier, the ferryman. It was his inseparable companion. After his death it used to go down to the Ferry—and wait for the boat—and go home looking forlorn" (p. 376).

fought with Bob. A wheel of the cart ran over Bob and he died. Mrs. Simpson told people "with kindly tears" that the dog's death was "well timed" as "within another fortnight she must have bought a new dog license for Bob" (Linder, 1971, p. 378). The carrier's children wrapped him in a sheet of newspaper and buried him beside the road.

The editor, Anderson Graham, rejected the story because he did not think it was "quite happy" (Linder, 1971, p. 376).

### The Mole Catcher's Burying (Sunday, October 29, 1911)

This little story consists of the conversation among a group of moles who are digging a grave (6 feet long and 6 feet deep) for the dying Jimmy Dacre beside the grave of his wife who had died a long time before. The man had killed thousands of moles and now the surviving moles are digging his grave in vengeance, while recounting the names and numbers of family members he had killed. By the time the sexton of the church arrived in the morning, Jimmy Dacre had died and his grave had already been dug.

The editor did not accept the story (Linder, 1971, p. 376).

### Pace Eggers (undated)

The third story describes an old folklore custom that Beatrix Potter had witnessed in which children recounted a series of historical incidents in sung verse. She commented that the version that she saw was confused and historically thoroughly garbled. She wrote, however, that: "For [her] part—in these days of semi-artificial folk-lore revival—we gladly bestow a whole shilling upon this genuine fragment from old times. . . . No amount of prompting will induce [the children] to remember the words; but their encounter with our turkey cock brings down the house" (Linder, 1971, p. 383).

*182*

The editor also rejected this story stating it was "not topical" (Linder, 1971, p. 376).


## The Fairy Clogs

The final story was published in the October 25, 1913, issue of *Country Life*.

(Hill Top Farm, Sunday evening, November 5, 1911)

One very cold winter day Mrs. Agnes Ann Hodgson and her sister, Mary Feirn, were at home housecleaning. Nearby was a very large frozen lake.[2] Agnes Ann had given her children a piece of bread and blackberry jam to "get shut of them" (Linder, 1971, p. 384). Mr. Carradus, driving a cart, came to their door and asked the two women if they had lost two little Herdwick lambs. Mrs. Hodgson responded that she had not nor had she missed them. With this a 3-year-old little girl and a 4-year-old boy raised their heads from a blanket that had been covering them in the cart. These were the two little "Herdwick lambs" to which Mr. Carradus referred. When he asked Mrs. Hodgson if she knew where her children had been, she replied that they were at Auntie Meg's at the Riddings. Mr. Carradus then told her that he caught them on the ice at Silverholme which was seven miles away by road and four miles across the water. Mrs. Hodgson did not believe him.

Mr. Carradus had seen the two little children on the ice behind the shelter of an island and had heard the boy's shouts in the gale. He went by himself on the glasslike ice, struggling against the wind, and, with difficulty, brought the two children to shore. They told him that they "had swimmed" from the top end of the lake, some four miles, a feat he realized a child could never accomplish as the little girl could hardly toddle. Wearing clog irons that were like skates, they had been blown down the

---

[2]Linder (1971) believes this was Lake Windermere (p. 376).

length of the lake by the fierce wind. After finding out who the children were, Mr. Carradus had interrupted his own errands to bring them home to their mother "who had never missed them" (Linder, 1971, p. 386). He had not even gone to find their father who was in the market because he thought that their father would be "unalarmed and unaware" about his children but that their mother, Agnes Ann, would be "distraught and truly thankful." Mr. Carradus's own child had died of a fever when she was 7 years old.

When Matthew Hodgson heard the story in the market he hurried home, very concerned about his children, and offered to call a doctor. Mrs. Hodgson, however, dismissed his concern, saying that Mr. Carradus's story was a pack of lies. Beatrix Potter writes: "When a person sets up for a monument of capability and good housekeeping, it is disconcerting to have two children strayed for five hours without ever missing them" (Linder, 1971, p. 387).

Mrs. Hodgson told him that the children were all right. They had had hot bread and milk and were in bed sleeping. Her husband went upstairs to look at them and then, after stabling his horse, had his tea silently. His wife "said no word about having failed to miss the children," but apologized for upsetting a bag of shot while she was housecleaning. Her husband "reddened to the tips of his ears. He had never in the course of his married life received an apology from Agnes Ann; he did not quite know how to take it. It seemed prudent to let the matter pass. He lit his pipe" (Linder, 1971, p. 388).

Later, when the children woke up, their father went to them and held them.

"It blew—it plew—it plewed!" said Tommy, "and it tatched her petticoats, and I hung on till her—" "Tatch em—tatchem! tatchem! Oh, zee pitty fairies!" crowed little Polly.
"Zur was leetle teeny weeny fairies dancing—the beech leaves they was *full* of fairies—they danced wiv us all the way across the lake—" (Fairies?—good angels, that kept them off the spring heads where the wild ducks swatter, and the ice skims thinly.) Matthew shuddered, and hugged them closer.

"Did ye none try to turn back, Tommy?" "Me *couldn't*, Dada;
me went with my legs, and my clogs *swummed* after the fairies!"
"Tis the clog irons, mother; they've slid up the ice before
the wind like a sledge" [Linder, 1971, p. 388].

This poignant little story was probably based on a real
incident. Impressive as it is, however, another factor in Beatrix
Potter's decision to write it up may have been some real or
fantasied autobiographical significance. From this standpoint it
is likely that through the story Beatrix Potter revealed how she
experienced her parents' relationship to each other, to herself,
and to her brother (compare with Mr. and Mrs. Hackee's marriage in *The Tale of Timmy Tiptoes*, written the same year). As
we have already seen, she viewed her mother as being cold and
indifferent, a person like Mrs. Hodgson who had set up "a
monument of capability and housekeeping." In this respect she
was like the figure of Mrs. Tittlemouse whom we described in
chapter 22. Beatrix Potter's characterization of the two father
figures, Mr. Carradus, who had lost his own child to fever when
she was 7 years old, and Mr. Hodgson as concerned and caring
fathers was her view of how caring a father could or should
be. The affectionate and caring attributes of a father, so clearly
presented in this story, are in marked contrast to Beatrix Potter's view of the mother figures, and undoubtedly presented
one aspect of her feelings about her own father. Although Rupert Potter was undoubtedly grouchy and critical, his daughter
loved him dearly.

It is significant that the four stories deal with aggression
from diverse, albeit related, standpoints. There is an internal
connection between the first story about Bob, the carrier's dog,
and the last one about Tommy and Polly who almost drowned.
The common denominator of these two stories is that both Mrs.
Simpson and Mrs. Hodgson, who are wives and mothers, are
represented as uncaring women: the former about her dog,
the latter about her children.

From the mole's standpoint, Jimmy Dacre is the quintes-
sential murderer, someone who has committed genocide. The

moles, symbolically viewed as small children, are united in their anger at this man and in their determination to be rid of him. They ready his grave next to that of his wife before he is even dead.

The story of *Pace Eggers*, while providing a somewhat comic relief in the quartet of stories by its childlike absurdity, expresses an aggression against important historical personages. Often such aggression, just because it is playful, is able to caricature people or situations that are basically not at all funny. Children especially delight in such behavior because it permits them to express their aggression against their parents in an acceptable fashion.

Taken as a group these four stories express Beatrix Potter's own highly conflicted relationship with her parents from her early childhood on. Now that her parents were aging, were not in the best of health, and needed her more, her resentment toward them was becoming more overt and was expressed in this series of stories. The fact, too, that Beatrix Potter's relationship to William Heelis was beginning to become more serious (he was to propose to her in the winter of 1912 [*Letters*, p. 203]) must have also contributed to the emergence of her aggression against them because she knew they would disapprove of her interest in him just as they had disapproved of Norman Warne.

## Llewellyn's Well (1911 or 1912)

Sometime in 1911 or 1912 Beatrix Potter wrote a story called *Llewellyn's Well*. The story is incomplete but the verses sketchily indicate the plan for the content of her story. It was never published, however. It is given in Linder (1971).

Morved Edwards Jones and her husband John had twin girls, Evadne and Myfanwy. One day Morved Edwards Jones went down the long hill to get some water out of a well, locking her house door and leaving her children to play outside on the door stoop.

The well was a wishing well, and its water was "fairy water" (Linder, 1971, p. 358), so many people came there to wish upon it and "sometimes" their wishes were granted. When Morved Edwards Jones came to the well, she expressed her wish for only one thing: money. Without waiting for her pitcher to be filled, and without any wishes for her children or for her husband, she left the well and went into town.

At this point the story becomes a series of incomplete verses in which the bubbling waters from the well express various predictions about the fate of Morved and her children. They foretell that for Morved money would be a curse; that she would have much sorrow, much trouble with aging and pain, and a protracted illness leading to her death. Ultimately, however, the bubbling waters predict that her tears will be pearls, and she will be forgiven. As far as the children were concerned, the bubbling waters predict that they will be gentle and pretty, that they will have joy, rest, and peace.

This little unfinished story may be viewed as a pendant to the story of *The Fairy Clogs*. It is a continuation of the basic theme of the woman who is uncaring of her children or her husband.

The bitter fate that the bubbling waters of the well foretell for Morved expresses Beatrix Potter's secret aggressive wishes for her mother. Yet, the bubbling waters, and Beatrix Potter herself, predict that ultimately she (the mother) will be forgiven.

And, just as the waters foretell happiness for the children, Beatrix Potter anticipated that now that her relationship to William Heelis was beginning to develop into something more than client-solicitor, the predictions of the fairies for "love in June, in some time soon; for *content* in July for *pleasure* in August" and for "joy, rest and peace" would come true for her (Linder, 1971, p. 359).

## Chapter 25

# Two Fairy Tales

# (1912)

In 1912 Beatrix Potter became very much interested in telling her own version of two of Charles Perrault's (1628–1703) fairy tales. They were not published but two of them are included in Linder (1971, pp. 360–374). The first of these is *Little Red Riding Hood*. Linder states that Potter rewrote her version of *Little Red Riding Hood* years later, intending to include it in *The Fairy Caravan* but it was not used.

In her 1912 version of *Little Red Riding Hood* Beatrix Potter indicates that the story is adapted from the French of Charles Perrault. It essentially follows Perrault's well-known version with a few minor modifications of the details.

The main difference between the stories of the two authors is that Perrault's version is followed by a moral whereas Beatrix Potter's is not. Perrault's moral is as follows:

From this story one learns that children, especially young lasses, pretty, courteous and well-bred, do very wrong to listen to strangers, and it is not an unheard of thing if the wolf is thereby provided with his dinner. I say wolf, for all wolves are not of the same sort; there is one kind with an amenable disposition, neither noisy, nor hateful, nor angry, but tame, obliging and gentle, following the young maids into the streets even into their homes. Alas! who does not know that these gentle wolves are of all such creatures the most dangerous! [Perrault, 1697, p. 77].

We may wonder why at this time in her life Beatrix Potter was interested in retelling this particular story, one that, according to Perrault, is essentially a cautionary tale warning pretty young girls to beware of being seduced by what seem to be harmless, caring, and attentive gentlemen. We have seen a similar theme expressed in *The Tale of Jemima Puddle-Duck*. The story seems to reflect her own anxiety about possible encounters with unscrupulous men. We do not know, of course, whether she was actually exposed to such temptations, but whether or not she was in reality is not as significant as her writing about such possibilities. It expresses her own concern that encounters with strange men (however nice) may prove disastrous. It was a warning that she must have heard many times: beware of a man, he will take advantage of you.

The other story that Beatrix Potter chose to retell was the story of *Cinderella*. There are many versions of the story but most people know the version written by Perrault. Linder (1971) states that although Beatrix Potter's version was based on Perrault's story it was considerably longer and "gives the setting in great detail" (p. 364).

A wealthy merchant lost his young wife within a year of their marriage. Her dying request was that their infant daughter be christened at the Chapel at the Palace where she had been married. After some time the merchant married a widow who:

> [R]uled the merchant's home with decorous hospitality and she reared his little daughter through childish ailments and the A.B.C. Above all she inculcated principles of truth, unselfishness, and joy in simple tasks well done, and thereby laid the foundation of a very lovable character. Perhaps she had

learned to teach through experience of earlier failure [Linder, 1971, p. 365].

This woman, however, had "two self-willed, disagreeable, nearly grown-up daughters" (Serina and Katinka) who were "offended by their parent's re-marriage," did not respect their mother, and "flouted her authority" (p. 365). The merchant made no attempt to control them as he was absorbed in his own business. An epidemic occurred and the merchant and his second wife died within a week of each other.

Even though the merchant's house and fortune should have passed on to Cinderella there was no one to assert her rights. The stepsisters became her guardians, took possession of all the property, and treated her shabbily.

Beatrix Potter introduces a mystery lady endowed with magical attributes who was known as Madame La Fée Marraine into the story. She was "a small erect little old lady who tap tapitted out of afternoons in the sunshine with an ivory-handled stick" (Linder, 1971, p. 367). She had been fond of the merchant's first wife and was godmother to Cinderella as well as to Prince Charming.

One day Madame La Fée Marraine appeared unannounced and invisible to all but Cinderella. She noted the treatment accorded to Cinderella by her stepsisters. While she approved of Cinderella's housewifely skills in the kitchen, she criticized her for having a dirty face and for not conducting herself in an elegant fashion, for not knowing how to dance or play the harpsichord, and for always being late with dinner. She then proceeded to instruct Cinderella in many social skills, teaching her how to dance the minuet as well as how to make a court curtsy. Although Cinderella was a willing pupil she did not learn to be punctual.

It came about that on one particular occasion when her godmother appeared, Cinderella informed her that her stepsisters were going to a ball at the palace the following night. She wished that she could go but realized that it would be funny if she appeared in her "dirty, sooty frock" (p. 370).

Cinderella was commanded by her stepsisters to help them dress for the ball after which they left for the palace in two sedan chairs, escorted by two fine gentlemen. While Cinderella was sitting by the fire wishing that she could go to the ball and dance just once, Madame La Fée Marraine suddenly appeared and ordered her to fetch a pumpkin, four white rabbits from a hutch, a mousetrap, a wire rat trap, and four lizards from under a flower pot. She then waved her ivory stick and turned the pumpkin into a gold coach, "harnessed by rabbits driven by a whiskered rat, attended by mouse link boys and on the back board hung four lizard footmen" (p. 371).

Madame La Fée Marraine told Cinderella that she would arrange for her to go to the ball but when the clock struck a quarter to eleven, no matter how pleasant things were, she had to return punctually. With this, she touched Cinderella's frock with her stick transforming it into a rose-colored silk gown, and gave her a pair of glass slippers. Beatrix Potter writes: "Cinderella got into her carriage, as though in a dream" (p. 371). When she arrived at the palace, the sentries saluted and, thanks to the godmother's instructions, her "deportment was perfect." Prince Charming invited her to dance and they danced repeatedly. After this he took her to supper. Everyone, including her stepsisters, was curious about who she was. At a quarter to eleven, Cinderella curtsied to the Prince and left. The gold coach took her home and then turned back into a pumpkin. When her stepsisters returned from the ball, a shabby Cinderella had to unlace them.

The Court of Nowara (clearly a pun for "nowhere") was puzzled by the fair, unknown young woman. The Prince was more than curious. He was lovesick. At the suggestion of the court chamberlain, another ball was announced. Things happened as before except this time Madame La Fée Marraine told Cinderella that she must leave the ball punctually at a quarter to twelve otherwise she would be turned into a dirty kitchen wench. The Prince was so entranced by her that everyone thought he would propose during the evening. As the clock began to strike, at first Cinderella thought that it was chiming the quarter hour but it was beginning to strike twelve o'clock. Frightened, she stopped dancing and fled but tripped over her ball dress and dropped a glass slipper. Recovering herself she ran on hearing more and more strokes of the clock. When she got outside no coach awaited her at the door and as she ran through the streets, there was a rush of mice, rats, and rabbits. She paused to take off her glass slipper and put it in the pocket of the dirty drab frock she was now wearing.

Her stepsisters returned later, excitedly discussing what had happened. The palace had been in a hubbub. No one had seen Cinderella go but someone commented on seeing a dirty looking beggar maid and a curious contraption of rats. The Prince was disconsolate but had found the glass slipper and vowed that he would marry none other than the unknown "charmer."

Accompanied by the Lord Chamberlain, sentries, and footmen, the Prince began to search the area carrying the slipper Cinderella had left behind. They tried it on the foot of every young woman including the stepsisters, but it fit no one. When the Prince noticed a very pretty, shabbily dressed girl standing in the doorway, he insisted that she be allowed to try on the slipper despite the disapproval of the Lord Chamberlain and the stepsisters. Then, the Prince tried the slipper on Cinderella himself, bowing low. Her foot slipped into it with ease and Cinderella, "smiling and blushing, drew the other little glass slipper from her pocket" (p. 374). Beatrix Potter writes, "nobody quite knew how—Madame La Fée Marraine stood amongst them, and touched Cinderella's dirty gown with her ivory-handled stick. The Prince married her within a week, and they lived happily ever after" (p. 374).

The two stories that Beatrix Potter chose to adapt from Perrault are thematically related in that both deal with a girl's relationship to a man. The story of *Little Red Riding Hood*, as we have seen, expresses a warning: "Beware of Men! They will kill you and devour you!" The story of Cinderella, by contrast, is thoroughly reassuring: "A relationship with a man can be thoroughly gratifying. You can fnd your Prince Charming, get married and live happily ever after!"

By her selection of these two stories Beatrix Potter is able to express her ambivalent feelings about a relationship to a man and also gives a clue to some of the underlying bases of her anxieties. Manifestly, these deal with her fear of annihilation by a man who, like the wolf, would kill and devour her as he did Red Riding Hood's grandmother and Red Riding Hood herself. The story, however, is set in motion by the girl's mother who sends her on the errand. Thus while the consequences are disastrous because of the girl's naiveté, there is the subtle implication that the girl's mother should have been more protective. Such a formulation would be congruent with the story about the uncaring Mrs. Hodgson, for example. The reference to the uncaring mother may also be seen more directly in the Cinderella story where the stepsisters functioning as the girl's mother surrogates demean her in every way. Negative feelings toward mother figures are more openly expressed in *Cinderella* than they are in the story of *Little Red Riding Hood*. In fact, for no specific necessity as far as the plot of the story is concerned, Beatrix Potter indicates that Cinderella's mother died within a year of her marriage (i.e., when Cinderella was still an infant) and that her stepmother also died to be replaced by her cruel daughters.

Positive feelings toward mother figures are also represented in these stories. They may be seen in the implied willingness with which Little Red Riding Hood went on her errand to see her grandmother who was "poorly" and above all by the totally benevolent and helpful attitude of Mme. La Fée Marraine, godmother of both Cinderella and Prince Charming. She is a supreme idealization of Cinderella's stepmother who "reared [her] through childish ailments and the ABC . . . inculcat[ing] principles of truth, unselfishness, and joy in simple tasks well done" (Linder, 1971, p. 365).

It is quite likely that in her story about Cinderella, Beatrix Potter identified the fairy godmother with an idealized view she had of her grandmother Jessie Potter whom she dearly loved and who entertained her with stories.

Beatrix Potter's story of Cinderella paints a beautiful picture of the fantasy life of every girl who wishes to be a princess herself, to live in a beautiful palace, and to be married to her own Prince Charming. These ubiquitous wishes express Beatrix Potter's own wishes which she too had had since her childhood. In her memories of Camfield Place (written around 1891, *Journal*, pp. 447–448), she describes her grandparents' house and specifically a part of the house that was a "delicate mystery" to her. There was a "stained yellow window" which did not open. She writes: "I used to sit there for hours looking into the stable yard and wondering if there was an enchanted prince below; but he made no sign."

Beatrix Potter writes that after Madame La Fée Marraine had touched Cinderella's "frock with her stick" and transformed it into a gorgeous gown she "got into her carriage, as though in a dream" to go to the ball. It was not only the realization of Cinderella's wish but it was also the fulfillment of Beatrix Potter's own wish as well. Now as a woman in her midforties, after years of waiting, her wish to attract her own prince might soon be fulfilled. Some years earlier it had also been her thought when she turned to read the last part of *Persuasion* after she received Norman Warne's letter of proposal (see chapter 12). While the warning to be wary of men probably still rang in her head, she felt once again that the old dream could become a reality. Her relationship to William Heelis was developing and she must have sensed that he would soon propose marriage to her. Love would conquer all.

## Chapter 26

# The Tale of Mr. Tod

## (1912) [1911]

From Beatrix Potter's letter to Harold Warne dated November 18, 1911, we learn that she had written *The Tale of Mr. Tod* some time before. The book, published in October 1912, was dedicated to "Francis William of Ulva—someday."[1]

A subtle but noticeable change had begun to take place in the content of Beatrix Potter's stories. In the writings discussed in the last two chapters we have been able to see her increasing openness in expressing the intensity and depth of her underlying feelings and conflicts.

In the manuscript that Beatrix Potter sent to the publisher she introduced her story by writing: "I am quite tired of making goody goody books about nice people. I will make a story about two disagreeable people, called Tommy Brock and Mr. Tod" (Linder, 1971, p. 210). As the publisher evidently did not like this beginning, Beatrix Potter deleted the initial phrase and altered the wording to read: "I have made many books about well-behaved people. Now, for a change, I am going to make

---

[1]Francis William was the newborn son of Beatrix Potter's cousin Caroline Hutton who had married the Laird of Ulva. The "someday" meant "when he would be old enough to enjoy the story" (Linder, 1971, p. 212).

a story about two disagreeable people, called Tommy Brock and Mr. Tod." The publisher was still not satisfied and suggested other changes. Her response to Harold Warne on July 14, 1912, was sharply critical. She wrote:

> If it were not impertinent to lecture one's publisher—you are a great deal too much afraid of the public for whom I have never cared one tuppenny-button. I am *sure* that it is that attitude of mind which has enabled me to keep up the series. Most people, after one success, are so cringingly afraid of doing less well that they rub all the edge off their subsequent work.
>
> I have always thought the opening paragraph distinctly *good*, because it gets away from "once upon a time" [*Letters*, p. 198].

She also informed Harold Warne somewhat impatiently, on November 20, 1911, that in "Saxon," Tod was a common name for a fox and that brock was a "country name" for a badger (*Letters*, p. 189).

Beatrix Potter tells her readers that Tommy Brock was essentially a "nasty person" who had a virtually perpetual grin. On occasion he ate rabbit pie but only when other food was scarce. He was friendly with Mr. Bouncer, an old rabbit who lived with his son, Benjamin Bunny, and his daughter-in-law, Flopsy (see chapter 8).

On this particular afternoon, Benjamin Bunny and Flopsy had gone out and had left old Mr. Bouncer in charge of their family of seven baby rabbits. Tommy Brock came by and Mr. Bouncer, forgetting about his charge, invited him to come inside. He was hungry, so Mr. Bouncer offered him a slice of seedcake and a glass of "Flopsy's cowslip wine" (Potter, 1912, p. 18). They chatted and smoked together, until finally Mr. Bouncer fell asleep.

When Benjamin and Flopsy returned, they discovered that the baby rabbits were gone. Quite understandably, they were very upset and angry with Mr. Bouncer. Initially, he did not admit that he had invited anyone into their house, but the smell of badger and the heavy footprints in the sand forced him to admit his error. Determined to rescue the baby rabbits, Benjamin Bunny started off to find Tommy Brock by following his footprints. After some time he met his cousin Peter Rabbit and the two rabbits followed Tommy Brock's trail which finally led them to a house belonging to Mr. Tod. There, on the kitchen table, they saw that preparations had been made for a meal for one person.

By this time it had grown dark, and as their eyes became adapted to the darkness, they observed through a bedroom window that Tommy Brock was asleep in Mr. Tod's bed still wearing his boots. They were also able to ascertain that the baby rabbits had been shut up in the oven which had not been turned on. They could find no entry into the house, so they dug a tunnel under the house, hoping to find some way to get into it.

At daybreak when they heard the fox barking, they hid themselves in the tunnel. Mr. Tod was in a vile humor, having had an unsatisfactory night hunting for food. When he entered his house he discovered the preparations that Tommy Brock had made for a meal and found that he was asleep in his bed. Actually, the badger realized that the fox was in the room, but he pretended to be asleep by snoring while he watched Mr. Tod's actions through one partially opened eye.

Mr. Tod wanted to beat up the badger either with his walking stick or with a coal scuttle, but decided not to. Instead he suspended a pail filled with water on a hook over the bed and ran a clothesline from it through a window. Then he went outside and attached the other end of the rope to a tree. During all this time the badger, pretending to be asleep, snored loudly while watching Mr. Tod's actions. After the fox went out to cut the rope so as to drench the badger, Tommy Brock quickly got up, and rolled Mr. Tod's dressing gown into a bundle which he put into the bed underneath the pail of water. He then went into the kitchen where he lighted a fire to boil some water, entirely unconcerned about the baby rabbits in the oven.

When Mr. Tod tried to gnaw through the rope, it suddenly gave way and "nearly pulled his teeth out." Hearing the crash and the splash in the house, he looked through the window and saw that water was dripping from the bed and that the pail had rolled into a corner of the room. He believed the object in the bed was the badger, and thought the pail had hit Tommy Brock and killed him. When he opened the door of his house, however, Tommy Brock threw a cup of hot tea at him and the two animals got into a terrible fight, upsetting and breaking everything in the house. Snarling and biting, they rolled outside, over the bank and down the hill away from the house.

In the meantime, when the coast was clear, Peter Rabbit and Benjamin Bunny rescued the little rabbits, which were still in the sack, and dragged them home. Flopsy and Mr. Bouncer were relieved and overjoyed when Peter Rabbit and Benjamin arrived with the baby rabbits. Flopsy forgave Mr. Bouncer and they all had dinner while Peter and Benjamin told their story.

In February 1913, four months after the publication of this story, Beatrix Potter received a letter from 6-year-old Harold Botcherby inquiring about the outcome of the battle between Tommy Brock and Mr. Tod. Beatrix Potter replied on February 17, 1913, as follows:

My dear Harold:

I have inquired about Mr. Tod & Tommy Brock, & I am sorry to tell you that they are still quarrelling. Mr. Tod has been living in the willow till he was flooded out; at present he is in the stick house with a bad cold in his head. As for the end of the fight—Mr. Tod had nearly half of his hair pulled out of his brush (= tail) and 5 bad bites, especially one ear, which is scrumpled up, (like you sometimes see nasty old Tom Cat's ears)—The only misfortune to Tommy Brock—he had his jacket torn & lost one of his boots. So for a long time he went about with one of his feet bundled up in dirty rags, like an old beggar man [*Children*, p. 164].

When we first became acquainted with Mr. Bouncer, in *The Tale of Benjamin Bunny*, he was depicted as a strict father figure who did not hesitate to whip his errant son and Peter Rabbit, and who attacked the cat with a great deal of fury. Now, Mr. Bouncer is a grandfather, an old gentleman, who is more interested in talking with a crony, smoking a cigar, and having a glass of wine than in paying strict attention to his charges, the bunny grandchildren.

Beatrix Potter sets the mood of the story at the very outset by declaring her intention to write about two disagreeable people. She depicts Tommy Brock as a nasty person without any redeeming characteristics, a description which she continues in her letter to Harold Botcherby. The theme of aggression, so obvious in this story, then proceeds in a sequential manner beginning with the neglectful grandfather whose lack of care results in his charges being abducted by the badger with the obvious implication that he will eat them.

The behavior of Mr. Tod, the fox, continues the theme of aggression. When he first sees Tommy Brock sleeping in his bed, he wants to beat him with his walking stick or with a coal scuttle. But then he changes his mind and determines to teach the badger a lesson. He decides to pour water on him by carefully manipulating the pail and the rope. The plan of having a pail spill on an enemy has all the characteristics of an adolescent prank, or a practical joke rather than a murderous assault. It hardly seems to fit in with the intense aggression expressed earlier by the threat of using the walking stick and coal scuttle to beat up the badger. Yet, when the fox goes to examine the unmoving bundle in the bed, he is pleased that his scheme "turned out better than he had planned," because he believes that Tommy Brock had been killed by the falling pail.

The fight that ensued between Tommy Brock and Mr. Tod was violent and destructive. Everything in the house was in shambles. Beatrix Potter mentions that in the course of the destruction "handfuls of Mr. Tod's sandy whiskers" were torn out, "the kettle fell off the hob. Tommy Brock put his foot in a jar of raspberry jam. And the boiling water out of the kettle fell upon the tail of Mr. Tod" (Potter, 1912, p. 75). The animals continued snarling and fighting outside, eventually rolling down the hill.

In her story Beatrix Potter carefully controls her description of the personal injuries the animals inflicted upon each other. Her letter to Harold Botcherby, however, is more specific about the extent of the damage as she tells him that nearly half of the hair had been pulled out of Mr. Tod's tail, he had five bites, and that one ear was "scrumpled." Tommy Brock's only misfortune was that his jacket was torn and that he lost one of his boots. The latter consequences may be regarded as symbolic: the jacket may refer to the skin and the boot may refer to one of his lower extremities.

Beatrix Potter provides an important determinant for the repetitive theme of aggression, one that we have seen before. This has to do with the matter of looking and observation which under certain circumstances may give rise to the liberation of aggression. In this story the act of looking is referred to repeatedly. When the rabbits approach the lair of the fox, they *peer* through the kitchen window where they *see* objects in preparation for a dinner. They look into the bedroom window and in the semidarkness they make out the figure of Tommy Brock asleep and snoring in Mr. Tod's bed. There are a number of illustrations in the published version showing the two rabbits peering into the window as well as pictures of Mr. Tod looking at the badger sleeping. The fact that the badger pretends to sleep while he is watching the activities of the fox is strongly emphasized.

We have said earlier (chapter 5, pp. 63–64) that the emphasis on looking is an expression of the scopophilic instinct, a powerful force which dominates a great deal of an individual's development. In the normal successful vicissitudes of this instinct, it becomes integrated with socially acceptable and sublimated activities. It is only where it has not been successfully integrated in the course of the individual's development that it becomes connected with activities which are asocial and punishable by law. While the instinct itself, like any other striving, is probably biologically or constitutionally based, any environmental or experiential force can serve to fixate the drive, either along healthy and sublimated lines or along pathological ones.

Beatrix Potter's remarks about the *Protection of Animals Act* give us a very important example of how the observation of a traumatic episode can bring about a subsequent pathological response. In explanation of the Act, Taylor quotes:

> Paragraph 7 in the First Schedule of the *Protection of Animals Act*, 1911: "No person who is under the age of sixteen years shall be admitted to, or permitted to remain in, the knacker's yard during the process of slaughtering or of cutting up the carcass of any animal." The penalty for failing to comply with the regulation was a fine "not exceeding ten pounds." The Act received the Royal Assent on 18 August 1911 and came into effect on 1 January 1912 [*Letters*, p. 191].

In response to this Act Beatrix Potter drafted the following letter. There is no indication, however, that it was ever published. She wrote:

> Under the amended law for the protection of animals it has become illegal for a "child" under 16 years of age to be present at the slaughter and cutting up of carcasses. It is unwise to allow little children of 4 or 5 years old to be present at a pig-killing. There have once or twice been serious accidents, where they have tried to imitate the scene in play. But do our rulers seriously maintain that a farm-lad of 15 1/2 years must not assist at the cutting up? One of the interesting reminiscences of my early years is the memory of helping to scrape the smiling countenance of my own grandmother's deceased pig, with scalding water and the sharp-edged bottom of a brass candle-stick. Pan lids were also in request. Lord Rosebery is right. The present generation is being reared upon tea—and slops [*Letters*, pp. 190–191].

We may add from our clinical knowledge that early traumatic observations may also result in emotional problems and pathological behavior in the adult.

Among the various possible traumatic observations that can take place, the observation of sexual relations is a common source of anxiety: its degree is dependent on many factors. Such observations may occur if the child witnesses the mating of animals, as on a farm, accidentally perceives the sexual activity of strangers, and especially if he or she observes parental intercourse. Children are often aroused by such sights and may experience them as fighting between the parents. They may even experience the episode as being intensely sexually stimulating to themselves and, being unable to deal with the flood of their erotic excitement, react in various ways (see chapter 5, p. 63ff). Among these reactions are aggressive or "naughty" behavior on the child's part or, specifically, some biological or physiological reaction such as wetting the bed, soiling, vomiting, and the like. It is of importance, too, that frequently children will experience the observations of their parents wrangling, bickering, or actually fighting as somehow sexual. In these instances the observations which are of a nonsexual nature may be given sexual significance by the child who does not understand what is going on.

Examining *The Tale of Mr. Tod* as Beatrix Potter presented it here we have seen a number of disparate elements that pertain to observation accompanied by anxiety. We are struck by the fact that there are certain specific details which seem to refer to humans rather than to animals. For example, there is the description of a male figure, lying in bed with his feet (in boots) protruding from under the covers. There is the towering figure of the fox whose complicated maneuvering to fill a pail with water without disturbing the badger who pretends to be sleeping, is a type of aggressive activity unlike anything an animal would do. There is the element of Mr. Tod's dressing gown which is rolled into a bundle and put into the bed. There is the subsequent element of the fallen pail and the water dripping onto the bed. Further, there is the fighting, wrangling, snarling which the two animals engage in while they roll on top of each other. And finally, there are the bunny rabbits in the oven who are frightened by the sounds of all this activity, as are Peter Rabbit and Benjamin Bunny. In the end, both Mr.

Tod and Brock are injured but survive, although the fox seems to have gotten the worst of it.

We should not be put off by the fact that the two protagonists of the story are both male, because this may have been a convenient distortion of the underlying significance of the story—and one much more acceptable to children than if the protagonists were a male and a female.

We are now in a position to understand something of the underlying significance of this story. At the very beginning Beatrix Potter announces that now she would make a story about "two disagreeable people" for "a change" (because she is tired of making "goody-goody books about nice people"). With this story she writes about an aspect of people's personalities that she had not been able to talk about before. Now, as she says, she can openly say what she thinks about some people.

She begins her story by describing old Mr. Bouncer as being negligent and inattentive to the children he is supposed to be caring for. Totally egocentric he fraternizes with the badger who is obviously an enemy, not seeming to realize the possible consequences of inviting him into his home.

Viewing this story as an expression of the personal concerns with which Beatrix Potter was involved at the time, we would suspect that the neglectful male figure, here personified by Mr. Bouncer, was her father Rupert Potter, who was beginning to show serious signs of deterioration. But, while Mr. Bouncer lacks concern for his grand-"children," Mr. Brock and Mr. Tod are the truly outwardly aggressive and totally malevolent figures. The antagonism between the two animals expresses a good deal of what Beatrix Potter felt and observed about the relationship of her parents to each other (see chapters 19 and 23). If even a fraction of the antagonism which the animals manifested in her story had been present between her parents, it must have seemed extremely terrifying to Beatrix Potter as a child. Not only was she frightened of their aggression, however, but she must have felt angry with them and resentful of them for making her life so unhappy by their behavior.

All in all, while the story is suffused with aggression, what seems to have been repressed are the erotic components of the relationship between her parents and her view of them.

Beatrix Potter's statement that she was going to make a story about "two disagreeable people," because she was tired of writing "goody-goody" books about "nice people," referred both to herself (I am tired of being a goody goody) and to her parents whom she viewed as "disagreeable." Her negative feelings toward them, strong to begin with, were intensifying, and she began to allow herself to express them.

## Chapter 27

# The Tale of Pigling Bland
## (1913) [1910]

In her letter from Sawrey on January 8, 1910, to Louise Ferguson of New Zealand, Beatrix Potter wrote: "I think I shall put *myself* in the next book, it will be about pigs; I shall put in me walking about with my old 'Goosey' sow, she is such a pet" (*Letters*, p. 173).

One of a series of Beatrix Potter's miniature letters to Andrew (Drew) Fayle (dated between 1909 and 1910 in the Sotheby sale catalogue of October 1950) was signed by Peter Rabbit. Writing as Peter Rabbit, she states that: "[Miss Potter] says that she has drawn enough rabbits. But [Peter goes on] I am to be put into one picture at the end of the pig book" (*Children*, p. 141). This would indicate that Beatrix Potter was already working on illustrations for *The Tale of Pigling Bland* at that time.

The story was completed in the early spring of 1913. On September 24th of that year she wrote to her friend Gertrude Woodward of the Natural History Museum in London that she had finally "got rid of the revised proofs" of the book the previous week and said: "it is disgracefully late. It has been such a nuisance all summer" (Linder, 1971, p. 213).

The dedication of the book was to Farmer Townley's two children: "For Cecily and Charlie. A Tale of The Christmas Pig" (Potter, 1913, p. 4).

The story begins with a mixture of fact and fiction. Beatrix Potter's old sow, Aunt Pettitoes, had eight piglings: four females and four males. The male piglets were named Alexander, Pigling Bland, Chin-chin, and Stumpy, who had had an accident to his tail. One or another of the piglets always seemed to be getting into some mischief. Beatrix Potter relates how she and Aunt Pettitoes dragged the frightened Alexander piglet out of the hoops of the pig trough where he had gotten stuck. In another incident she had whipped Cross-patch and Suck-Suck who were rooting up carrots. Cross-patch, she added in the final version of the manuscript, tried to bite her, presumably when she led her out by her ears. Finally, Beatrix Potter, critical of the piglets for eating too much and for drinking "bucketfuls of milk," decides that they must be given away. Her description of the piglets' prodigious appetites had a factual basis as she had written to Millie Warne (November 17, 1909) from Hill Top farm that: "The two biggest little pigs have been sold, which takes away from the completeness of the family group. But they have fetched a good price, and their appetites were fearful—5 meals a day and not satisfied" (*Letters*, p. 172).

After a number of the pigs were disposed of, she and Aunt Pettitoes began to get Pigling Bland and Alexander ready to go to the market. Beatrix Potter writes: "*we* brushed their coats, *we* curled their tails and washed their little faces, and wished them good-bye in the yard" (Potter, 1913, pp. 18–19; emphasis added).

Aunt Pettitoes gave the two little pigs instructions. She said: " 'Pigling Bland. . . . Take your brother Alexander by the hand. Mind your Sunday clothes, and remember to blow your nose. . . . Beware of traps, hen roosts, bacon and eggs; always walk upon your hind legs' " (pp. 19–20). Then, Beatrix Potter, speaking for herself, added impressively: " '[I]f you once cross the county boundary, you cannot come back. . . . Here are two

licences[1] permitting two pigs to go to market in Lancashire. . . .
I have had no end of trouble in getting these papers from
the policeman' " (pp. 22–23). She (Beatrix Potter) "pinned the
papers, for safety, inside their waistcoat pockets" (p. 24). Aunt
Pettitoes gave each of them eight "conversation peppermints
with appropriate moral sentiments in screws of paper" (p. 25).

The two piglets started out. After they had gone about a
mile, Alexander wanted Pigling Bland to give him one of his
peppermints as he had already eaten all of his own. He refused,
stating that they should be reserved for emergencies. They got
into a fight and "the papers got mixed up" (p. 28). They made
up again and continued along the road singing:

> "Tom, Tom, the piper's son, stole a pig
>    and away he ran!
> But all the tune that he could play,
>    was 'Over the hills and far away'!"[2] [p. 28].

---

[1]Beatrix Potter included an illustration of herself giving a license to one of the
pigs.
[2]Evidently there are several versions of the little poem. The one quoted by the
Opies (1951) is as follows:

Tom, he was a piper's son
He learnt to play when he was young,
And all the tune that he could play
Was, "Over the hills and far away";
Over the hills and a great way off,
The wind shall blow my top-knot off.

Tom with his pipe made such a noise,
That he pleased both the girls and boys,
And they all stopped to hear him play,
"Over the hills and far away."

Tom with his pipe played with such skill
That those who heard him could never keep still;
As soon as he played they began for to dance,
Even pigs on their hind legs would after him prance [p. 408, No. 508].

The Opies write:

These verses make up the second part of chapbooks titled *Tom, The Piper's Son*
and appear to form a version of the old metrical tale "The Friar and the Boy,"
the nearest British approach to the story of the Pied Piper of Hamelin. The first
part of the chapbook includes the rhyme, "Tom, Tom, the piper's son" with
which the present song is sometimes confused, as by Pigling Bland, in Beatrix
Potter's story, who went off to market singing,

Suddenly a policeman appeared and asked the pigs for their licenses. Pigling Bland was able to produce his promptly, but Alexander was not, having somehow mislaid it during the scuffle with his brother. The policeman forbade him to continue without it and insisted that he return home with him. Although Pigling Bland wanted to go back with his brother, the policeman would not allow him to do so.

Once more Beatrix Potter puts herself in the story saying that the policeman came to their house around teatime and that *she* "disposed of Alexander in the neighborhood" (p. 32).

Pigling Bland went on alone toward Market Town, knowing that the hiring fair would be the next day. It was raining, however, and he had never wanted to go anyway. He wished that he had a little garden and could grow potatoes. He wandered about and got lost. It got dark before he finally came to a henhouse where one of the hens clucked: "Bacon and eggs, bacon and eggs!" (p. 39). Although Pigling Bland was frightened, he did not heed Aunt Pettitoes' warning and determined to sleep there until daybreak.

Shortly afterward, the owner, Mr. Peter Thomas Piperson, an offensively ugly, elderly man, appeared. He took six of the

---

Tom, Tom the piper's son, stole a pig and away
  he ran!
But all the tune that he could play, was, "Over
  the hills and far away!" [p. 409].

The actual rhyme is given by the Opies:
  Tom, Tom, the piper's son,
  Stole a pig and away he run;
    The pig was eat
    And Tom was beat,
  And Tom went howling down the street [No. 510].

Children are often concerned about the stolen pig being straightway eaten; modern illustrators, however, depict the scene incorrectly. The pig was not a live one but a sweetmeat model sold by a street hawker, as is narrated in the chapbooks. . . .

The only live pigs with which Tom had anything to do are in the quite separate song (No. 508) in which Tom's musical ability is said to be such that "Even pigs on their hind legs would after him prance" [p. 411].

fowls and put them into a hamper to take to the market the following morning. Seeing Pigling Bland, he put him into the hamper too and took him into the house where he fed him some porridge.

After consulting an almanac and feeling Pigling's ribs, he determined that it was too late in the season to cure bacon and ordered the pig to sleep on the rug. In the morning, a neighbor who was giving Mr. Piperson and the hens a lift to the market whistled for him. Mr. Piperson told Pigling to shut the door behind him and not meddle with anything, threatening to come back and skin him if he did.

Beatrix Potter writes that "it crossed Pigling's mind that if *he* had asked for a lift, too, he might still have been in time for market" but he distrusted Mr. Piperson (p. 49). He ate some potato peelings and washed the porridge plates. As he worked, he sang another verse from the poem we quoted about Tom, the piper's son. Suddenly he heard a voice chime in "Over the hills and a great way off,/ The wind shall blow my top-knot off!" (p. 50) but he could find no one else in the kitchen.

Later, Mr. Piperson returned and made a lot of porridge. When he retired for the night, however, he did not properly shut the cupboard door. Pig-wig, a little black, Berkshire pig, suddenly appeared and asked Pigling to make her more porridge. He asked her how she got there to which she replied that she had been stolen. In reply to his question, of "What for?" she cheerfully replied: "Bacon, hams." When he asked her why she did not run away, she replied that she would do so after supper. Pigling Bland told her that she could not go in the dark. In reply to her question, he said that he was going to market and that he had two papers. He said that he might take her to the bridge if she had no objections.

After singing three or four verses that had to do with little pigs, Pig-wig fell asleep.

Early the next morning, Pigling tied up his bundle and woke Pig-wig, telling her that they had to leave before the hens awakened Mr. Piperson. With this, they left very carefully. As they came in sight of Westmorland, Pig-wig began to sing and dance, "Tom, Tom, the piper's son, stole a pig and away he ran!" When Pigling urged her to hurry, she asked him why he wanted to go to the market. He replied that he didn't; he wanted to grow potatoes. He warned her, however, to keep "under the wall" because there was a man plowing.

They were within sight of the bridge leading to the next county when suddenly a grocer driving a tradesman's cart came up the road. Pigling pretended to be very lame and held onto Pig-wig's arm. When the grocer noticed the two pigs, he asked them whether they were going to market. Pigling nodded assent but the grocer informed them it had been the day before and demanded to see their licenses. Pigling handed him the papers but the grocer was suspicious of Pig-wig as she was a female and the name on the license was Alexander. He consulted an advertisement in his newspaper and saw a notice of a reward for a lost, stolen, or strayed animal which he thought might be Pig-wig.

Ordering the two pigs to wait for him, he drove ahead to talk to the plowman. While he was suspicious of pigs, he did not think that a very lame pig could run away. When he got to the plowman he noticed that his horse was lame also, having gotten a stone in its hoof. It took some time to get the stone out.

In the meantime, however, Pigling wasted no time in urging Pig-wig to run as fast as she could. They ran over the bridge and over the river, hand and hand. "Then over the hills and far away she danced with Pigling Bland!" (p. 84).

There are many determinants to this story, which are, in part, based on a number of factors in Beatrix Potter's life. We have already indicated that she did have pigs that were sold because they had big appetites.

There is also some real basis for Pig-wig. Beatrix Potter's caretaker at Hill Top, John Cannon, had ordered some pedigreed baby pigs from Farmer Townley. As he was unable to get them himself, Beatrix Potter went to pick them up. At the Townley farm she saw a tiny baby black female pig and wanted to buy it. Townley did not want to let her have it, perhaps because it was the wrong color or had no pedigree. With considerable misgiving, however, he finally relented and let her take the pig saying: "You must tell [Cannon] I refused you, but you took it and I couldn't stop you" (Linder, 1971, p. 214).

According to Linder: "Cannon was shocked to see the black girl-pig, and refused to have it anywhere near the others. Then she [Beatrix Potter] was really cross, found a basket, put the little black pig in it in a blanket, got a feeding-bottle and put it beside her bed and fed it herself night and day, until in the end it became her pet, and followed her everywhere indoors and out" (p. 214).

Thus, in the story of Pigling Bland Beatrix Potter combined one reality—that she did have a male pig named Pigling Bland who had been disposed of, with another reality—that she did have a little black female pig. She then embellished a fantasy in which the two pigs became romantically involved and escaped to another area (county) "over the hills and far away" where they would be safe.

At the time this story first came into existence Beatrix Potter was determined that her life would change. She had expressed this intention in her opening remarks in *The Tale of Mr. Tod* when she wrote that she was tired of writing "goody goody books about nice people." She was in fact saying that she herself was "quite tired of being goody good and nice." She was a nice, well-behaved person but she was tired of living a life so constrained by the wishes, demands, and critical opposition of her parents. She wanted to be free, to be married in spite of their opposition.

It was not only Beatrix Potter's parents who were opposed to her wish to be free and to be married, however. She must have recognized by now that there was a part of herself, her superego, that resisted such an idea, and it was this part of herself with which she was in conflict. In *The Tale of Pigling*

*Bland* Beatrix Potter provides the reader with a vivid description of how a severely critical superego is in part derived from extreme demands for very high standards of behavior which are then internalized. At the very beginning she places herself directly into the story as an auxiliary parent or governess to the piglets, thus actively playing out the way she herself had experienced being treated. She is critical of the piglets and how they had been brought up. She complains that they eat too much and drink too much milk, that they get dirty and in trouble, and worst of all, that one of them even tried to bite her and had to be whipped. Some of the piglets, moreover, are given away (i.e., they are sold or gotten rid of). Pigling Bland and Alexander, after being instructed on how to behave are strictly warned that once they cross the county line (i.e., leave home and are independent) they can never return. Their departure implies the penalty of permanent rejection. While there is a loving note expressed by Beatrix Potter and Aunt Pettitoes by their giving the piglets some peppermints as a farewell gesture, and there are tears shed by Aunt Pettitoes, the message is painfully clear: education and proper breeding is initially established on the basis of threat and punishment by maternal figures. These early determinants of superego formation are reinforced by subsequent experiences with authoritative male figures. Throughout the story of Pigling Bland, we see references to such threatening figures as the policeman who demanded to see their licenses or the "offensively ugly" elderly Mr. Piperman whom Pigling Bland did not trust, or later the threatening grocer.

In the characterization of Pigling Bland, Beatrix Potter is able to express her own wishes. The pig says that he does not want to go to the market to be "stared at and hired by some strange farmer." The way the story is written he would be a "helper" to the strange farmer and do necessary chores for him. But this is, of course, a total absurdity and a denial of his fate, because all pigs are raised for the one purpose, which Pigwig expresses directly: to be killed and turned into bacon and ham. They would not become helpers to a farmer. The frightening Mr. Piperson feels Pigling Bland's ribs and concludes, after he consults the almanac, that it is too late in the season for curing bacon. This was a clear and direct confirmation of what Pigling Bland's fate would be. For him to go to the market was to actively do what frightened him most.

Pigling Bland's wish, à la Voltaire, was to cultivate his own garden and "grow potatoes." Translated, this expressed Beatrix Potter's own wish that she would not be sacrificed for the wishes of her parents, but that she would become independent so that she could live out and gratify her own personal needs and wishes. Her wishes are openly expressed at the very end of the story where Pigling Bland and Pig-wig dance together as they cross the bridge, "Over the hills and far away" into freedom. The story then is a testimonial of Beatrix Potter's hope and determination couched in the metaphor of animals, a metaphor with which she was most adept.

In the late summer of 1912,[3] William Heelis proposed to Beatrix Potter and, despite her parents' disapproval, she agreed to marry him. Her parents had many objections, not the least of which was that they were aged (her father was 80) and they needed her to take care of them. Rupert Potter had been ill but then he improved and his nurse, who apparently had difficulties with Beatrix Potter's mother, left.

Even though her parents objected to her engagement to William Heelis, they did invite him for a weekend. She wrote to Gertrude Woodward on September 24th that: "They never say much but they cannot dislike him" (*Letters*, p. 212). Yet they continued to disapprove and complained, as they had about Norman Warne: that William Heelis was not good enough for her.

To make matters worse fate once more dealt Beatrix Potter a bitter hand. She became seriously ill with influenza. The letter

---

[3]Taylor (1986) says the engagement took place toward the "end of 1912" (p. 130). In Taylor, Whalley, Hobbs, and Battrick (1987) the date is given as "late summer" (p. 27). In *Beatrix Potter's Letters* the time of the engagement is simply stated as "during the winter of 1912" (p. 203).

to Harold Warne dated March 3, 1913, not even written by her, contained the following message. "I have been resting on my back for a week as my heart has been rather disturbed by the Influenza. I am assured it will recover with quiet. My chest has been quite well for some time" (*Letters*, p. 203). Four days later, her letter was again written by someone else but the postscript "was added shakily by Beatrix." "The doctor has just been & he is so much pleased with my progress that I am going to keep flat a few days longer. My heart now feels quite comfortable" (*Letters*, p. 203). On April 7th she wrote that she was "well but not able to walk uphill yet" (p. 204).

Evidently she had somewhat of a setback because she wrote to Harold Warne on April 19, 1913, that she had taken a "bilious turn" but was hopeful she would be better, stating that it seemed to her to take a long time to get strong again. Ten days later, on April 29th, she said that one of her front teeth was coming out. By June 4th, however, she wrote that she was feeling stronger and very much interested in farming matters.

There seems to be little doubt that while her ill-health was determined by physical factors, the stress of her troubled relationship with her parents contributed to her physical condition. We may well imagine that having lost Norman Warne because of his illness, she was depressed over the fact that now she was ill herself, just at the time that she was looking forward to being married to William Heelis.

In her conflict with her parents about marrying Heelis, Beatrix Potter found that she had support from her cousin Caroline Clark to whom she had written telling her of the situation and asking her advice. " 'I advised her to marry him quietly, in spite of them,' Mrs. Clark remembered: 'they thought a country solicitor much beneath them . . . and she had the (now) old-fashioned ideas of duty from children to parents, and to excuse them wrote, 'I see their objections, as we belong to the Bar and the Bench' " (Lane, 1946, p. 110).

But in addition to Caroline Clark, Millie Warne (Norman's sister) had also been encouraging after Beatrix Potter told her that she and William Heelis were engaged. Beatrix Potter wrote in reply to Millie Warne's letter:

> Thank you for your kind letter. . . . I have felt very uncomfortable and guilty when with you for some time—especially when you asked about Sawrey. You would be only human if you felt a little hurt! Norman was a saint, if ever man was good. I do not believe he would object. . . . I certainly am not doing it from thoughtless light-heartedness as I am in very poor spirits about the future. We are very much attached and I have every confidence in W. H. but I think it can only mean waiting and shall never be surprised if it were for the time broken off [Lane, 1946, pp. 110–111].

There was further support from Bertram who now revealed to their parents that he had been married since November 28, 1902.[4] At the time of their marriage he was 30 and Mary Walsh Scott, the daughter of Michael Scott, a wine merchant, was 29.[5]

With all of the pressures exerted on Beatrix Potter's behalf, her parents finally relented and she and William Heelis were married October 15, 1913, at St. Mary Abbot's, Kensington. Beatrix Potter was 47 years old and William Heelis (born December 2, 1871) was 42 years old (Letter to Joseph Moscrop, December 26, 1941). She and her husband went to live in Castle Cottage, which was on her property at Castle Farm.[6] Her wish for freedom and marriage was finally realized. From then on Beatrix Potter signed her letters as Beatrix Heelis or H. B. Heelis or H.B.H. (Helen Beatrix Heelis).

---

[4]Bertram had become a farmer in Ancrum, Scotland and seldom returned to England. He died suddenly in 1918.

[5]This information was made available to me through the kindness of Judy Taylor who sent me a copy of their marriage certificate.

[6]Beatrix Potter purchased this farm in 1909. It had "a small house facing Hill Top and affording a grand view of her land" (Taylor, 1986, p. 127).

## Chapter 28

# The Tale of Kitty-in-Boots
# [1914]

Shakespeare wrote: "When sorrows come, they come not single spies, but in battalions" (*Hamlet*, Act IV, Scene 5, Line 78). This was surely true in Beatrix Potter's life at this time. For a number of years she had been having difficulties with Harold Warne about her royalty checks. His ambiguous answers to her queries about late or missing royalty payments and his failure to send her an accurate accounting were extremely irritating to her.

On August 2, 1911, in the postscript of her letter to Harold Warne she wrote: "I must confess. I sometimes regret the times when cheques were smaller but *punctual*. I do not like overlapping of seasons so late as August, unless there is some serious inconvenient reason for it, which I trust not" (FW unpublished).

A week later, on August 9th, knowing that Harold Warne was on a holiday, she wrote to his brother, Fruing, openly stating her dissatisfaction with how her royalty payments were being made.

Dear Mr. Fru,

As Mr. [Harold] Warne is in Jersey, perhaps you are in charge—(though I hope for your own sakes that you are all away at the seaside! 82 in shade here on the hills).

Would you mind telling me—without sentiment—& I trust without the slightest irritation—does FW&Co mean to pay the first installment of the 1910 royalties in *Aug* or *Sept*? The winding up cheque of the 1909 royalties was July 29th (nominally) (paid in Aug 5th).

I am *not* short. I am *not* of opinion that the circulation of the books is smaller than it ought to be, or any other of Mr. Warne's etcs. His letters are enough to drive anybody mad. I only want to know as a matter of banking arrangements whether the next cheque is going to be inside August, or whether it means Sept 15th. You had better *not* tell him I wrote; it is very annoying that he always thinks I am complaining about the *amount* of the money, whenever I ask about the *date*. I think the books sell & pay more than enough. The difficulty of getting cheques at the time promised has sometimes rather perplexed and alarmed me; but that is not the same thing, as he tries to make out [*Letters*, p. 188].

From Beatrix Potter's candid letter we can see that she had been annoyed with Harold Warne about the matter of payment for some time but her vexation had only surfaced in this particular letter.

The next year she again had problems regarding her royalty check and on September 15, 1912, she wrote to "Mr. Warne": "I have suffered no inconvenience from waiting, but I hope it will be convenient to give me a cheque when I get back or I shall be getting anxious, it has never been so much in arrear" (FW).

It appears that a portion of her 1912 royalties were still unpaid a year later. In her letter of September 13, 1913, she wrote to Harold Warne that she was "rather disturbed" that the check had not come and asked if there was going to be any delay in "keeping to the plan of settling the 1912 account, & beginning to pay the 1913 account in October" (*Letters*, p. 210). She goes on to say: "I am not short but I am spending money on building, and I ought to cut my coat according to my cloth! When one knows there is money overdue one is tempted to spending" (*Letters*, p. 210). But this whole issue was not settled at that time either.

## The Tale of Kitty-in-Boots

On February 23, 1914, using her married name, Beatrix Potter wrote to Harold Warne from Sawrey that she had not yet decided on a name for her next book but was using "the working title [of] *The Tale of Kitty-in-Boots*." She apologized for the delay but explained that she had been busy as she had "inhabited 3 houses" since her marriage (*Letters*, p. 216).

About a month later on March 20, 1914, she wrote him from 2 Bolton Gardens that her father, who was ill with cancer, was weaker and "seem[ed] to have taken another step downhill in these last two days." She added that: "He may last a good while, but it is scarcely to be wished" (*Letters*, p. 217).

On May 9, 1914, some two and a half months after that letter, Beatrix Potter wrote to Harold Warne again, telling him that she had been busy because of her "father's ill-ness . . . dropsy from internal cancer" and informed him of his peaceful death the previous evening. She wrote: "I do not think he ever had acute pain, but it has been rather a ghastly illness. We are very thankful it is over, as we feared he might drag on for weeks longer—he went suddenly at the end" (*Letters*, p. 217). In a postscript she told him that there had never been a case of cancer in the family except one old female cousin who had recovered. The official death certificate, certified by A. R. H. Bland, indicates that the cause of his death was malignant disease of the abdomen and exhaustion and states that Helen Beatrix Heelis was present at his death.

On July 12, 1914, she informed Harold Warne that she had been occupied with getting her mother settled and could not leave her alone. As a result, she had been unable to complete the book, *Kitty-in-Boots*, but added that she was a "good deal damped" that neither he [Harold] nor Fruing "seem[ed] to care much for the story, & then it was too late to think about another" (*Letters*, p. 218). Perhaps her general dissatisfaction with the Warne firm also contributed to her not completing the story. At any rate it was never published but appears in Linder (1971, pp. 219–224).

Kitty was a "serious," young, black cat who called herself Miss Catherine St. Quintin. She belonged to an old lady who, fearing that the cat might be stolen, kept her locked up at night in a washhouse. She believed that her cat was very well behaved, although on some mornings, when she came to let her out, Kitty's fur was "draggled and wet" and "her tail seemed thicker, and she scratched" (Linder, 1971, p. 219). Actually, there were two cats. During the night, a black tom cat named Winkiepeeps came to the washhouse, unlocked the window, and took Kitty's place while she went hunting.

One night Winkiepeeps was late and defiantly refused to climb through the window and take Kitty's place in the wash-house. Kitty, who was already wearing her coat and boots in preparation for going hunting, threatened to scratch him. Win-kiepeeps "changed his tone, and began to purr and coax[ed]" (p. 220) Kitty into letting him go hunting with her. Her gun (a pop or air gun) was in the possession of Cheesebox, another cat.

After giving her the gun, Cheesebox criticized Kitty for poaching along with "dirty ferrets" (p. 220), and warned her that Mr. Tod had been setting steel traps.

Kitty's use of the gun was erratic and at times the gun went off unexpectedly. For a while she stalked behind trees. She aimed and shot at a mouse but at that point, her gun was not loaded. On another occasion she was going to shoot at some sheep and crows but then was frightened away by them. She accidently shot Slimmy Jimmy, a white ferret, but did not hurt him very much. When his cousin, John Stoat-Ferret, demanded the gun and bullets, the two ferrets fought for possession of the gun. Kitty, however, painfully scratched both of their faces. Although they managed to take her gun away from her, she would not relinquish the bullets.

The two ferrets "got" a few young rabbits until they were suddenly pursued by a rabbit in a blue coat, carrying an um-brella. A fight ensued during which Kitty grabbed back her gun. While following the rabbit, the ferrets walked into one of

Mr. Tod's steel traps, but Miss Kitty, a "born poacher," continued to follow him. Finally the rabbit took a long jump, but when the cat jumped too, she caught both toes across her boots in another one of Mr. Tod's traps. Beatrix Potter writes: "It was very sad; but Miss Kitty ought not to have gone out on the sly, poaching. It served her right. It seemed plain she would have to remain in the trap till the person who had set it, let her out" (p. 222).

When Mr. Tod finally arrived he showed her half of "a fine thick black cat tail" (p. 222). As he approached Kitty, however, she pointed her gun at him. Although he promised to "release [her] from [her] uncomfortable position," she shot him through his coat sleeve. They argued and finally Mr. Tod went off, telling her that "perhaps [she] may have come to [her] senses before morning" (p. 223).

Mr. Tod had dropped his bag, but he had not claimed it as he was afraid that Kitty would shoot him. After he left, the bag began to move and a voice, belonging to Mrs. Tiggy-winkle, begged to be let out. Kitty, in turn, asked Mrs. Tiggy-winkle to free her from the trap, promising her that she would not eat her. Although the hedgehog succeeded in freeing Kitty from the trap, the cat lost one toe and had to leave her boots in the trap. Kitty then threw away her coat and gun, vowing never to poach again.

She limped home and found Winkiepeeps lying upon the hearth rug, wrapped in a shawl, with a sticking plaster on what was left of his tail. Blaming Winkiepeeps for her misfortunes, Kitty attacked him and the two cats fought all over the room.

For the rest of her life Kitty remained a little lame but stayed at home catching mice and rats in the yard, "varied by tea-parties with respectable cats in the village, such as Ribby and Tabitha Twitchit" (Linder, 1971, p. 224). Winkiepeeps, on the other hand, lived in the woods.

In her letter to Harold Warne of February 23, 1914, mentioned earlier, Beatrix Potter, briefly summarizing the plot of this story, wrote: "It is about a well-behaved prim black Kitty cat, who leads rather a double life, and goes out hunting with a little gun on moonlight nights, dressed up like puss in boots. As the gun is only a pop gun (which continually goes off) the bag is neither large nor painful." The letter is signed: "H. B. Heelis" (*Letters*, p. 216).

Later, on March 20, 1914, writing to Harold Warne about the book, she commented: "Of course there is a question of the sentimental dislike of traps. I haven't much pity for poaching cats myself; but traps are ghastly if not looked at regularly. Still I don't think this story is extra harassing" (*Letters*, p. 217).

As Beatrix Potter developed her story, she modified her original plan. Not only did Kitty lead a "double life," but there were actually two cats, one female and one male. The two cats were not distinguishable in the eyes of Kitty's owner, so Beatrix Potter affirmed her statement to Warne that Kitty was leading a "double life."

The two cats, viewed as one by their owner, represent the basic bisexuality of any individual. The cat's double, Winkie-peeps, a kind of "Doppelganger" for Miss Kitty, expresses the masculine aspect of her personality. Kitty's dressing herself in the coat and boots and carrying a gun, which she could not properly control, points to a kind of masquerade of masculinity.

The reference in Beatrix Potter's letter of February 23, 1914, to the working title of the book as *Kitty-in-Boots* is a modification of the well-known story in *Grimms' Fairy Tales* entitled "Puss-in-Boots." The cat in that story is definitely male and basically delinquent. He lies and threatens people for the benefit of his master (also male).

In Beatrix Potter's story, however, the cat does nothing for her mistress but is also a delinquent. Her "crime" is poaching, and the punishment for it is being caught in a trap and losing one toe, her jacket, and her boots, which Beatrix Potter says, "served her right." The familiar theme of losing a part of the individual's anatomy is continued in the fate of Winkiepeeps who loses half of his tail ("a fine thick black cat tail")—presumably as a consequence of his fight with the fox.

By now, we have seen this theme repeated several times in Beatrix Potter's stories, indicating her preoccupation with it. The idea of loss of a body part appears consistently, although the portion of the anatomy that is lost, or its symbolic equivalent (fishing rod, boots, jacket, etc.), varies from story to story. The manner in which the loss occurs is usually traumatic: it was taken away, torn away, shot off, or given away. The basis for such a notion, common in the fantasies of children, is that at one time *every* individual did indeed possess a penis but that it was lost as a result of some inflicted injury. Generally, these thoughts or fantasies are associated with the idea that the loss was a punishment for something the child did or thought—that it "served them right," so they had better be good or it would go even worse for them (i.e., they will be killed).

As the material in the story is presented, the punishment meted out to Kitty, the loss of a toe, is perceived by her as a punishment for poaching, which is illegal behavior. Consequently, she voluntarily gives up this way of life and embarks on a life of domesticity "catching mice and rats; varied by tea parties with respectable cats in the village such as Ribby and Tabitha Twitchit" (see chapter 11). This represents Beatrix Potter's mother's life-style, and perhaps Beatrix Potter was concerned at this time about the future of her newfound independence and freedom. Now that she was a married *woman* would she have to pursue a life-style of domesticity like her mother's, and have to give up the pleasures associated with freedom?

From another standpoint, we may also view Beatrix Potter's initial description of a story about a cat with a "double life" or, in its final version, the two similar cats, as expressing two aspects of her personality that were in conflict with each other. The story continues to express the conflicts with which she was concerned in the story of *Pigling Bland*. In this story, Kitty, which her owner knew as a good, well-behaved cat, may be considered as one aspect of herself: the good (or "goody goody") Beatrix

Potter, the view that she presented to her parents and to their friends. But there was another part of Beatrix Potter which she viewed as bad, the part that wanted to rebel against the values and dictates of her parents' social circles. It was for these forbidden wishes and fantasies that she felt she would be severely punished. Yet, ultimately she was able to brave the threat and pursue the life-style she wanted, incorporating her wish for freedom while adopting those rules of society that were congruent with her own high ethical and moral standards.

## Chapter 29

# New Directions
# ("Aesop in the Shadows")

Beatrix Potter's feelings of frustration about the way she was being treated by the Warne publishing firm continued to rankle her. Around December 18, 1915, she wrote to Fruing Warne informing him that Harold Warne had written to her that the accounts for 1913 (the year of *Pigling Bland*) were ready; but she had never received them. She wrote:

> I also should like a statement of the payments in the spring of 1914, as I do not know which season they were on account of, or exactly how we stand.
>     I promised not to ask the firm for payments while times were so difficult; but I think you will allow that the failure to send any statements at all is a trial of patience; and the overlapping and unpunctuality had begun *long before the war* [*Letters*, p. 222].

In addition to her problems with Harold Warne regarding royalty payments and accounting statements she was also displeased by the terms of her agreements with and assignments to her publisher. She went on to tell Fruing Warne:

> Your bookkeeping seems so elaborate & careful, I expect you could write them up to date with time—but if it *is* past unravelling, I think it would be better for someone to see you on my

227

behalf and get at some compromise; and also make some new arrangement with the firm about the copyright.

You know the letter of the agreements is not being kept, they were assigned upon certain terms, and conditions.

You will be busy just now with the Christmas season—such as it is. If the matter of the accounts is not gone into satisfactorily by the end of January, I shall have to take some steps about it—not in any unfriendly spirit, but to put the matter on a more businesslike footing. For one thing I should instruct my London solicitor to alter my will; I cannot leave this muddle to go on accumulating. I am writing this without any consultation with my husband; for reasons which you may guess I feel a repugnance to his intervening in any business between me and your family.

I am not likely to be in London at present; and I confess if I were I have no inclination to call at the office, it results in nothing but talking. I have done no book this season; and I should not have sent it if I had.

I am not out of temper; I am very sorry for you all, in the struggle that you must be having. But I am tired of the muddle, and it is *not* all due to the war. Neither is it *all* due to Harold; I think it would have been courteous if *you* had sent a line of regret about the half yearly interest [*Letters*, p. 222].

On June 12, 1916, almost six months later, Beatrix Potter wrote to Harold Warne stating in part:

I do not like the indefinite term of the assignment to F. W. & Co their heirs and assigns—in view of the uncertain future for all trade.

You could not help the circumstances, but you will admit I have been forbearing & patient; the agreements are virtually a dead letter.

It is unthinkable that I should ever quarrel with you & your family but if there were ever a reconstitution of your business in the uncertain future I think I ought not to be in that indefinitely tied up position, in view of my easyness in the past [*Letters*, p. 225].

The situation with Harold Warne was obviously very tense.

In April of 1917 Harold Warne was arrested. *The Times* of London reports this on Tuesday, April 3, 1917:

## ALLEGED FORGED BILL.
## CHARGE AGAINST A PUBLISHER

At the Mansion House yesterday, before the Lord Mayor, HAR-
OLD EDMUND WARNE, 56, publisher, was charged with ut-
tering a bill of exchange for £988 10s 3d., [to Mr. William Henry
Notley] knowing it to be forged. . . .
The LORD MAYOR adjourned the further hearing of the
case until Tuesday, April 10 [p. 3].

Mr. Robert Humphreys, for the prosecution, said he "was told
that the amount involved by the charge was something like
£15,000 to £17,000." As a consequence, the Lord Mayor did
not grant bail.

About a week later on April 11, 1917, *The Times* reported:

## A PUBLISHER'S BILLS.
## ALLEGED EXTENSIVE FORGERIES

At the Mansion House yesterday, before Alderman Sir Charles
Johnston, HAROLD EDMUND WARNE, 56, publisher, was
committed for trial on charges of uttering two bills of exchange
for the payment respectively of £988 10s. 3d. and £985 14s.
knowing them to be forged.
Mr. Robert Humphreys, solicitor, who prosecuted said the
bill for £988 10s. 3d. was drawn in the name of Messrs. William
Fruing and Co. (Limited), Jersey, and purported to be accepted
by Messrs. Nicholson and Co., merchants, East India-avenue
On March 8 the bill was discounted by Messrs. Reeves, Whitburn
and Co., bill brokers, Clement's-lane for the defendant, and a
cheque for the proceeds was given to him, and paid into the
account of his firm, Messrs. Frederick Warne and Co. It was
subsequently ascertained that the acceptance of Messrs. Nicholson and Co. on the bill was a forgery. The defendant was then
arrested. . . . In addition to those two bills there were 12 bills
outstanding, and they were all forgeries, their value, after de-
ducting the discount, being something like £12,000. . . .
Recently the defendant [Harold Warne] has retired bills
before they arrived at maturity, stating as his reason for doing
so that the insurance money had been paid on cargoes which
had been torpedoed and he wished to take the bills up before
maturity as he had the funds, and would not have to pay interest. . . .
In reply to Mr. Huntley Jenkins, who appeared for the
defence, the witness said his firm had had business transactions

with the defendant during the last 20 years. The defendant was a gentleman of the highest possible standing and respectability. All their transactions with him were perfectly satisfactory down to last year. The witness allowed him to draw bills on goods in transit—dried codfish for the Brazilian market, and also goods to be shipped from Canada to Brazil. The transactions were in relation to William Fruing and Co.

The charges having been read over to the defendant, Mr. Huntley Jenkins said the defendant did not desire to make any statement or to call any witnesses [p. 3].

On April 27, 1917, about two weeks later, also from *The Times*:

### £20,000 BILL FORGERIES.

At the Central Criminal Court yesterday, before the Recorder, HAROLD EDMUND WARNE, 56, publisher, was sentenced to 18 months imprisonment with hard labour [to be served at Wormwood Scrubs Prison in London] on a charge, to which he pleaded "Guilty," of forging and uttering an acceptance to a bill of exchange for £985 14s. and the acceptance to another bill.

Mr. TRAVERS HUMPHREYS, for the prosecution, said the total amount the prisoner had obtained by means of forgeries was £13,623.

Mr. HUNTLEY JENKINS, appearing for the defence, said that in addition to the bills mentioned by Mr. Travers Humphreys the prisoner wished it to be stated that he had uttered seven other bills of exchange, amounting to £6,495.

Mr. Huntley Jenkins said he wished to state that the prisoner's brother [Fruing] was in no way implicated in the forgeries and knew nothing whatever about the matter [p. 3].

At the time Wormwood Scrubs prison, a large institution, was used to confine men who were first offenders and had been sentenced for a variety of crimes. Because the philosophy of the prison was to rehabilitate prisoners under the sentence of hard labor, their training, occupations, and abilities were considered. There were many different activities to which they could be assigned such as "gardening, tailoring, wood-chop-ping, laundry, shoemaking, brush-making, carpentry, canvas-bag making, baking, cooking, work connected with stores, ad-ministration, library and cleaning of the prison" (Crew, 1933, p. 123). I have not been able to ascertain to what type of labor Harold Warne was assigned. Prisoners, after a certain time, could receive mail and visitors for specified periods.[1] From the material in the Frederick Warne Archives that I was able to examine, it is evident that Fruing Warne was in contact with his brother during his incarceration.

Fruing Warne became the head of the family publishing business which was rapidly becoming bankrupt. In order to raise enough money to avert foreclosure, he was forced to sell everything, including his home in Surbiton.

He also sought help from Beatrix Potter. Taylor writes:

> [Fruing Warne] turned . . . to Beatrix, the creator of the com-pany's most valuable assets—and the person to whom the com-pany owed the most money. The merchandise needed to be sorted out and resuscitated and perhaps Beatrix could even be persuaded to do a new book? [*Letters*, p. 233].

Beatrix Potter wrote to Fruing Warne on June 21, 1917, suggesting that they put the Appley Dapply rhymes into a book. Having found that she could "scrape together" sufficient old drawings to fill one book, she commented that "the old draw-ings are some of them better than any [she] could do now" (*Letters*, p. 141).

The genesis of *Appley Dapply's Nursery Rhymes* actually goes back to 1893 when Beatrix Potter first illustrated the rhyme "The Old Woman Who Lived in a Shoe." She had prepared a book-let illustrating another rhyme in the 1890's but it was not pub-lished. Although she had used a number of the well-known rhymes in *Appley Dapply*, others were her own invention (Linder, 1971,

---

[1]I was also unable to ascertain who visited Harold Warne during his imprisonment. The Home Office indicated that those records were not kept.

p. 225). As time went on, Beatrix Potter, more or less in her spare time, worked on plans for a book illustrating the nursery rhymes. On January 1, 1904, she wrote to Norman Warne and told him that "one *might* fall back on the rhymes—'Appley Dapply' (*Letters*, p. 85). About a year and a half later she wrote to Norman Warne about the rhymes but shortly after that he died and the book was put aside.

"In October 1917 an abridged edition of the work was published which contained six of the original rhymes together with one new one" (Linder, 1971, p. 228).

After Beatrix Potter's death the original dummy for the 1905 version of *Appley Dapply* was discovered. The thirty verses she had sent to Norman Warne for his approval are reprinted in Linder's (1971) book.

Beatrix Potter had been sympathetic to the serious troubles of her publishers and had compiled the *Appley Dapply* book to help their financial distress. Yet her resentment of the way the publishers handled their financial obligations to her had not abated. In a postscript to her letter, dated November 10, 1917, she told Fruing Warne: "Also—do not be vexed with this—I was getting so annoyed & puzzled by H's [Harold's] prevarications—that I really think if the crisis had not come you might have seen a new book by a new author HBH and Arris [sic][2]—but it most certainly would have steered quite clear of FW & Co's 'Peter Rabbits'' (*Letters*, p. 240).

## The Tale of Johnny Town-Mouse (1918)

On February 26, 1918 Beatrix Potter, wrote to Fruing Warne that a few years before she had amused herself by "writing out several of Aesop's fables, this is one that got rather longer than

---

[2]Ernest A. Aris had published a number of illustrated booklets strikingly similar to Beatrix Potter's works. The most recent was *The Treasure Seekers* which "featured a rabbit called Peter. Warne asked Beatrix to allow them to protest" (*Letters*, p. 239).

the others" (*Letters*, p. 246). The story she was referring to, *The Tale of Johnny Town-Mouse*, was based on Aesop's fable, "The Town Mouse and the Country Mouse" (Linder, 1971, p. 243). The original title of "The Tale of Timmy Willie" was altered several times. On March 18, 1918, she said that she didn't like the name Jimmy Willie and, as such a person existed, she was "inclined to call it 'The Tale of Johnny Town Mouse' " (*Letters*, p. 246). The book was published in 1918 and was dedicated to "Aesop in the shadows" (Linder, 1971, p. 244). Beatrix Potter wrote that she had had "an awful scramble to do this little book" in time for Christmas sales (p. 244).

The story is about a country mouse named Timmy Willie, who was born in a garden and went to town in a hamper "by mistake" (Potter, 1918, p. 9). What had happened was that the gardener had left the hamper, which he used to send vegetables to town, by the garden gate. Timmy Willie crept into it, fell asleep, and awakened when the hamper was lifted onto the carrier's cart. After a jolting journey, the carrier arrived in town. The street noises frightened Timmy Willie a great deal. He found himself in a house where he was terrified by the cook's screams. He scurried away, ran down a small hole, and dropped into a mouse dinner party.

Johnny Town-mouse introduced him to nine other mice with long tails and white neckties. Beatrix Potter makes the point that Timmy Willie's own tail was "insignificant" (p. 22). She writes that the friends of Johnny Town-mouse noticed this but "they were too well bred to make personal remarks; only one of them asked Timmy Willie if he had ever been in a trap" (p. 22).

Even though the mice treated him well, Timmy Willie was unhappy and felt ill. The continual noises in the house gave him a good deal of anxiety and he could not tolerate the food. Nor, for that matter, could he accept Johnny's recommendation of a soft pillow to sleep in because the sofa smelled of cat. He lost weight and was homesick. When Johnny Town-mouse asked him about himself, Timmy Willie told him about the garden. Johnny Town-mouse said: "It sounds like rather a dull place. What do you do when it rains?" (p. 33).

Finally Timmy Willie eagerly seized the opportunity to return to his home in the country. As the hamper went back and forth on a regular basis, he hid there and in due time arrived safely in his own garden. Nor did he ever try to go back to the city again.

In the spring Johnny Town-mouse arrived at the garden carrying a brown leather bag. He complained of the dampness, was frightened by a cow and the sound of the lawn mower. He had come to visit because the family in whose house he lived had gone to the seaside for Easter holidays and the cook was doing spring cleaning, being particularly dedicated to clearing out the mice. Besides there were now four kittens and the cat. It was his turn to be disappointed, however, and he went back to the city in the hamper at the next opportunity.

In conclusion Beatrix Potter writes: "One place suits one person, another place suits another person. For my part I prefer to live in the country, like Timmy Willie" (p. 59).

In Aesop's fable of "The Town Mouse and The Country Mouse," the town mice were frightened when someone comes into the room where they are starting their meal. The field mouse decides that he did not care if he had to go hungry and says good-bye to his friend with the remark: "You may eat your fill and enjoy yourself. But your good cheer costs you dear in danger and fear. I would rather gnaw my poor meals of barley and corn without being afraid of having to watch anyone out of the corner of my eye." The moral is: "A simple life with peace and quiet is better than faring luxuriously and being tortured by fear" (*Fables*, No. 41, p. 43). We may note, of course, that even in the country mice have to watch out for predators.

While Beatrix Potter's story was based on Aesop's fable, the setting and illustrations were very personal. Her picture of Johnny Town-mouse carrying a bag of golf clubs was clearly based on Dr. Parsons, and was identified as such by Mrs. Susan Ludbrook[3] (see Linder, 1971, p. 243). Mrs. Ludbrook wrote that Dr. Parsons and Mr. Heelis used to play golf together. She said:

> "When anyone wanted the doctor in the village, the villagers would say, you must find Mr. Heelis, they have gone out together with bags of sticks, and where one is you will find the other. Golf was very new then, and few knew anything of the game, but Dr. Parsons and Mr. Heelis had a private golf course constructed for their own use at Sawrey and played together there" [Linder, 1971, p. 243].

What is of particular note is that this story, written after her marriage, confirms Beatrix Potter's judgment that she preferred her life in the country to her life in London. The words of Johnny Town-mouse, who found the country "dull," expressed her mother's views and not her own.

The idea of illustrating Aesop's Fables and retelling them in her own words, with her own cast of characters, must have greatly appealed to Beatrix Potter. With these stories as a basis which she could elaborate upon using her own imagination and interpretation, she would be able to express her pleasure in retelling stories and illustrating them. She wrote a number of stories and sent them to Fruing Warne. The stories were: *The Folly of Vanity* or *The Tale of Jenny Crow*, which was her version of *The Fox and the Crow*; *Grasshopper Belle and Susan Emmet*, her version of *The Grasshopper and the Ant*. In addition to these she planned to include *The Frog's King*; *The Idle Shepherd Boy, Sour Grapes, The Hare and the Tortoise*; and *King Stork* (Taylor, Whalley, Hobbs, and Battrick, 1987, p. 66). Only *The Folly of Vanity* and *Grasshopper Belle and Susan Emmet* were included in Linder (1971, pp. 247–248). The remainder have never been published.

---

[3]Custodian at Hill Top.

## Grasshopper Belle and Susan Emmet
## (The Ant and the Grasshopper)

Beatrix Potter presents an interesting variation of Aesop's story.

After working hard collecting provisions for the winter, Susan Emmet, the industrious ant, ignores the grasshopper's pleas to let her into the house. Emmet convinces herself that it is the wind which is rattling the latch of her door. When Susan Emmet asks who is at her door, the loud wind whistles and the grasshopper's sobbing voice cries: " 'Susan Emmet, Susan Emmet, let me in! . . . Let me in, let me in, I am dying, Susan Emmet' " (Linder, 1971, p. 250). The ant deliberately did not open the door to see what made the sound. After she ate her supper and collected the dishes, Susan Emmet says: "She has had her lesson, I suppose I must let her in; she can sleep on the door mat" (Linder, 1971, p. 250). It was only then that the ant opened her door and saw the grasshopper lying dead on the doorstep.

Beatrix Potter's story follows Aesop's moral lesson that one should work and provide for the rainy or cold day when food is not available. Actually, there are several versions of the moral in the Aesop Fables but in each the ant refuses to give the insect (in one case a bettle, and in another case a cicada) any food.

Of special interest in Beatrix Potter's version is the fact that both the ant and the grasshopper are female. By structuring the story in this way she seems to allude to a mother (or governess) who neglects her daughter's needs by insisting that she work and who maintains a harsh, primitive attitude to teach her a lesson even if it means she will die.

Fruing Warne was not satisfied with the stories. He wrote on May 19, 1919:

I should rather say the proper title of the book was "Tales of Mr. Tod," 2nd series or perhaps "Aesop's Fable applied to Mr.

Tod." The "Jenny Crow"[4] part of the story is exceedingly interesting and entertaining, but unfortunately it is short. If the whole book could have been made out of the Jenny Crow incident, it might have been a different thing, but you introduce grapes, and then frogs, and then King Stork and then finally the fox and the stork. Practically you have adopted the idea of putting together five of Aesop's tales into modern language for children—with the result that your Publisher is disappointed; it is not Miss Potter, it is Aesop. Why, he added, could not they have her pigeon story (The Faithful Dove), which was brilliant? [Linder, 1971, p. 245].

Beatrix Potter was thoroughly annoyed by the criticism. She wrote categorically against doing *The Faithful Dove*: "I do bar the rather namby-pamby pigeons for this season" (May 23, 1919, FW, unpublished) and suggested that the title of the book would be *The Tale of the Birds and Mr. Tod.*

Her irritation with Fruing Warne continued and several days later, on May 29, 1919, she wrote to him from Sawrey:

> You do not realize that I have become more—rather than less obstinate as I grow older; and that you have no lever to make use of with me; beyond sympathy with you and the old firm, nothing else would induce me to go on at all. You see I am not short of money. I have never cared tuppence either for popularity or for the modern child; they are pampered & spoilt with too many toys & books. And when you inferred that my originality is more precious than old Aesop's, you *do* put your foot in it! I'm not at all sure after this indecision & interruption that I could get Jenny Crow finished this year at all. . . .
>
> I will try & do you the pigeons some day [referring to *The Faithful Dove*], but this season I can't & *won't.* . . . I could not possibly "dress up" the pigeons. Some creatures lend themselves to "dressing up" (= clothes) but birds don't. . . .
>
> I should have been drawing today but this has put me off . . . [*Letters*, pp. 257–258].

Beatrix Potter continued to seethe about the criticism of her work on Aesop's Fables. On November 3, 1919, she wrote:

---

[4]Note the similarity to "Johnny Crow" the name by which she referred to Norman Warne (see chapter 9, p. 87).

I have not been ill. . . . if I have neglected correspondence it has not been through idleness! It is absolutely hopeless & impossible to finish books in summer. I will try and get one done by next spring—But I rather doubt the policy of going on with this one; I *did* begin it earlier than usual, but was put out of my course by your evidently not caring about it—otherwise I was in full swing to finish it last May—and even now I note you are asking for the *title*—I called it the "Tale of the Birds & Mr. Tod"—was that unsatisfying? I think you had better send me back the three or four drawings which I forwarded in July, and when I see them altogether, I can consider what it looks like—I hardly remember which I have done [*Letters*, p. 259].

Further in the same letter, she wrote angrily:

I am glad you are having a good season—apart from my misdeeds—which you will have to put up with sooner or later—for you don't suppose I shall be able to continue these d . . . d little books when I am dead and buried!! I am utterly tired of doing them, and my eyes are wearing out. I will try to do you one or two more for the good of the old firm; but it is quite time I had rest from them—especially as there is still other work that I should like to finish for my own pleasure.

    I remain with kind regards and very moderate apologies yrs sincerely [*Letters*, p. 259].

Six months later, on May 7, 1920, she wrote to Fruing Warne: "I got out the half finished last year's book [*The Tale of the Birds and Mr Tod*] to look at; but alas I found such a very unenthusiastic letter put away with it. . . . I put all back in the wrapper" (*Letters*, p. 261).

A month later, on June 12, 1920, Beatrix Potter wrote from Sawrey to Fruing Warne: "I think it is only honest to tell you that book is not getting on yet . . . but I seem as if I can't screw it out, and my eyes are always tired. I am afraid you will be much vexed" (*Letters*, p. 262). The book was never completed. We can see from this that the problems with her eyesight while real could be pressed into service for other purposes.

It is understandable that Beatrix Potter responded to Fruing Warne's rejection of her adaptations of the Aesop stories with irritation and anger. While the decision of the firm was presumably guided by its judgment of what the public wanted and the prospect of sales of her works, Fruing Warne's comment about her book as being insufficiently original must have thoroughly infuriated her. Beatrix Potter knew perfectly well that many artists, composers, and writers often used the works of others for their inspiration and elaborated them in accordance with their particular creative talents. Although Beatrix Potter recognized that her abilities to paint and draw were being thwarted by changes in her vision over which she had no control, she attempted to continue to be creative by retelling, in her own unique fashion, stories that Perrault and Aesop had originated. From her unpublished stories, to be found in Linder (1971), and her drawings from this period, we may see that Beatrix Potter's work had great merit, if not by her standards comparable to her earlier work. When her stories were rejected, she lost interest in writing the book and for several years virtually gave up supplying the publishers with creative works.

It is of special interest to note that when she was almost 76, she began to rewrite the story of *Grasshopper Belle and Susan Emmet*. Evidently she was still convinced that her ideas did have merit and warranted her working them out. Linder (1971) writes that "unfortunately her revised version was never finished" (p. 246).

It was not until 1922 that Beatrix Potter published *Cecily Parsley's Nursery Rhymes* which were based on earlier material using some of the drawings she had done in 1893 and 1897. The success of *Appley Dapply's Nursery Rhymes* made the Warne Company ask for a sequel. Beatrix Potter wrote to a friend that " 'people worry me for just one or two more books,' " but, she continued, " 'My eyes are getting weak and I am tired of doing them . . . and since the war there is so much to do. . . . I have a big farm as well as my housekeeping; so I seldom sit down except to meals and necessary letters' " (Linder, 1971, p. 252).

Despite these feelings, on November 12, 1922, she wrote to Fruing Warne: "I found time, somehow, to collect some old drawings and piece them together with some additions for a little book of nursery rhymes" (Linder, 1971, p. 252). This was *Cecily Parsley's Nursery Rhymes.*

It is in this collection that we find the well-known nursery rhyme about the three blind mice which was mentioned in the first and second editions of *Peter Rabbit.* There, it will be re-called, Peter hears someone singing the song about three blind mice (see chapter 4, p. 53). Beatrix Potter's illustration for this nursery rhyme depicts two of the mice wearing glasses and playing violins. The third mouse, obviously blind, has a cane with which he is feeling his way as he runs, and a hat in his paw which is extended as though collecting alms. All three mice, however, have complete tails. We are able to see in this picture the return to a subject we have considered before: the fre-quency with which castration significance is symbolized in her stories. While in the poem the tails of the mice are cut off, in this particular illustration they are *not* cut off, the mice are not really castrated, so it would seem that the castration is undone or the damage has been restituted. Yet the mice still remain blind (i.e., symbolically castrated). Thus even though Beatrix Potter attempts to offer reassurance that the farmer's wife, or any other female, is no longer to be feared for bringing about such a horrible fate, the anxiety nonetheless persists. To con-firm this, we see that in the first printing of the story hearing the song about the three blind mice "sounded disagreeable to Peter; it made him feel as though his own tail was going to be cut off: his fur stood on end."

Beatrix Potter was not very happy about having to continue to produce books "on demand." On February 6, 1924, she wrote to Fruing Warne:

> I understand your feeling from the business point of view—but I doubt if I could ever explain *mine* to you. You as publishers like the Peter Rabbit Series; naturally enough; and pressed me to go on with them after I was sick of them—there only were about 5 I ever cared about—The clay-faced paper & over-much-colour-illustrated has always been against my taste, but [a] new

line might sell less well, and is not encouraged by you. I have always been too loyal to think of another publisher; but sometimes when I get hold of other peoples [sic] books I feel how pleasant (and expensive) it would be to be privately printed just as one liked without having to think of travellers & shops [*Letters*, p. 286].

The blows to her self-esteem that she had incurred over the years from Harold Warne, and more recently from Fruing Warne, provided her with the determination to develop her interests more fully in other directions.

## Chapter 30

# The Fairy Caravan

## (1929)

Initially, although Beatrix Potter had no intention of producing another book, she was ambivalent about it. She wrote to Henry P. Coolidge who had come from Boston with his mother to visit her: " 'Sometimes I feel I don't want to print the stories at all, just keep them for the private edification of Henry P. [Coolidge] and me. I guess we will keep some of them private and unprinted; they are more and more peculiar; I wonder what makes me spin such funny spider webs' " (Taylor, 1986, p. 169). Alexander McKay from Philadelphia persuaded her to have them published by the David McKay Company, however, and *The Fairy Caravan* appeared in the United States in October 1929.

The stories in the original version, entitled *Over the Hills and Far Away*, were written in " 'the homely idiom of the old north country speech' " (Linder, 1971, p. 294). In the copy of the privately published edition which Beatrix Potter presented to the Alexander McKay family, to add to their enjoyment of her story, she told them "more about the places and characters" by adding "copious notes neatly pencilled in the margins," and writing on the end-paper that the 'children might like some "explains" about the pictures' " (Linder, 1971, p. 295). Eventually the book was published in England. A copy of the privately published edition of the book, bearing the date October 25, 1929, was deposited at the British Museum.

On November 20, 1942, in a letter to Bertha Mahony Miller, editor and founder of *The Horn Book* magazine, Beatrix Potter wrote:

> My reason for arranging publication by another publisher in America . . . was that they were stories of a rather different sort which I have no wish to publish in this country (too personal—too autobiographical—what do you call it?) You may ask "Why print them at all then?" I suppose vanity and the desire to see them in the dignity of printed type without the expense of myself paying for printing!! . . . I have always disliked the idea of the *Fairy Caravan* being on sale here . . . [*Americans*, p. 192].

*The Fairy Caravan* is a collection of short stories, episodes, and word pictures that Beatrix Potter wrote at different times over the years and then put together in the present volume.

The first story is about Tuppenny, a short-haired guinea pig. We have already discussed this work in chapter 7. The original version of the story had been written in 1903 but was never published. Beatrix Potter modified it for purposes of this book. Tuppenny had become a part of Alexander and William's Circus, a traveling circus, a "fairy caravan," invisible to humans but visible to the animals who attend its performances as it travels from place to place.

Tuppenny represents a kind of unifying or organizing figure throughout *The Fairy Caravan*. In many of the stories he appears as the one who asks questions, and then becomes the listener when the different animals recount their experiences.

Among the prominent characters in the book are: Sandy, a West Highland terrier; Xarifa, a dormouse; Paddy Pig; Jenny Ferret; Iky Shepster, a starling; and Billy, or Pony William.

The animals, including some sheep that they meet, relate incidents that are either based on actual events that Beatrix Potter had witnessed on her farm, or on episodes about animals that her friends and neighbors related to her. On February 20, 1929, she wrote to Alexander McKay: "Every anecdote is fact—except possibly: the fairies?" (*Letters*, p. 314).

A year before she died, Beatrix Potter described how she first became "aware of the Fairy Caravan" (Linder, 1971, p. 293). One day when she was alone near Troutbeck Tongue she had watched some wild fell ponies cantering around a tree and wondered to herself if they too had seen Pony Billy. She then went on the reminisce that on an earlier occasion:

> In a soft muddy spot on the old drove road I had found a multitude of un-shod footprints, much too small for horses' footmarks, much too round for deer or sheep. I wondered were they foot marks of a troupe of fairy riders, riding . . . away into Fairyland and the blue distance of the hills. . . . The finding of those little fairy foot steps on the old drove road first made me aware of the Fairy Caravan [Linder, 1971, p. 293].

Various cats figure in the series of stories in *The Fairy Caravan*. In one, two cats, Louisa and her sister, Matilda, run a milliner's shop. One day Matilda's face was swollen because she had gotten a fishbone stuck between her teeth. She was persuaded to allow Sandy, a dog, to extract the fishbone with a pair of sugar tongs. She had to be restrained, however, to prevent her from kicking and scratching. Although she felt better, she stated that she hated dogs.

On the basis of many personal references to her dental problems in Beatrix Potter's letters, we may suppose that this story was a caricature of her own experiences with her dentist.

Many of Beatrix Potter's stories contain detailed descriptions of flowers and birds, and the beauties of nature. It is as though she were painting pictures with words by finding the most precise and accurate ones for the particular scene that she was describing. In her stories, she sought to imitate the sounds of animals and birds by using onomatopoetic words or expressions. "Birds' Place," which she described so beautifully, had been the garden of an old manor house in Hertfordshire. It had completely fallen to ruin and was the home of wild flowers, small animals, and birds (*Journal*, p. 146). She wrote to a friend (Mrs. M. C. Grimston) on February 12, 1938, nine years later: "If all the chapters had been as charming as 'Birds' Place'—it would have been a fine book!" (*Letters*, p. 386).

In one story Xarifa, the dormouse, tells Tuppenny that she was born in Birds' Place (*Journal*, p. 146), in a nest thatched with brown chestnut leaves and that she had a sister and a brother. Although he repeatedly asks her what their names were, she ignores his question and does not answer it. Pony William tells Tuppenny not to ask Xarifa questions about her siblings: "She suffered from a distressing want of appetite—when she first travelled with us. It is unwise—to remind her of Adolphus" (FC, p. 64).

As neither Xarifa nor Pony William would answer Tuppenny's questions about Xarifa's siblings, we may wonder whether this is an allusion to Beatrix Potter's own search for enlightenment, specifically sexual enlightenment. What the story implies is that when she was a child, neither parent would allow her to ask such questions and, if she did, no answer would be forthcoming.

The following chapter of *The Fairy Caravan* contains an account of the members of the circus putting on a performance in which they display a Pygmy elephant. To do this, they dress up Paddy Pig and, since he had no trunk, they shaped white peeled sticks to look like tusks, and for a trunk they attached a black stocking that had been stuffed with moss to his snout (FC, pp. 66–67). At one performance Paddy Pig sneezed so violently that he sneezed off the stocking. The pig's worst fault was forgetting to let his tail hang down. Tuppenny rode on the elephant's neck in front of the howdah inside of which was Princess Xarifa. Some little pigs in the audience believed that the "elephant" was a fraud and insisted on getting back their admission fee of peppercorns.

We may wonder whether this particular story referred to some games which Beatrix Potter either participated in or observed as a child. It is frequently observed in nursery schools, or learned from parents' reports, that little girls will play at putting various objects around the region of their genitals to play out their wish to be boys.

Habbitrot, a ewe, tells a story about twin lambs who were chasing the foam in a stream. They both fell into the swirling waters and were carried away. Frightened and cold, they called desperately for their mother. A fox, wearing a woolly shawl pulled over its ears, and leaning on a stick, attempted to entice them. When a dog suddenly appeared, the fox ran away. A shepherd rescued the two lambs and carried them to their mother.

While the incident described in this story was probably a fictionalized account of a real occurrence, we may see it as the expression of a rescue fantasy which Beatrix Potter may have entertained at one time. A similar theme is expressed in the story of Jemima Puddle-duck who was rescued from the fox by dogs.

One of the longest stories in the book relates the adventures of Paddy Pig when he wandered off into Pringle Wood. There were many strange and magical things of a frightening nature in these woods. Paddy Pig had been warned not to eat anything in the woods, but despite this warning, he ate "Tartlets" which were toadstools. As a consequence, he became very ill, delirious, and virtually psychotic. Not knowing what to do for him, the animals sent for Mary Ellen, a cat, who was knowledgeable in prescribing medications such as rue, an antidote for poisonous toadstools for sick pigs. Mary Ellen talked to the pig in such a condescending manner, however, that rather than being comforted, Paddy Pig became infuriated and violent.

Finally a veterinary retriever was brought in. Beatrix Potter cleverly uses this situation to satirize doctors. A humorous scene takes place in which the retriever "dognoses" Paddy Pig's condition. For example, the pony suggests that to take Paddy Pig's pulse they feel his tail, and, as the retriever has no watch, he suggests that they use the thermometer for that purpose. He recommends giving the pig a laxative, so they give him castor oil. The next morning the pig is better and vows that he will never again eat toadstool tartlets.

The story about Paddy Pig gives Beatrix Potter the opportunity to do more than describe the agony, the depression, the delirium of the sick pig, and the ministrations that were tried to cure his illness. She combines her sharply honed wit with a stinging bite of sarcasm to describe the roles of the simperingly sweet cat nurse, who is well meaning but inept, and the veterinarian dog, a totally ignorant physician who can only cure by means of giving the patient a laxative. It would appear that Beatrix Potter may have used some of her own personal experiences with illness to ridicule the various treatments that were instituted by physicians, whom she may have regarded as being totally incompetent. We have seen a similar idea expressed in *The Pie and The Patty-pan* in her characterization of the magpie, Dr. Maggotty.

The final story of the book, *The Fairy in the Oak*, is about an old English oak tree in which a fairy lived. It had been decided by the authorities that the oak tree had to be cut down in order to widen the road. The "Surveyor of the District Council has no sentiment and no respect, either for fairies or for oaks!" (FC, p. 219). In the end the tree was felled with much difficulty and the wood was cut up in a sawmill. The fairy, now depressed and homeless, wandered about all winter. When spring came she found that a new bridge had been built on the road and its timbers were made of the fairy's oak tree. This made the fairy happy again and she made her home in the bridge.

There seems to have been an early determinant of this story. On Friday, June 8, 1883, she noted in her *Journal*: "They cut down the old walnut up the new road. Poor old tree, I remember it almost as long as I remember anything hereabouts. They are cutting a road across the field, preparatory to building. It is the last bit of the orchards left" (p. 47).

In the story of *The Fairy in the Oak* the fairy was depressed because the oak tree was cut down and she was homeless. Yet, the chapter and the book end on a very optimistic note as the fairy finds that the oak tree served a useful purpose for society: being used to make a safe bridge for children and for vehicles. Beatrix Potter writes: "The good farmhorses bless the bridge that spares them a weary road; and Something leads them over, and helps to lighten their load" and "Something guards" the footsteps of children "by the bank of the flowery pool" (FC, p. 224).

At the time Beatrix Potter wrote *The Fairy Caravan* she had achieved success in many areas of her life. The depression she experienced in earlier years had been alleviated by the pleasure she gained from her accomplishments. She had become like the good fairy in her story and was optimistic about the amount of pleasure that her efforts would provide.

## Chapter 31

# The Tale of Little Pig Robinson
# (1930) [1893, 1894, 1901, 1902]

The writing of this story has a long history. On November 5, 1943, six weeks before her death, Beatrix Potter wrote that she had "found an old draft of Pig Robinson's first chapters dated 1893!" (*Americans*, p. 202). At that time it had been entitled *The Tale of Poor Pig Robinson*. In October of 1943, she wrote that the book "was invented very long ago" and recalled writing the first part in 1901. Inside of one of the three exercise books containing early versions of the story Linder (1971) found a note indicating that it was originally written at Falmouth in 189__, then at Sidmouth in April 1901, and "copied again" in April of the following year. In her pencil note of October 1943, Beatrix Potter stated that she did not think that "Robinson's subsequent adventures were committed to paper until the story was wanted (?) for publication . . . " (p. 257).

Linder (1971) writes that after the publication of *The Fairy Caravan* Alexander McKay asked Beatrix Potter for another book (p. 257). She showed him the story of Pig Robinson in December 1929 (see *Letters*, p. 330). It is not clear, however, whether she showed him the entire story or only what she had written many years before.

The present book was published in the United States by David McKay and in England by Frederick Warne. The American edition was dedicated to Margery, Jean, and David McKay. The Warne edition had no dedication (*Letters*, p. 330).

Beatrix Potter begins her story by telling the reader about going to the seaside for the holidays when she was a child and watching the fishing boats and the fishermen in the harbor.

There was a white cat named Susan who always met the boats. She belonged to Sam, an old fisherman and his wife, Betsy, who suffered from "rheumatics." Betsy would send Susan to the harbor to bring back some herrings. While Susan was hurrying down to the harbor one day, she met Stumpy, a large dog with a short tail who lived with Bob, a retriever, who was lame because his foot "had been trapped under the wheel of a milk cart." (We may be reminded here of "Carrier's Bob," the dog that had been run over by a cart.) On arriving at the harbor, Susan observed a cat sitting in the rigging of a ship called the *Pound of Candles*, and a small pig running around the deck of the ship.

Following this introduction, Beatrix Potter reminds the reader of Edward Lear's poem *The Owl and the Pussy Cat*, and quotes a portion of it. She states that she will tell the story of how Pig Robinson, who had a silver nose ring, came to live on the island with the Bong tree.

When he was little, Pig Robinson lived on a farm in Devonshire with his aunts, Miss Dorcas and Miss Porcas, who "led prosperous uneventful lives, and their end was bacon" (Potter, 1930, p. 22). The "carrier man" had had an accident with his donkey cart so he was unable to bring them supplies from the town and they were unable to send anything to the market. After some hesitation the two aunts decided to send Robinson to Stymouth, some distance away, to sell a few of their farm products and to bring back a number of items that they needed. All the people he met were critical of his aunts for sending him on such an errand. They were concerned about his welfare and urged him to go home before it got dark.

Down near the quay, Robinson met a sailor who invited him to look at his ship, named the *Pound of Candles*, commanded by Captain Barnabas Butcher. Although the ship reminded Robinson "of tallow, of lard, of crackle and trimmings of bacon" (p. 73), he went along anyway, not knowing that the sailor was the ship's cook.

As they boarded the ship, a large yellow cat on the deck who was blacking the captain's boots made some extraordinary faces at the pig and the cook threw a boot at it.

Robinson was fed muffins and crumpets until he fell asleep. When he awoke, the ship had already set sail and was out at sea. He tore about the deck, shrieking and finally singing a song about "Poor Pig Robinson Crusoe." After a time the sailors, tired of his singing and rushing about, got angry. The ship's cook told him that if he did not stop singing through his nose, he would make him into pork chops. At this, "Robinson fainted and fell flat upon the deck of the 'Pound of Candles' " (Linder, 1971, p. 256). The original 1893 version of the story ended at this point.

Robinson was well treated on board ship and as time went on he became fat and lazy as the ship sailed south. The cat, however, disapproved of his greediness and tried to warn him of his eventual fate on Captain Butcher's birthday. Robinson seemed not to understand and disregarded these warnings.

The cat was depressed because of being separated from the owl, "that sweet hen-bird, a snowy owl of Lapland," who "had sailed upon a northern whaler bound for Greenland" whereas the *Pound of Candles* was headed for the tropics.

One day they were becalmed and the sailors went fishing. As Robinson slept on the deck, he overheard the first mate tell the cook to cover Robinson because he did not want him to die of sunstroke in the hot sun because it scorched the skin and spoiled the "look of the crackling" (p. 93). They hoped that the captain's temper would improve before the following Thursday or he would not enjoy the roast pork.

Later, the cat found Robinson crying bitterly, terrified by what he had overheard. Calling him a fool for not paying attention to his warnings, the cat told Robinson of a plan to save him. From the crow's nest on the main mast, he had seen the top of the Bong tree on an island of the archipelago, not too far away. Moreover, he told him that the straits of the archipelago were too shallow for the *Pound of Candles*.

Then, "actuated partly by unselfish friendship, and partly by a grudge against the cook and Captain Barnabas Butcher" (pp. 99–100) the cat helped Robinson collect some necessities for his trip. In addition, the cat, using a gimlet, bored large holes in the three boats on board the ship. He pushed Robinson over the side of the ship to slide down the rope into the jolly boat tied to the stern of the *Pound of Candles*. The cat then went up the rigging and pretended to sleep.

Presently, the captain and his crew discovered that the pig was missing and with him many items such as tools, telescope, compass, provisions, and even an armchair. Moreover, they soon realized that because the three boats leaked so badly they had no way to capture the pig.

Rowing steadily, Robinson finally came to the island with the Bong tree "where a stream of boiling water flowed down the silvery strand" (p. 110) and delicious, abundant food was everywhere. It was truly a pig's paradise.

Beatrix Potter tells the readers that if they wanted a more detailed description of the island they should read *Robinson Crusoe*. She goes on to say that "the island with the Bong tree was very much like Robinson Crusoe's, only without its drawbacks." Although she had never been there herself, she states that the Owl and the Pussy Cat who visited eighteen months later had spent a delightful honeymoon on the island. They were enthusiastic about the climate, although it was a little too warm for the Owl.

Later, Robinson was visited by Stumpy and another little dog who found him "perfectly contented, and in the best of good health" (p. 111).

Beatrix Potter ends the story by stating: "For anything I know he may be living there still upon the island. He grew fatter and fatter and more fatterer; and the ship's cook never found him" (p. 111).

It is quite probable that the urging of her American and English publishers to produce another story, as well as her wish to generate further income for herself, had much to do with Beatrix Potter's going back to her earlier versions and pictures to complete *The Tale of Little Pig Robinson* in 1930. But even then she only did this after she was convinced that it was "wanted (?) for publication," having called it "most dreadful rubbish." On June 21, 1930, she indicated that "everyone will be tired of [Robinson] before the last chapter" (Linder, 1971, p. 257).

Beatrix Potter often worked on more than one story and had more than one story in mind at the same time. This seems to have been the case with *Pig Robinson*. Beatrix Potter was in Falmouth both in 1892 and in 1893, and had told Mrs. Miller that the old draft of *Pig Robinson* chapters was written in 1893 (*Americans*, p. 202), so we may suspect that at least a portion of the story was written in Falmouth. On March 28, 1894, she sent a picture letter about the story of Pig Robinson to Noel Moore's brother Eric from the Pendennis Hotel in Falmouth. Beatrix Potter's complete letter and illustrations may be found in *Letters to Children* (pp. 26–27).

What is of special interest is that about six months earlier, on September 24, 1893, she had written the *Peter Rabbit* letter to Noel Moore. It is significant that the early version of *The Tale of Pig Robinson* was written or at least conceived at about the same time. As we have seen in our discussions of other stories that were written at about the same time, it is likely that these two stories were concerned with similar or related topics with which Beatrix Potter was trying to deal at the time.

Let us compare *Peter Rabbit* and *Pig Robinson*. In both stories the animal is put into a situation of life-threatening danger. In both stories there is a male villain. In *Peter Rabbit* it is Mr. McGregor; in *Pig Robinson*, it is the cook. In both instances the animal is warned that he would be killed and eaten. In the case of Peter Rabbit, his mother, Mrs. Bunny, warns him and his siblings that their father had had an accident and been put in a pie by Mrs. McGregor. In the case of Pig Robinson, he is urged to return home, and later when he is on board the ship, he is warned by the cat that he is in mortal peril.

An atmosphere of anxiety pervades both stories. A picture accompanying Beatrix Potter's letter to Eric shows the cook waving a knife and fork. She writes that the cook wants to make the pig into sausages and that the pig is squealing as he is rowing away from the sailors. The epitome of anxiety and sheer terror is evident in the 1893 version of *Pig Robinson* when Beatrix Potter writes that "Robinson fainted on the deck of the 'Pound of Candles.'"

In both *Peter Rabbit*, and in the final version of *Pig Robinson*, however, the frightened animal is finally able to make his escape. In the case of Peter Rabbit, the animal demonstrates a counterphobic attitude by deliberately defying his mother's warning and going into a situation which is clearly dangerous. Pig Robinson follows the cook to the ship despite its reminding him of "tallow, of lard, or crackle and trimmings of bacon," and, ignoring the cat's warning, consumes large quantities of food. Both animals attempt to master their anxiety by following their instinctual urge to eat large quantities of food, Peter to the point of having a stomach-ache, Pig Robinson until he is fat. The behavior of both animals is based on a denial of the danger and also uses a method of coping with anxiety—doing actively what was done (or might be done) to one passively. In this case the animal eats a great deal rather than be eaten himself. This mechanism is continued to the very end of the story of Pig Robinson where he has gotten "fatter and fatter and

fatterer" with apparently no ill-effects and was "perfectly contented" and "in the best of good health."

The role of the cat is subject to considerable development.
In *Peter Rabbit* the cat is potentially a dangerous figure. In the
1893 version of *Pig Robinson* the cat is only mentioned in connection with Edward Lear's poem. In the final version of *Pig
Robinson*, however, the cat plays an important role in saving the
pig's life.

There is an interesting example of the plasticity of Beatrix
Potter's creativity in connection with the cat. It is curious that
*at no point* in Lear's poem does he indicate the gender of either
the cat or the owl. In keeping with this, Beatrix Potter's illustrations seem to be remarkably inconsistent about the gender of
the owl. In her letter to Noel Moore on March 4, 1897, she
comments about her picture in which she has the owl eating
out of a dish after they were married, "it is funny to see a bird
with hands, but how could *he* play the guitar without them"
(emphasis added). In the final version of the story of *Pig Robinson*, however, she writes that the cat was morose and gloomy
because of the separation from the owl and refers to the owl
as: "that sweet *hen-bird* [emphasis added], a snowy owl of Lapland" (p. 88). Thus, in the final version she specifies that the
owl is a female.

Beatrix Potter informs the readers that if they wanted to
have a more detailed description of the island with the Bong
tree, they should read *Robinson Crusoe*, a work with which she
was obviously familiar. Although in her letter to Eric Moore
she wrote that the pig landed *on* "Robinson Crusoe's island,"
in her final version she does not land him there but rather on
an island "very *like* Robinson Crusoe's [island] only without its
drawbacks" (emphasis added). The drawbacks, of course, refer
to the dangers that were present there and the work that he had
to do to make the place habitable. She described Pig Robinson's
island as a place where true gratification is a daily occurrence.
Unlike Robinson Crusoe, Pig Robinson need not do anything
but enjoy his life there.

In a letter to Helen Dean Fish on September 19, 1930, Beatrix Potter wrote, after receiving a book about Dr. Dolittle and "his fascinating ship's company:

> I also have taken a voyage, in imagination, and sent my Pig Robinson to the southern seas; but I think my adventures are cribbed from *Robinson Crusoe*, "per" Stevenson's *Kidnapped*. There is nothing new under the sun; and in the making of many books there are bound to be coincidences; it is probably that many plagiarisms are quite involuntary [*Americans*, p. 39].

Beatrix Potter's reference to *Robinson Crusoe* is particularly interesting. There are a number of ways in which Pig Robinson is identified with Robinson Crusoe. The hero of Defoe's story defied his parents' warnings not to go to sea. From his first sea voyage on, Robinson Crusoe firmly believed that he was being punished for his disobedience. His adventures culminated in his being shipwrecked on the island for more than twenty-eight years. When he discovered that the island was used by cannibals who feasted upon human flesh, he realized that he was in mortal danger and his anxiety fully erupted. Like Robinson Crusoe, Pig Robinson also defied the advice of various people who told him to return home promptly, and of the cat who told him not to eat so much. His anxiety broke out fully when he overheard that he was going to be killed and eaten. The theme of disobeying a parent's warning with the terrifying possibility of being killed and eaten is also prevalent in the story of *Peter Rabbit* written, as we have noted, at about the same time. In all instances the hero manages to escape: Robinson Crusoe from his island and the savage cannibals; Pig Robinson from the *Pound of Candles* and the cook and Captain Barnabas Butcher; and Peter Rabbit from the garden and from Mr. McGregor.

Another important theme with which Beatrix Potter was concerned in 1893 is also taken up in the two stories (*Peter Rabbit* and *Pig Robinson*). This theme had to do with the relationship of the mother or her substitutes to her offspring. The views that Beatrix Potter presents are contrasting. Mrs. Bunny is portrayed as the concerned mother who warns her offspring of the dangers of going into Mr. McGregor's garden. Diametrically opposed to the manifestation of maternal devotion of Mrs. Bunny is the attitude of the aunts Dorcas and Porcas who function as surrogate mothers for Pig Robinson. While they are cognizant of the dangers inherent in sending him on the errand, they decide to let him go nonetheless. That they themselves realize that their decision was unwise is borne out by their being "uneasy about Robinson" after he left. It is evident that they were less concerned about his welfare than about their own needs. Their remark about the carrier man is a reflection of their general attitude: "Why could not he keep out of the ditch (with the donkey cart) until after market day?"

From our consideration of the antithetical position of the two stories we are led to surmise that Beatrix Potter viewed her mother and/or the governesses as being like the selfish, unempathic Dorcas and Porcas. She expressed the wish that her mother had been as concerned about her welfare as Mrs. Bunny was about her offspring, and specifically about her errant and disobedient Peter to whom she lovingly gave the camomile tea.

It may be of some interest to note that as an "intermediary" story between the initial version of *Pig Robinson* and the final version, Beatrix Potter wrote *The Tale of Pigling Bland* (1913). In certain respects, it deals with a similar subject. In both stories the chief protagonist is a pig who is in danger of being killed and eaten. In *Pig Robinson* the "villain" is the cook, whereas in *Pigling Bland* it is Mr. Piperson, and later, the grocer. In both instances the pig is able to escape: Pig Robinson to the island; Pigling Bland to another county. In both instances the animal is able to achieve happiness with a gratification of his instinctual needs. Pig Robinson's are solitary and totally oral in nature; Pigling Bland's imply marriage and heterosexuality. It would seem that after Beatrix Potter was able to gratify her own instinctual needs through her marriage, she was able to return to and complete her story of Pig Robinson where in the final version there is an allusion to the consummation of a heterosexual relationship by the reference to the Owl and the Pussy Cat who are married and spend their honeymoon on Pig Robinson's island.

By the time Beatrix Potter sent the book to Alexander McKay for publication in 1930, her life situation had changed enormously from what it had been when she first conceived the story of *Pig Robinson*, more than thirty-five years before. She had become successful and independent in her own right and was happily married. Whereas in the story the cat was sufficiently concerned about Pig Robinson's fate to function as a deus ex machina to rescue him or, specifically, to provide a means for his escape, in real life it had been her success, her marriage, and her husband's counsel that had helped her establish her freedom.

Chapter 32

# Sister Anne

## (1932) [1929]

Although intended for inclusion in *The Fairy Caravan*, the story of *Sister Anne* was withdrawn because it was too long. Alexander McKay suggested publishing it as a separate book. Beatrix Potter told him that someone else would have to illustrate it, so he arranged to have Katherine Sturges do the drawings.

*Sister Anne*, the longest of Beatrix Potter's published works and the last story published during her lifetime, resembles a classical Gothic novella.

Much of the story takes place in an old castle that belonged to Baron Bluebeard. He had been married seven times and following the death of his seventh wife he looked for an eighth. Some distance away, in another community, lived a wealthy woman with her two daughters, Anne and Fatima, and her two sons, John and Henry. Bluebeard wanted to marry the mother for her wealth and possessions but she refused, stating that she was too old to change her way of life. Instead, she offered Fatima, her favorite daughter, to him with a sumptuous dowry.

Seventeen-year-old Fatima was a fun-loving "high-spirited girl" (SA, p. 12), who in the past had danced "down thirty couples" with Lancelot Lackland. She had seen the Baron only once, thought his beard was "lovely," and that "it must be fine to live in a castle" (SA, p. 13). In obedience to her mother's wishes, she agreed to marry Bluebeard. They left for his castle immediately after the wedding, with Fatima riding behind him on his horse. In her baggage was a basket containing a pair of pet doves or pigeons, capable of carrying messages home from the castle. The bridal couple was followed by a retinue of some ten dirty and villainous appearing troopers, riding on horses that were in very poor condition.

Five days after the wedding one of the cock pigeons flew back with a letter from Fatima to her sister Anne, asking her to visit because Fatima was lonely, and telling her to bring another dove. Sister Anne suspected that Fatima's invitation was based on more than just loneliness. She told her brothers that if the other pigeon came back while she was not there to look for a letter, and if the third pigeon came home, to come quickly to the castle, implying that their armed help would be desperately needed.

On her way to the castle Sister Anne heard many stories about strange happenings that took place there. She found the adjacent town deserted, the people having huddled furtively out of sight behind closed doors because they were afraid Bluebeard and his henchmen would pillage the town.

A brave woman, Sister Anne was determined to help Fatima. As she walked toward the castle, an old woman approached her with a "cackling laugh," making some comment about "more wives" (SA, p. 29). Another old woman, while cursing and sobbing, kept asking: "Where's Marion? Where's Marion?" (SA, p. 31).

When Sister Anne finally came to the gate and the portcullis, Wolfram, a one-eyed porter, answered her knock, called her "a pretty lass," and asked if anyone was with her (SA, p. 32). Calling him a varlet, she boldly ordered him to conduct her to her sister.

Beatrix Potter depicts a scene of dreary solitude, emphasizing the gloomy labyrinth and the dusky chambers in the castle.

Piled in with some rubbish there was a spinning wheel and broken cradle "that had rocked the first wife's child" (SA, p. 43). Worms had eaten through silken gowns, bats flitted through the gloom, and "there was a sickly smell" (SA, p. 43).

In reply to Anne's questions about her marriage, Fatima told her that Bluebeard was absent a good deal of the time, riding away with his henchmen. She described him as kind and generous to her with gifts of jewelry but a "little jealous" at times, even though there was no one for him to be jealous of. As the pikemen were rough and uncivil, Fatima had not dared to descend into the courtyard below. She had been spending her lonely days walking the battlements and bastions. Her only companion was an old hound named Rollo.

The women were suddenly frightened when they heard Wolfram's hoarse voice singing:

> What did he do with her breast bone?
>   Down, down, hey down,
> He made him a violl to play thereon;
>   Down, down, hey down! [SA, p. 45].

Sister Anne determined to go down one of the stairways. When she descended, the smell of roast meat as well as "mouldy seaweed; dead crabs, and live cats" (SA, p. 49) assailed her. Presently she came to an area where a woman named Elspeth was roasting half a sheep on a spit over a fire. When Anne approached, the terrified woman urged her to leave promptly if she would live. She repeated Marion's name saying, "Seven of them and Marion, and many another, many another. Get you gone, young woman!" (SA, p. 52). Marion, Elspeth's niece, the nurse for Bluebeard's first wife's child, had been shot when she attempted to escape. When Anne appealed to her to save her sister and herself, Elspeth told her of an unused postern door that opened into a ditch. She said that she could steal the key to it but it was useless without outside help. Sister Anne

told Elspeth that she would send her a sign after she had sig-
naled her friends. As Anne left at the old woman's insistence,
they again heard Wolfram's voice singing.

> What did he do with her tongue so rough?
> Unto the violl it spake enough!
> What did he do with her nose ridge?
> Unto the violl he made it a bridge.
>   Down, down, hey down.
> What did he do with her fingers small?
> He made him pegs to his violl withall [SA, p. 55].

A day later Sister Anne and Fatima heard Baron Bluebeard
and his henchmen arrive on horseback. When the two sisters
went to greet him, Bluebeard demanded that they serve him,
saying that he had such an appetite he could eat Anne's horse.
After supper, he asked Anne many questions about her possessions "as though he were inquiring whether it could furnish
forth another dowry" (SA, p. 65). Bluebeard was evidently very
wealthy. His chests contained many gold pieces and jewels obtained by extortion and other crimes.

One day Bluebeard returned in a terrible temper, striking
Fatima and swearing at Anne. He and his men had stopped at
an inn where they met a party of men returning from a funeral.
He joined their carousal and learned that they had just buried
a wealthy landowner who had died suddenly. This man, who
had lived nearby, had been a bachelor and "his vast inheritance"
(SA, p. 72) went to his ugly looking, spinster sister. Although
she had already received five offers of marriage she had refused all of them. Bluebeard was angry with himself for having
come too late to attend the funeral and pay his respects to the
wealthy spinster. What he did do, however, was to bribe Roger
Darkness, the heiress's confidential steward, to arrange a liaison
of some kind. As Fatima was in the way of this "suitable marriage," the implication was that he had to get rid of her.

The next day Bluebeard told Fatima and Anne that he intended to ride again and would be back at five o'clock "to sup off a rump of mutton" (SA, p. 74). Ordering Fatima to clean the silver, he gave her his keys with instructions to unlock nothing except the cupboard, not to pry or peep. He arrived promptly and "ate hugely of the rump of mutton" (SA, p. 76). The following morning he left again, telling Fatima that he must meet Roger Darkness on pressing business. Again, he gave Fatima his keys with the same instructions. After he left, it was Anne who took the keys.

When Bluebeard returned, "His voice was loud, his nose was red, his temper was vile, and his beard was blue" (SA, p. 89). He asked about his keys which Fatima brought him and he carefully examined them.

Then he informed them that he would be absent for three days, and that he expected company for dinner. " 'Roast beef and carrots for the steward, Wolfram! And a beef bone for old Rollo, and the cow's hide for a winding sheet!' Wolfram guffawed with his master, and made derisive gestures behind the chairbacks of Fatima and Sister Anne" (SA, p. 91).

Before he left the following morning, Bluebeard slipped his keys into the pouch that hung at Fatima's girdle without his usual threats and admonitions. After he was gone, the two women prepared for a siege by stocking up on provisions. They went twice to the courtyard to get water. The third time Anne went alone while Fatima stayed above guarded by the dog. When Anne returned with the last bucket of water, however, Fatima was gone. She released the dog whom Fatima had closed up in the bower and followed him through the passages of the castle to find her. As she went, she heard in the distance Wolfram singing:

What did he do with her two shins?
Unto the violl they danced Mall Simms!
   Down, down, hey down. etc. [SA, p. 105].

Finally Anne stepped into a dark chamber where her foot touched a bunch of keys on the floor and she saw her sister lying on the floor, like one dead. The candle had gone out. "Her eyes were glazed upon the nameless horror that its light had made visible" (SA, p. 109). Anne picked up the keys and dragged her sister out of the room.

Beatrix Potter then interrupts her story with a parenthetical comment, evidently preserved from the original version. When *Sister Anne* was to have been inserted into *The Fairy Caravan*, there was an introduction stating that the story was told by the second of three little mice, cousins, while they sat to spin. At this point in the story she wrote: "(Then the First and Third Cousin Mice, with nerves and fur on end, fell upon the Second Cousin Mouse and bit him)" (SA, p. 110). The story then continued.

No matter how much Anne tried to calm her sister nothing availed because she dreaded the Baron's return, fearing the worst. Anne dispatched one of the doves but it was intercepted by a peregrine falcon and never reached its destination.

Anne made further preparations for a siege, and arranged a signal with Elspeth to open the postern door.

Presently, the Baron returned. Fatima shivered with so much anxiety that Anne told him that she had the ague. Bluebeard ordered Sister Anne to open the cupboard and give him his keys. When he examined and smelled them, he shouted: "Faugh! Grease! tallow grease! and a stain; a stain that smells like blood" (SA, p. 118). When he tried to attack Fatima, she fell moaning at his feet. He kicked her and cried that she had been "peeping and prying. Since you have seen them once, you shall see them again!" (SA, p. 118). As he was dragging her, he tripped and fell over a stool that Anne had thrown in his path. Rollo jumped at his throat as he was clutching his poniard ready to kill Fatima. Suddenly Wolfram appeared informing him that Roger Darkness had just arrived. Sheathing his dagger, and promising to deal with them shortly, Bluebeard ordered the women to go to their bower and be silent or he would skin them.

After he left to discuss a marriage treaty to the red-haired spinster with Roger Darkness, Anne urged Fatima to climb with her to their bower in the turret while she carried further provisions for them. For the time being the sisters were left undisturbed. Anne gathered some material and sent up a smoke signal for her brothers and watched for an answering smoke signal from them but none was forthcoming. She sent up another dove but it too was killed by a peregrine falcon.

Three days passed. Fatima developed a fever and became delirious, continually asking whether anyone was coming.

When Bluebeard and his troop of men went out to ride again leaving only Wolfram behind, Anne went to the hall below with Rollo intending to get more wood and a loaf of bread. Meaning to kill Anne, the porter shot an arrow at her but missed and killed Rollo instead. That evening Anne released her last pigeon but did not dare to watch to see if it would also be killed. The pigeon arrived at its destination where a fire was set as a return signal. Anne, however, did not see it.

During the night Anne's brothers, Henry and John, rode to the castle on horseback. Old Elspeth opened the bastion door for John and he entered the castle. She warned him that Wolfram was there and would kill them. John, however, saw Wolfram and shot him. He was then able to join Anne and Fatima. They gave Fatima "warm mulled ale—and hope, and life" (SA, p. 149).

More messages were exchanged by smoke signals. Forty men on horseback with long bows, led by Lancelot Lackland, his brother, and Anne's brother, Henry, came into the castle, joined by men from the town. When Bluebeard and his robber men returned in the afternoon, they saw nothing to arouse their suspicions. As the Baron rode up the causeway and blew his horn, "He fell, shot through the heart by an arrow at his own gate" (SA, p. 153). The townspeople and the bowmen killed all the men of the infamous band and burned the castle to the ground.

The town prospered. Fatima married Lancelot and became a happy wife and mother. Thus ended the story.

While the story of Bluebeard is based on a folk tale, common to many European cultures and told in essence in *Grimm's Fairy Tales* under the title of "Fitcher's Bird," Linder (1971) writes that Beatrix Potter followed the story of Bluebeard written by Charles Perrault.

In contrast to Beatrix Potter's version, Perrault's story is rather brief and very much to the point. According to his account, Blue Beard was a wealthy man who owned several town and country houses. Perrault writes sympathetically that "the poor fellow had a blue beard, and this made him so ugly and frightful that there was not a woman or girl who did not run away at sight of him" (Perrault, 1697, p. 78).

Blue Beard asked a lady "of high degree" (p. 78) for the hand of one of her beautiful daughters. The girls raised objections, however, largely because of the man's blue beard and because he had been married several times before. No one knew what had become of his former wives.

So that they might become better acquainted, Blue Beard invited the two girls, their mother, and three or four of their friends to meet a party of young men from the neighborhood at one of his country houses. They spent eight days there enjoying themselves a great deal. As everything went so well, the younger daughter began to think "the master of the house had not so very blue a beard after all, and that he was an exceedingly agreeable man" (p. 80). As soon as they returned to town, they were married.

At the end of a month Blue Beard told his wife that he had to attend to some important business and would be gone at least six weeks. He suggested that she invite some of her friends to his home in the country. He gave her the keys to his storerooms and strong boxes plus the master key to all of the apartments. He also gave her a small key with the strict injunction that she was not to open the door at the end of a passage with it. He said: "I forbid you so seriously that if you were indeed to open the door, I should be so angry that I might do anything" (p. 80).

Her friends came and wandered about the house admiring the evidence of wealth before them. The girl, however, wanted to see what was in the little room so she left her guests and, despite the prohibition, opened the door. Then,

> At first she saw nothing, for the windows were closed, but after a few moments she perceived dimly that the floor was entirely covered with clotted blood, and that in this were reflected the dead bodies of several women that hung along the walls. These were all the wives of Blue Beard, whose throats he had cut, one after another [Perrault, 1697, p. 81].

Terrified, she dropped the key to the room but then picked it up, closed the door and left. Noticing that the key was stained with blood, she wiped it several times but the blood did not go away even though she washed it and rubbed the key with sand and grit. Perrault writes: "For the key was bewitched, and there was no means of cleaning it completely. When the blood was removed from one side, it reappeared on the other" (p. 82) (compare with Mrs. Tiggy-winkle, chapter 10).

Blue Beard returned early from his journey. When he demanded the keys, he asked her why the key to the little room was not with the others. He insisted that she bring it to him and then asked her why there was blood on the key. Although she denied any knowledge of it, he exclaimed that she knew well enough—that she had entered the little room. He said: "Well, madam, enter it you shall—you shall go and take your place among the ladies you have seen there" (p. 83).

Although the girl, whose name is not given, begged her husband's pardon, he insisted that she die at once, but finally gave her a quarter of an hour in which to say her prayers. The girl called her sister Anne to go to the top of the tower to see if their brothers were coming as they had promised they would visit her that day. Three times, the terrified girl begged Blue Beard for more time, but each time Blue Beard insisted that she come to him at once. Presently, when Sister Anne reported that there were two horsemen coming, the frightened girl came down in response to Blue Beard's shouts, again begging for mercy as she cast herself at his feet. As he raised his cutlass to cut off her head, she begged him for one more moment to collect her thoughts. Just then her two brothers dashed in, caught Blue Beard, and plunged their swords into his body.

Blue Beard had no heirs, so his wife became mistress of his wealth. She arranged a marriage between Sister Anne and a man with whom she had been in love, purchased a captain's commission for each of her brothers, and used the rest of the money for a dowry for her own marriage "with a very worthy man, who banished from her mind all memory of the evil days she had spent with Blue Beard" (p. 87). That is the end of Perrault's story.

Let us now compare the two versions of the Bluebeard story.

In Perrault's version, Blue Beard asks the mother, a lady "of high degree," for the hand of one of her daughters but does not seem to care which one. In Beatrix Potter's version, Bluebeard *first* asks for the *mother's* hand but she refuses him and instead "offers him" (p. 12) her favorite daughter for a bride. Fatima, thinking Bluebeard's beard is lovely and that it would be fine to live in a castle, "like an obedient daughter" consents to an early wedding.

Perrault's story continues on a rather playful, cheery note with Blue Beard encouraging his young wife to invite her friends to his home to enjoy themselves and to keep her company while he is away. None of this is evident in Beatrix Potter's version in which Fatima sends Sister Anne a note asking her to come because she is lonely. The Gothic atmosphere of the castle, suffused with gloom, imbues the entire story with horror, desolation, depression, and despair.

In both versions the consequences of violating Bluebeard's prohibition against looking are disastrous. In Perrault's version what the girl sees is very specific. There is blood on the floor; the women have been hanged; their throats have been cut. It is a terrifying sight. Beatrix Potter's version, however, in a sense, is even more horrendous for she does not say specifically what Fatima saw, but only alludes to it, and leaves it to the reader to imagine the worst. Linder (1971) writes that with a "few well-chosen words she effectively conveys the spine-chilling atmosphere: 'The guttered candle had gone out and fallen from her hand. Her eyes were glazed upon the nameless horror that its light had made visible' " (p. 325). It was as a result of this revelation that Fatima collapsed.

While the sight that greeted Fatima's terrified eyes is not specifically named, the horror is expressed by the gruesome verses that Wolfram, the one-eyed porter, sang. ("What did he do with her breast bone?" etc.)

In addition to what Bluebeard did with the bodies of the women he slaughtered, which was entirely her own invention, Beatrix Potter takes the trouble to mention Bluebeard's threat to skin Wolfram and describes Bluebeard's prodigious appetite. "He ate hugely of the rump of mutton" (SA, p. 76); "he was so hungry that he could eat Sister Anne's horse" (p. 62). His voracious appetite, together with his sadism and his mutilation of the bodies of the women, point to cannibalism, a virtual endpoint of a psychotic type of oral sadism. This idea is further emphasized by the destruction of the innocent pigeons by the peregrine falcons. Moreover, in the parenthetical remark that Beatrix Potter chose to retain in her story connecting it with *The Fairy Caravan*, the story-teller mouse evokes so much anxiety by the oral sadistic nature of the material that one of the mice bites the other. The mention of biting by the animals, who are noted for their biting behavior, continues the animalistic attributes of Bluebeard. It is highly doubtful that, as she stated later, "the mice afforded comic relief" in the story (letter to Mrs. Coolidge dated April 29, 1932, *Letters*, p. 346).

As the final literary work published during her lifetime, *Sister Anne* is a masterful document in which Beatrix Potter, at the age of 63, reveals some of the underlying bases of the anxieties and emotional problems that had troubled her since childhood. She no longer needs to resort to metaphors. The dramatis personae are people.

The setting of the story, Bluebeard's castle, may be viewed as virtually a caricature of her home at 2 Bolton Gardens in London. It will be recalled that one of her Potter cousins called it a "dark Victorian mausoleum." As a child the house must have seemed very large to her, replete with the kind of foreboding and Gothic gloom that she was able to recreate in *Sister Anne*.

While Beatrix Potter took Perrault's story as the inspiration for her book, she utilized her own experiences, both real and fantasied, in its creation. Her need for companionship with a contemporary, and for a protector, someone who would shield her from her parents, was realized when Anne Carter, three years her senior, was engaged to be her governess. It is somehow fortuitous that the true heroine of Beatrix Potter's book bears the name of Sister Anne.

Anne Carter essentially rescued Beatrix Potter from the atmosphere of 2 Bolton Gardens. The close friendship that developed between them lasted her lifetime. Beatrix Potter's devotion to her and then to her children was in large part due to Anne Carter's having provided a necessary relief from the abject loneliness and depression from which she suffered. The story of *Sister Anne* clearly implies that without Anne's help Fatima would have been killed as Bluebeard's other wives had been.

By choosing to elaborate this particular story of Perrault's, Beatrix Potter revealed that at one time, or in her unconscious, her conception of marriage and of sexuality was that the woman would be horribly tortured, beaten, and killed by the man.

While such ideas or fantasies probably contributed to her depression, it appears that at this time in her life she was able to put such thoughts aside and write about them from a distance, so to speak.

It is important that Beatrix Potter selected this particular story to relate at this time of her life, because it was one that she had initially planned to include in *The Fairy Caravan*, a book essentially designed for children. She did have some question about having it published, however. In a letter to Mrs. Coolidge on April 29, 1932, Beatrix Potter wrote:

I remarked to Mr. McKay that the book seemed likely to be over weighted by the tale of the Second Cousin Mouse; an absurd and grisly version of Bluebeard which grew to a big length. I suggested throwing it out. Which he has done. But he suggested printing it first and as a separate book under title of "Sister Anne;" and "eliminating the mice." Alright [sic]; it will suit me well. Only if the mice are "eliminated" the tale becomes deadly serious. I am recopying it and trying to improve the writing; but I am uncertain whether it is a romance or a joke. It certainly is not food for babes. He will get it illustrated in USA, which will relieve me from the difficulty of trying to illustrate human figure scenes. I think it had better have a blood curdling picture on the cover to warn off the babes! As it stood originally, the mice afforded comic relief; for instance after Fatima's discovery, the chapter ended—"Then the First and Third Cousin Mice with nerves and fur on end, fell upon the Second Cousin Mouse and bit him." I leave the responsibility intirely [sic] with Mr. McKay. But I am not sure whether he is right. It wanted alteration, taking out of the framework of the Caravan; but I am not sure how it will stand by itself. . . . it will be a queer book [*Letters*, p. 346].

From its very beginning the setting of *Sister Anne* in a medieval castle warns the reader of the "blood-curdling" events that are to follow. The description of the castle apparently was based on some actual observations. In her letter to Marian Frazer Harris Perry dated December 13, 1933, Beatrix Potter wrote in a postscript thanking her for some books:

["T]here is nothing new under the sun;" and not so often plagiarism. There are sentences of description in the first chapter of *Otto* [*Otto of the Silver Hand* by Howard Pyle] that are singularly like the description of the Castle in *Sister Anne*. I suppose we each unconsciously repeated some old description. I went to Lancaster Castle one day this summer and it was much as I remembered and had tried to describe it. All old castles are much alike [*Americans*, p. 53].

In her travels around England and Scotland Beatrix Potter had seen other castles. We do not know exactly when she had first seen the one in Lancaster before her visit there in 1933. We do know, however, of her description of visiting another castle from the entry in her *Journal*, written in Lennel, dated Wednesday, August 29, 1894, when she was 28 years of age. She described a journey that she had taken to Edlingham with her father to do some photography. She wrote that "the only fault of the expedition was the amount of time wasted on the trivial journey" and her father's insistence on "a full half hour at two stations" which resulted in the day having been spent more or less on the railway (p. 341).

In the same entry, after describing the town, she mentions that they visited a castle, probably the one known as Edin's Hall Broch. She writes that "[she] never saw a more romantically silent spot for a castle, and in itself it is well worth seeing . . . " (*Journal*, p. 341). Although "all old castles are much alike" her description of this castle must have made an impression on her so that she used some of her observations in her description of Bluebeard's castle. She wrote of "heavy black cattle" and black bullocks around the castle that were "inoffensive but bothered with the flies, and ran right round the tower like the beasts guarding the castle of *The red Etain of Ireland*." Then she quotes the following: " 'The red Etain of Ireland, once lived in Ballygan, and stole King Malcolm's daughter, the King of fair Scotland. He beats her, he binds her, he lays her on a band, and every day he dings her with a bright silver wand. Like Buliane the Roman, he's one that fears no man' " (*Journal*, p. 341).[2]

---

[2]It may have been a typographical error or Linder misread Beatrix Potter's secret code. In this well-known poem the word should be "Julian the Roman" not "Buliane

The poem that Beatrix Potter quoted is to be found in a number of fairy tales and Scottish folk stories. It is well known and the content, with some variations, has been used as the basis for several different fairy tales and folk stories.[3]

The essence of the story is as follows. A widow who had three sons told the oldest to bring water in a can from the well so that she could make a cake. By the time the boy returned, however, most of the water had leaked out through a hole so the cake was small. His mother then asked him if he would take half the cake with her blessing, or the whole cake with her curse. Seeing that the cake was small, he took the whole cake with her curse. Before he left, he gave his brother his knife to keep until he returned with the injunction to look at it every morning and if it had turned dim and rusty, then some ill had befallen him.

The young man went forth to seek his fortune and on the third day he met an ancient shepherd who was tending his flock. When he asked him to whom the sheep belonged, the man replied:

The Red-Etin of Ireland
   Ance lived in Bellygan,
And stole King Malcolm's daughter,
   The King of fair Scotland,
He beats her, he binds her,
   He lays her on a band;
And every day he dings her
   With a bright silver wand.

---

the Roman" as it is in *The Journal of Beatrix Potter*, p. 341. See Westwood (1985, pp. 363–364).

[3]Although the story was originally told by Chambers in his *Popular Rhymes* (1842), it probably goes back at least to the sixteenth century.

Westwood (1985) further states: "This old fairy tale, with its web of traditional lore, has become attached . . . to Edin's Hall Broch, on the northeastern slope of Cockburn Law. . . . Its massive appearance as well as its name probably helped attract to it the belief that it was the castle of the monstrous Red Etin . . . " (p. 367).

Like Julian the Roman,
He's one that fears no man.
It's said there's ane predestinate
  To be his mortal foe;
But that man is yet unborn,
  And lang may it be so
[Westwood, 1985, pp. 363–364].

The boy continued on his journey and eventually encountered a multitude of dreadful beasts, each with two heads, and every head with four horns. He ran away and came to a castle on a hill. Inside of it he found an old woman and asked her to hide him from the terrible beasts. She agreed to do this but warned him that the castle was a bad place because it belonged to Red Etin, a three-headed orgre who "spares no man on whom he can lay his hand" (p. 364). When the Red Etin came in, he cried:

Snouk[4] butt, and snouk ben,
I find the smell of an earthly man;
Be he living or be he dead,
His heart this night shall kitchen my bread
[Westwood, 1985, p. 364].

The ogre found the boy in his hiding place, pulled him out, and asked him three riddles. When the boy could not answer them, the Red Etin knocked him on the head with a mallet and turned him into a stone pillar.

The following morning the widow's second son looked at his brother's knife and found that it had rust on the blade so he left home to search for him. The same series of events befall him, and he too is turned into a pillar of stone in Red Etin's castle.

---

[4]"Snouk signifies, to search for with the nose like a dog . . . ," and the Red Etin is clearly a traditional ogre, able to sniff out the flesh of man—how like his rhyme is to "Fee, fi, fo, fum," the one which Shakespeare knew (*King Lear*, III. iv, 180–181) (Westwood, 1985, p. 366).

The widow's third son heard what had happened and determined to find and help his brothers. His mother also gave him a can to go to the well but a raven overhead warned him about the hole in the can. He patched it with some clay and brought enough water home for his mother to make a large cake. In response to her question, he took half the cake with her blessing.

After a time he met an old woman (a fairy) who begged him for a piece of his cake, and even though he only had half a cake, he gladly gave her a piece of it. In return she gave him a magic wand, told him the answers to the Etin's riddles, and then vanished. "When the lad comes to the place of the beasts with the two heads he does not run away but strides bravely through them" (Westwood, 1985, p. 365) and he strikes them with his wand killing them instantly.

On reaching the Red Etin's castle, he is also warned by the old woman. When Red Etin came in he repeated his threat to eat the intruder's heart, and asked the young man the three riddles which he answered promptly.[5]

With this, the Red Etin's power is broken. The young hero chops off Red Etin's three heads. After that the old woman leads him upstairs where there are many doors and out of every door comes a beautiful lady who had been imprisoned. Among them was a beautiful princess, the daughter of the king of Scotland. The old lady then leads him to a dungeon where there are two stone pillars. He touches them with his wand and immediately his two brothers are restored to life. The next day they all start out for the King of Scotland's court. As a reward, the king gives the boy his daughter and nobles' daughters to his two brothers in marriage. They all live happily ever after.

---

[5]The three riddles which the Red Etin asks were as follows: (1) Whether Ireland or Scotland was first inhabited. (2) Whether man was made for woman or woman for man. (3) Whether men or beasts were made first. The answers to the riddles given in Spence (1948) were that Ireland had been peopled with folk before Scotland; that man and woman were made for each other; and that the beasts were created before men.

We can readily see that this story closely resembles the familiar story of *Jack and the Beanstalk* and other similar tales (see also Rank, 1912; Opie and Opie, 1974, pp. 47–65).

What is important about Beatrix Potter's associations in her *Journal* entry is that she reveals the nature of her own emotional struggles at this time. She was photographing with her father and was annoyed with him. She comments twice that it was hot. With regard to the castle, she writes: "I never saw a more romantically silent spot for a castle, and itself it is well worth seeing." While she was angry with her father and disappointed with him, the scene was romantic and there was an implied reference to some erotic feelings which were engendered in her. She ends the description of the visit by stating the following:

> There is a curious turret-stair round and round, with a graceful pillar where it comes out into the upper air. I went up to the first window; there is a gap above which an active person might pass, but the upper part of the sandstone stairs looks unsteady. It must be a solemn place on a moonlight night [p. 341].

The entire situation which Beatrix Potter dutifully recorded in her *Journal*, at the age of 28, alludes both to frightening and erotic associations involving her father (for whom "the sandstone steps look[ed] unsteady"). In the main, the reference in her *Journal* suggests that Beatrix Potter's conception of her father and of men in general at certain times must have been similar to her descriptions of the loud, fearsome ogre, the Red Etin. I want to stress, however, that I do not imply that in reality Rupert Potter's personality was identical with that of the ogre. The context of the material strongly suggests that, like many girls, Beatrix Potter did have such fantasies about him at one time.

There are a number of parallels between the stories of *Sister Anne* and *Blue Beard* and the poem about the Red Etin. In the poem, the girls are beaten daily with a silver wand whereas in the story of Blue Beard they are tortured and killed.

278

We have been able to see from our clinical work that such stories, as well as the poem quoted by Beatrix Potter in her *Journal*, have a sexual, sadomasochistic significance, a common element in many fantasies of children of both sexes.[6]

It may be noted that there is a noticeable parallel between the Oedipus myth and the poem about Red Etin, in which the young man is able to answer the three riddles posed by the ogre, who then loses his power and is killed, after which the young man is awarded the princess by the benevolent King of Scotland.

Both in Beatrix Potter's *Sister Anne* and in Perrault's *Blue Beard*, the women are subjected to a strict prohibition. They must not look into the forbidden room, and, by implication, must not know what it contains. The admonition not to look, or not to know, in itself evokes and heightens curiosity. By handing the girl the key to the forbidden room, the temptation is further enhanced. Despite the strictness of the prohibition expressed by Blue Beard in Perrault's version, forbidding the girl not to look into the room "so seriously that if [she] were indeed to open the door [he] should be so angry that [he] might do anything," she is drawn by a virtual compulsion to defy his command and disobey him, especially since he has provided her with the key.

We know that developmentally the need to look and to know is present in all children and is often associated with a curiosity to learn about the parents' personal life (Nunberg, 1961). Children will rummage through drawers, boxes, closets, and cabinets[7] looking for evidence of their parents' sexuality or another secret about either of their parents. So great is the drive that in Perrault's story the girl leaves her guests because she was so "impatient to go to inspect the little room" (p. 86). Bettelheim (1975) provides further suggestions as to the significance of this story (pp. 299–303).

---

[6]While the only meaning of the term *ding* that I have been able to ascertain is to beat or thrust violently, I have heard it used colloquially to indicate sexual relations, and the term *dingus* used to refer to the male genital.

[7]Beatrix Potter writes that, after the destruction of Bluebeard's castle, the children in the village called its "tottering moldering turret" "Bluebeard's Cupboard."

The juxtaposition of the depressive, anxious setting in which Fatima finds herself, the incredible feeling of loneliness that pervades her days in Bluebeard's castle, with the material dealing with the violent, primitive oral sadism, provides us with an important clue to the psychological aspects of Beatrix Potter's own early depression. We have seen the reference to this theme in a number of her stories, and especially in *The Tale of Little Pig Robinson*. We may understand this theme clinically as being connected with a regression in which Beatrix Potter turned her own very early oral aggressive impulses against herself. The angrier she felt toward her parents and their surrogates, the more intense was the regression. As the pathways to regression became established and fixed, she became increasingly able to revert to feelings of depression associated with oral sadism whenever circumstances in the world of reality proved unduly strong, as when she felt unloved, or guilty, or incapable.

There is another aspect of Beatrix Potter's anxiety expressed in this story. While she blamed Fatima's mother for turning her over to Bluebeard, in both the Perrault version and in her story, the girl herself was intrigued by the idea of marrying a man like Bluebeard. His reputation was well known, and yet mother and daughter, in both versions, agreed to the match. By Beatrix Potter's allusion to this material we are drawn to the conclusion that there were powerful masochistic strivings in Beatrix Potter's own personality which were enormously frightening to her (compare with chapter 12, pp. 113–114; *Letters*, p. 121).

We are able to see a split in Beatrix Potter's attitude about sexual matters if we view Fatima and Sister Anne as representing two contrasting views of her own makeup. From this standpoint, Fatima represents Beatrix Potter's struggles with her own intense masochistic strivings while Sister Anne expresses a healthy defense against such impulses.

In the end of the story the problem of Fatima's masochistic tendencies is resolved. Bluebeard and his henchmen are killed and she is able to lead a normal life, marrying Lancelot Lackland, who succeeds in banishing "from her mind all memory of the evil days she had spent" with Bluebeard (Perrault, 1697, p. 87). She becomes a happy wife and mother. The town prospers and Bluebeard's castle crumbles. Fatima's masochistic relationship to Bluebeard with which she entered marriage had to have been dealt with before she could have a normal relationship to Lancelot. From the standpoint of Beatrix Potter this would imply that she had had to deal with her own masochistic tendencies to make it possible for her to marry and to be happy.

It will be noted that in both versions Fatima's and Anne's rescue is achieved with the help of their brothers. This may also have autobiographical significance for Beatrix Potter may have viewed her brother, Bertram, as having rescued her from the anxieties that she had in her relationship to her parents. As may be recalled, when she wanted to marry William Heelis, Bertram took her side and revealed to their parents that he had been married for more than ten years. Perhaps, he was even able to mitigate her parents' disapproval about her marriage to some degree.

In the final paragraph of *Sister Anne* Beatrix Potter states that in time "the castle crumbled" into ruins on the hillside. Her written words presaged by years the destruction of her own "unloved birthplace" at 2 Bolton Gardens in London during World War II. Her reference to it in the story signifies the diminishing of her early attachments, inhibitions, anxieties, and depressions. It was a hard-won battle for Beatrix Potter, now as Beatrix Heelis author of *Sister Anne*, who had succeeded in working through many of her problems. It is almost as though in her story she splits her identity between the frightened Beatrix Potter that she was, as represented by Fatima, and the competent mature woman that she became as Beatrix Heelis, represented by Sister Anne.

It is impressive that while Beatrix Potter's earlier stories dealt with *flight* as a defense against anxiety (e.g., Peter Rabbit ran away from Mr. McGregor), in the final work published in her lifetime, Sister Anne does not flee but (with help) is able to triumph over the vicious Bluebeard.

## Chapter 33

# Sequel to *The Fairy Caravan*

Beatrix Potter was delighted with the American edition of *The Fairy Caravan* published in October of 1929. She wrote to Alexander McKay: "Thank you for turning out such a handsome book, and I hope it will give satisfaction to both of us—and I may add—to my most exacting critics—my own shepherds and blacksmith. I do not care tuppence about anybody else's opinion" (*Americans*, p. 28).

On December 9, 1929, she wrote to Mrs. J. Templeman Coolidge regarding the story in her book about the Herdwick sheep. "That chapter made my old shepherd cry with pleasure; that is appreciation worth having" (*Letters*, p. 324). She then went on to write:

> Now I am very glad that you and Henry P. [Coolidge] and Mr. McKay—amongst you—extracted the book! It would have been rather a pity if I had shuffled off this mortal coil with most of those chapters inside my head. And it surprises myself that some of the late written chapters are as good as any, for instance the sheep anecdotes, and the woods by moonlight. It seems I can still write and invent. I think I had better write down some more, not necessarily for publication, but to preserve them. . . .
>
> Very funny. I could not judge it in the least. Sometimes I thought parts of it must be real fine. Other times I thought it was dreadful rubbish. I like the pig the least. He was rather an afterthought; his losing himself and & [his] illness was used to string the chapters together [*Letters*, pp. 324–325].

A few days later, December 12th, she wrote to Samuel H. Hamer, Secretary of the National Trust, that she thought that she had better write another book. "They say in Boston they sell as many autographed sketches as I can send, but it takes time" (*Letters*, p. 326).

Five days later she wrote to Alexander McKay, presumably about his suggestion that she do another book. Remarking that she was glad to hear that the "Caravan" was doing well, she then said:

> I will think things over. Only you must remember that I am *not* a prolific scribbler. I wrote myself out on the rabbit series. We must talk over the future of the caravan and consider where its wheels can travel without upsetting—not "most haste worst speed." My present inclination is to appease my English public and publishers with an inferior book next season; and make a sequel to the caravan the year following, if spared; which would give time for more adequate illustrations [*Letters*, p. 327].

Almost a year later, on November 5, 1930, Beatrix Potter wrote: "There are a good many other stories of the Caravan in existence. I will think the matter over. . . . I would like to do another volume some day; but I would not put so much crammed into it, as there was in the first one. And perhaps rather more pictures" (*Americans*, pp. 40–41).

While the sequel to *The Fairy Caravan* was never published, Beatrix Potter did begin working on several stories for it. Linder (1971) includes three of them that Beatrix Potter "had in mind" for this book. The first of these, *The Old Farmhouse at Hill Top*, has no plot. It features a conversation between Xarifa, the dormouse, Sandy, and Pippin. The animals refer to Mistress Heelis and describe her collection of glass as well as a warming pan and old steel candlesticks that belonged to her grandmother. Beatrix Potter used the discussion between the animals as a means to describe in detail the house and furnishings at Hill Top that were so important to her.

The second story, *A Walk Amongst the Funguses*, consists of a conversation between Xarifa, the dormouse, and Tuppenny, the guinea pig, who went for a walk "hand in hand" when the Fairy Caravan stopped at Cherry Tree Camp. Beatrix Potter contrasts the personalities of the two animals. Although the dormouse suffered from somnolence she had a "presence of mind" superior to the guinea pig who is described as "twittersome and nervous." The two animals stood under the shade of a bracken fern near which there was a colony of yellow funguses. Beatrix Potter writes:

> Tuppenny . . . staring seriously at the funguses, [asks]: "Are they made of butter, Xarifa?"
>
> "Certainly not" [she replied]. "Why do you think so?"
>
> "There are mooly cows in the field," [he says].
>
> "Cows do not leave butter lying about. It comes out of a churn. Those are funguses called Boletus."
>
> "Are they alive?" inquired Tuppenny, peeping round the fern. . . .
>
> [Xarifa did not reply, however.]
>
> "Can they walk about, Xarifa?" Tuppenny [asked], throwing a nut at the nearest Boletus.
>
> [Xarifa criticized him for throwing the nut saying]: "It is injudicious to throw nuts at things which we do not understand."
>
> "I beg your pardon, Boletus, sorry, I am not to do that, not to throw nuts again," twittered Tuppenny—"Xarifa, let us go away! I am sure the smallest Boletus shook its head at me!"
>
> "I can perceive no movement," said Xarifa [Linder, 1971, p. 314].

Tuppenny left but continued to be in a twitter. Xarifa told him that according to Petronella some mushrooms danced at night. "Do you think they are fairies? Xarifa?" asked Tuppenny. "Hush," said Xarifa.

She continued to point out various fungi, telling him some of their characteristics, and warning him not to touch one kind because it was poisonous.

This charming little story expressed in the anthropomorphic medium of animals and fungi allows Beatrix Potter to

285

return once more to her own childhood questions about enlightenment and the activities of the adults in the moonlight or
at night.

In this instance she portrays Tuppenny as a child asking
for information about the world around him. Xarifa, in turn,
functions as a parent, or governess, supplying him with information and educating him not to throw nuts at something he
does not understand. It is only when Tuppenny asks her if the
funguses are fairies that Xarifa tells him to keep quiet. In this
interchange we may see the familiar allusion to a child's curiosity about the parents' intimate life. Confused about what happens in the moonlight when the seemingly immobile Boletuses
and other fungi dance, Tuppenny wants to know if they really
are fairies. Yet, the adult finding the question too embarrassing
or too personal refuses to answer it and tells the child to hush.

When Tuppenny, again as the child, persists in his questions and thinks that one of the mushrooms shook his head at
him, Xarifa disagrees, saying that she perceived no movement.
Yet Xarifa felt that she could not or did not want to express
her personal opinion. Petronella then speaks a fairy rhyme
about the mushrooms.

> Nid, nid, noddy, we stand in a ring
> All day long and never do a thing!
> But nid nid noddy, we wake up at night,
> We dance and we sing in the merry moon light!"
> [Linder, 1971, p. 314].

The rhyme, if taken in the context of sexual enlightenment, acknowledges that such activity does indeed take place
at night. The metaphor is continued further as Tuppenny asks
whether Cantharella danced too. Xarifa again says that she
cannot tell him and can only quote Petronella who had said
that mushrooms danced in the merry moonlight. The entire
story thus expressed a child's early curiosity and continuing
attempts to learn about sex, an allusion most probably to a

phase in Beatrix Potter's early development. We have already seen evidence of this type of material in some of her previous stories.

The third story in this series is entitled *The Solitary Mouse*. This is the longest of the three stories and once more deals with the Fairy Caravan.

One April the caravan battled its way through rain and sleet to come to a stop behind Troutbeck Park and find shelter in an empty stable at the High Buildings in Hagg Ghyll. Noticing that it was in good condition, Pony William remarked that there were frequent repairs "when Mistress Heelis takes over another sheep farm" (Linder, 1971, p. 316). Sandy, the West Highland terrier, says: " 'This building has been used at lambing time. I have found two lamb jackets and I recognize that macintosh; it is the property of Joseph [Moscrop]. But shepherds do not use cork soles. Some of these things belong to Mistress Heelis.' " He goes on to say, after expressing a wish for some tea: " 'Mistress Heelis never minds anything, until she loses her temper' " (p. 317). The animals found two large biscuit canisters and remarked about the "smell of cheese" in the air.

While Xarifa and Tuppenny were preparing tea for everyone, suddenly a small mouse appeared lured by the smell of cheese. Although initially frightened, he became more friendly as time went on. In reply to Xarifa's question, the mouse said his name was Joseph Moscrop. The shy, frightened mouse whisked in and out of his hole but was able to tell them that he called himself by the name of one of the shepherds. Asked what was his own name, the mouse replied that he did not know, he was the last of his family: "There is no one left to call me anything." The mouse shed a tear and washed his face with it. Asked why he lived in the stable, he replied that it was a "long and melancholy story." He appreciated the warmth of the stove which had not been lighted since "Mistress Heelis and the shepherds went away" (p. 318). He states that if he had been a she mouse he would have called himself Beatrix after

Mistress Heelis. At this point the mouse asks if they knew any she mice saying: "There are no lady mice up here" and that he was the last mouse in the valley. He had no interest in field mice or voles, as "they have short tails."

The mouse went on to say that he did not come to that area but was born at High Buildings. "Until the shepherds came and Mistress Heelis, I had never heard of cheese, much less tasted it. My parents and my great grandparents lived in this barn, eating hay seeds and wild fruits. Gradually we dwindled. I am the last mouse left" (p. 318).

Asked why there were no house mice in the far away building, he replied that his grandmother told him before an owl caught her that their "fore elders lived at the Mill" some distance away which had burned down and nothing was left of it. He said that there might be other mice at the farm but he did not dare to run out there in daylight because he was afraid of buzzard hawks, nor could he go there in the moonlight because he was afraid of the horned owl. So he lived alone, a solitary mouse.

When Xarifa suggested that there were mice in villages, he said that he was afraid that villages were a great way off. He did like the taste of cheese and he was certain that " "Mistress Heelis would give [him] a taste if she were here' " (p. 319), but he could not get the lid off the canister. Sandy opened the canister, took out a piece of cheese from which the mouse nibbled off a tiny piece. He divided the small piece of cheese into two half thimbles and gave Xarifa one piece. Once more he asked whether she knew any lady mouse who would like to live up there. Xarifa thought that some mouse might. Suddenly Joseph asked: " 'Will you marry me?' 'I??!' said Xarifa, 'I?' 'Mrs. Joseph Mouse-trap!' 'I marry you! I would as soon think of marrying a guinea-pig' " (p. 319).

While everyone burst out laughing, Tuppenny twittered with embarrassment. The mouse was "so much upset by Xarifa's contempt, by the general merriment and by the mention of mouse-trap—[that he] whisked into the wall, and he did not come out again until next day dinner-time" (p. 319).

Beatrix Potter discusses Troutbeck Tongue in considerable detail and says that she used to go back to the High Buildings herself. She relates that one day when she was eating her bread and cheese, a mouse took some of the cheese from her fingers. On another day she brought him some cheese again. He would not come out until she had left but then the cheese disappeared.

Beatrix Potter brings herself into this charming little story at various times. In certain respects she seems to identify with some aspects of the animals, thereby revealing a great deal about herself and her emotional state at the time. This is especially evident in her description of the sad mouse who calls himself solitary, "the last mouse of his line," "the last of his family." Beatrix Potter, like the mouse, must have felt that she too was the last of her family. She was childless and her brother Bertram, who had lived in Scotland with his wife, had also been childless. He had died suddenly at the end of June 1918 "after a few hours illness" (*Letters*, p. 250).

Like the mouse, Beatrix Potter felt lonely and depressed at times. The degree to which her feelings of depression were present are epitomized in a letter to Mr. Samuel H. Hamer on October 20, 1929, when she wrote, simply but poignantly: "I am a rather forlorn person" (*Letters*, p. 318). Two years later, on February 27, 1931, she signed her letter to him: "I remain sincerely B. Heelis (depressed, but still arguing & spending)" (*Letters*, p. 343). Thus, even though she was married, had a great deal of freedom in her life, and gratification from her work, an undertone of sadness and loneliness persisted. To some extent this may have been constitutional, or endogenous, or it may have been a continuation of her struggle with her early emotional problems.

The use of the word *forlorn* chosen by someone who knew the English language as well as Beatrix Potter did constitutes a major confession. She virtually blurted out how she really felt as every connotation of the word refers to being lost or abandoned, deserted, forsaken, bereft, or wretchedly miserable (Webster). It is in connection with this undercurrent of depression that she allows herself to indulge in a bit of wistful humor by having the lonely mouse propose to Xarifa. But then she discarded the fantasy by having the group of animals laugh and be totally critical of the entire far-fetched idea.

Beatrix Potter's naming the mouse after Joseph Moscrop is interesting. By 1926 Beatrix Potter had a large flock of Herdwick sheep on her farms and needed additional help at lambing time. It was for this purpose that she hired Joseph Moscrop and his dogs from 1926 to 1942. Taylor writes that he was a 40-year-old bachelor who came from the Border Country where he lived with "the family of his brother Richard" (*Letters*, p. 302).

Beatrix Potter's letters to Joseph Moscrop reveal much about her own personality as well as the very friendly nature of their relationship. Typically, she would write to him sometime in January, expressing how she longed to see him, how she valued his cheerfulness, his smile, and his ability to get along with other people. Arrangements would be made for him to come early in the spring and assist in the work of lambing. He would bring a dog to herd the ewes into the area where the lambing took place. Her letters to him cover a wide range of topics including news items, the weather, politics, economics, the labor situation, as well as personal comments about her mother's health, her own health, and that of her husband.

The following excerpts are a small sample of some of her letters to him. The earliest letter that we have is one dated June 14, 1926, in which Beatrix Potter writes:

I was very pleased to get your letter. You will be thinking I was a long time in writing to thank you. And now I scarcely know what to say about the colley [sic]. I was *so disappointed* not to get a few days holiday during that fine weather; I wanted a rest; and for years I have wished to make an excursion over the country between Carlisle and Hexham, and the Roman wall remains, which I have never seen. It would have been pleasant to go over the Border and visit Allanwater.

She reminds him about the farm and its condition.

[O]f course I know that it is in a sad state—You and I won't forget the difficulties we had with fences and water last April!! . . .
I was sorry when you had gone; you just smiled and jogged on quietly. It is not a bit of good getting into a fuss and clashing about [JM].

Three years later there may have been some uncertainty about his coming for we learn from her letter to him on April 11, 1929: "It is a mercy you have written—I wrote ten days ago to Allery Bar, thinking you might have moved from Rowelton. . . . Martin was inquiring anxiously if I was sure you were coming; we concluded you would just be walking in without warning" (JM).

The following year, on January 22, 1930, she wrote: "I am looking forward to seeing you again, it is always something to look forward to with satisfaction—Never did I see such a spot for quarrels, but *you* have the sense and good temper to get on with everybody pleasantly" (JM). Further in that letter she speaks of the Herdwick shepherds as being "very annoying men." But evidently she respected Joe Moscrop's ability to get along with them.

On May 26th of that year she wrote that she thought his home address would be in Lewinshope, Yarrow, "at least you gave me that address in 1929 unless your Father has moved again. . . . I am going to send you a silly—rather pretty—book for bairns. I thought about giving it to you, but in some ways it is such nonsense that I am shy about it. There are some pictures of Troutbeck that you may recognize." And as a postscript, she added: "I shall post the book to Lewinshope as you won't want to cart it about—There are only about 60 copies of the English edition so it is a curiosity" (JM). Apparently, this was the English edition of *The Fairy Caravan*.

On January 15, 1931, she wrote to Joseph Moscrop thanking him for "the compliment of reading the Caravan with careful attention—not merely skimming, but digesting the immortal work(!?)" (*Letters*, p. 337).

Important and relevant to what follows later in another letter (see below), Beatrix Potter wrote to him on March 25, 1936, about Lassie's puppy, Matt, who had found dozens of sheep under the snow. She said that he was, "a valuable dog with a good nose for buried sheep under drifts, he has not missed many, only those 2, and 3 or 4 smothered. I look forward to seeing you—what shall we call you? A Harbinger of Spring!" (JM).

Four years later, on January 9, 1940, she wrote to thank him for having thought of sending New Year's Boxes. "There are still some kindly folk left in this unkindly world. I have a toffee in my mouth and I think of Joseph." She says that, "We look forward to seeing Joe and dog—again" (JM). In the letter she tells him that she and William have not had a good New Year "apart from apples and good wishes! He has been in bed with a chill, and I have sciatica. I felt the cold in my bones, it will go when a thaw comes. I wish Mr. Heelis would get right, he has not been so grand this winter—I think there is a sort of flu that gets hold" (JM).

In the summer of the same year (July 30, 1940) she wrote to Nancy Dean, a 7-year-old girl who expressed her pleasure at having her grandmother, Bertha Mahony Miller, read *The Fairy Caravan* out loud to her. In the course of her letter she mentions Joseph Moscrop. "He is wonderful with lambs and dogs; we all love Joseph. I do not think he would approve of me calling a mouse 'Joseph Mouse-trap' " (*Letters*, p. 421).

In a letter to Joseph Moscrop two years later (June 11, 1942), after having been bedridden for a month with influenza and bronchitis, she wrote: "So you have got a wee bit housie! well done Joseph! Will you have a cat or a colley [sic] or an old woman for company? I'm not sure—I think the colly [sic] is best company only it cannot cook the parritch [sic] or wash. If there's going to be no soap the washing doesn't count [it was war time]" (JM).

But in addition to her kind and friendly attitude toward Joseph Moscrop, Beatrix Potter reveals that she was a tough negotiator in their business dealings. On February 25, 1937, she wrote to him that she was "rather 'staggered' " by his asking for an increase in his salary from what it had been in previous years. She writes: "I really think you ought to be content with £15 Joseph! You are a hard nut!" (JM).

The following year he had apparently asked for a raise again and she firmly remarked: "I should be very sorry not to see you as usual, but it seems a high wage!" (JM). Then, on January 23, 1939, in consideration of the economic situation she wrote rather sternly: "You must be an incurable optimist if you think this as a suitable time to make jokes—I do *not*. . . . I shall be very glad to see you again at the Park, all being well. But you will please come down a pound Joseph—take it or leave it! not even King Canute could control the tide—or the—slump" (*Letters*, p. 394).

On other occasions Beatrix Heelis seems to have been rather generous and considerate. On January 18, 1941, she wrote: "Now about the wage Joseph. I think you should be satisfied with £20—but if you aren't—why you have us fast! for we cannot do without you—that's fact; more than ever (JM).

On February 26, 1942, she wrote:

> Will you please write again and tell me exactly what you are asking for the 4 weeks lambing? . . . It would be better if you would tell me "in black & white" exactly what you want—? . . . As you know very well I want you to come! But please write and tell me plainly and exactly what you are wanting—and with my very kind regards . . . [JM].

Evidently things improved for on March 11, 1942, she agreed to pay Joseph Moscrop £22.10 for four weeks lambing (JM).

One can gather from her letters that Joseph Moscrop must have been a remarkable person. His warmth and sensitivity come through from her comments to him.

The undercurrent of depression and loneliness from which Beatrix Potter suffered throughout her life is clearly apparent in her stories and in her correspondence. Her iron-clad superego dominated her behavior and condemned her to a rigid adherence to the principles of hard work and a strict ethical and moral code of conduct. There were advantages, however, for she was able to use its inexorable demands to achieve literary and financial success.

The creativity with which she was endowed found expression in the many letters she wrote. Her fertile and inventive mind was able to incorporate her experiences from either her recent or her remote past as material for her letters. An outstanding example of this ability of hers can be found in her letter to the "Dear Children Friends in Denver," dated July 12, 1936. It begins: "What can I say to you so far away? I can send my love, and thank you for still remembering Peter Rabbit. It was written more than 40 years ago for a little lame boy" (Denver Public Library). She then goes on to say that the previous week Noel Moore, now a "middle aged active man, a clergyman," had visited her.

She continues:

> I cannot think of more tales to write. There is no scuse for going on writing stories when I have nothing more to say. So I will just tell you a true account of my sheep dogs; and you may be interested, because I remember when I was very little I used to love a tale about a colley [sic] called "Sirrah"—how he went out by himself at night and saved a flock of sheep.
>
> I have a dog called "Matt;" his mother is my favourite colley [sic] "Lassie," a very pretty black & white colley. Matt is an ugly dog; but very wise. Last winter was terrible for snow and gales of wind. We had many sheep covered by drifted snow—"snowed over" as the shepherds say. Matt saved nearly 50—He seems able to smell a sheep buried underneath a 6 foot drift, and he

will not leave it. He scratches the snow and barks until help comes, when he assists to dig it out. And in summer he is just as clever, finding sick sheep. Such a dog is worth his weight in gold [unpublished, Denver Public Library].

Thus, several months after her letter to Joseph Moscrop on March 26th, quoted earlier, Beatrix Potter wrote again about her dog Matt's ability to rescue sheep buried in the snow.

Continuing her letter to the "Children Friends in Denver" she writes:

A friend of mine owed his life to his sheep dog. He is a farmer, and he was in the hay loft, cutting out hay from the hay mow (the hay stack) inside the loft. He had carelessly cut too far underneath, and the whole heap of hay toppled over on him. He tried to call help, but he was suffocating, when his old dog heard him and came and dug frantically. And Joe [Joe Gregg, *Americans*, p. 49] says she had the sense to clear the hay off his face so that he could shout! Indeed I would believe any cleverness of a colley [sic].

Beatrix Potter goes on to state:

I grieve to say that bad men sometimes put honest dogs to very bad uses. Which seems to me to be exceedingly mean—setting on an innocent dog to do their dishonest work. The sheep in this country are often feeding on Commons—open land without fences, and there is a lot of sheep stealing. The thieves have a clever quiet dog that does not bark; they carry it with them in a motor van and when they see a fat sheep near the road in a quiet spot, they stop and the dog catches it for the thief.

Although she extols the faithfulness and virtues of sheep-dogs and blames their masters for the dog's delinquent behavior, she does acknowledge the existence of "bad dogs."

Occasionally there are bad dogs who take to sheep stealing, or worrying, on their own account. They are so sly that it is most difficult to detect the culprit. They do not kill their own master's sheep, but go for miles away. And if there is any blood about them they will wash themselves in a river. I once saw a dog that had been in mischief, washing himself. He was rolling in a pool, and ducking his head under.

But it is a rare case. As a rule the sheep dogs are most faithful [Denver Public Library].

She signs her letter: "I remain your affectionate friend. Beatrix Potter."

What is so striking about this letter to the Children Friends in Denver is her introduction. It is remarkably similar to the beginning of her letter to Noel Moore on September 4, 1893, when she wrote: "I don't know what to write you, so I shall tell you a story" and proceeded to write *The Tale of Peter Rabbit*. To my knowledge, at no other time until this letter did Beatrix Potter ever use this particular introduction. Perhaps she found it appropriate to do so because she had recently had a visit from Noel Moore and because the "Children Friends in Denver" remembered Peter Rabbit.

While *The Tale of Peter Rabbit* was completely fictitious, the story about the dog, Matt, as well as her other story about the sheepdog who saved the farmer (Joe Gregg), was true. Just as when she was little she used to love a tale about a collie called Sirrah, who did a heroic thing, she was now able to tell a story about her own dog, Matt, who also does heroic things.

Besides extolling the virtues and usefulness of dogs as man's best friend, Beatrix Potter points to an important difference between the dogs and Peter Rabbit. In the *Peter Rabbit* stories, she speaks of the animals as being naughty, a matter that we have already discussed. In this instance, however, she makes the point about "bad men" using dogs for bad purposes, "setting on an innocent dog to do their dishonest work."

It is in connection with this that we are able to see an important change in her understanding and communication. Although Beatrix Potter acknowledges the existence of "bad dogs" (presumably on a constitutional basis), the significant thrust of her remarks is that she allows herself to state that the determinants of other "bad" dogs is based on their training. It is their masters who are at fault. By adopting this position she expresses an understanding that she would not have allowed herself to mention at the time she wrote *Peter Rabbit*. It is no accident that she could write this letter after both of her parents were dead (her mother died on December 20, 1932).

We may view her letter to the children of Denver as a confession of the intensity of her aggressive feelings toward her parents. It is as though she can now say in a letter, at the age of 70, that she too is really worth her weight in gold and that it was they (her parents) who had been responsible for wrecking her brother's happiness as well as her own.

## Chapter 34

# Helen Beatrix Heelis

As we examine the progression of Beatrix Potter's artistic output, we are struck by how much is revealed about the development of her personality. Her earlier struggles are graphically apparent in her *Journal*—her depression, the problems with her health, her insecurities, her problems with her parents—as well as her interests in so many different subjects (art, literature, politics, etc.). Probably the one single event that gave her a tremendous boost of self-confidence was the acceptance of her artwork by Hildescheimer and Faulkner—fortunately before she was subjected to the humiliating attitude of the Linnean Society. In addition, an outgrowth of her ability to draw and write were the picture letters to the Moore children, including the letter of Noel (September 4, 1893) that became so famous.

The acceptance of *The Tale of Peter Rabbit* by Frederick Warne and the subsequent acceptance of her other works ushered in a completely new phase in Beatrix Potter's development and did much to consolidate her self-confidence. This positive response from the world away from her family in an area of her greatest interest and ability was a testimonial that not only dramatically confirmed her sense of worth but also provided her with financial independence. But apparently this was not all.

At some point in her dealings with Frederick Warne she became emotionally involved with Norman Warne. There can be little doubt that as time went on she became deeply in love with him and that he served as a profound source of inspiration for the direction of her creativity. While her parents, and especially her mother, actively opposed the relationship, Beatrix Potter persevered and, as we know, on July 25, 1905, Norman Warne proposed to her and she accepted. Her falling in love with Norman Warne and daring to break away from her parents' domination and control were major steps toward establishing her self-worth as a woman in her own right. That Beatrix Potter was able to master the tragedy of his death and her loss proved to her that she could rise above the anguish of bitter disappointment and accomplish something significant in her life.

After Norman Warne's sudden death she continued the literary work that they had planned. For awhile, as in the *Jeremy Fisher* story, she was still very much under the spell of his inspiration. The completion of *Jeremy Fisher* was in essence the fulfillment of a promise she had made to Norman Warne. Undoubtedly it was written for him and in his memory.

In her subsequent works the content touched on many facets of her wishes and fantasies about what she had hoped for in their relationship. As may be expected, her writing involved the painful work of mourning Norman Warne's death. Woven into the material, her bitterness at her parents' critical, unempathic attitude about her relationship to him is readily discernable. Virtually coincidental with her mourning was the continued inspiration that she had derived from her relationship with Norman Warne as her works clearly had him in mind. Some of these revealed her wishes and fantasies of having a family and children. But, as time went on, there was a subtle diminution in the power of their joint collaborative efforts. One senses that with the notable exception of *Peter Rabbit*, written before she met Norman Warne, the quality of her work, although magical, never quite achieved the intangible sparkle it had when they worked together and it was the work of love.

During a period of several years following Norman Warne's death, Beatrix Potter gradually entered the next phase of her development. Her attachment to her parents diminished as her attachment to her house at Hill Top and her investment in her farmland increased. The life-style she adopted was that of a countrywoman, a farmer, one far different from what her life had been in London.

In time she became involved with William Heelis and began to blossom again, entering another phase in her life. But now it was a different kind of relationship. Both the change in her life-style and the physiological changes in her body as a consequence of her being older, brought about a different, perhaps imperceptible change in her literary productions.

By the time Beatrix Potter married William Heelis in 1913 she was 47 years of age and was financially independent. As far as her writing was concerned, Lane (1946) states that "all the best of her creative work was done." She became:

> Mrs. Heelis of Sawrey, who for the next thirty years was to be known as a dominant, shrewd, good-humoured and salty character of the Lake Country [who] was absorbed in the life that Beatrix Potter had always wanted, and had achieved only by snatches in her possession of Hill Top, and expressed with love and poetic truth in her art [p. 113].

With regard to Beatrix Potter's literary productions following her marriage, Lane (1946) writes:

> Of the four story books which appeared after her marriage, only one, *Johnny Town-Mouse*, which was published in 1918, can be compared in style and spirit with her earlier work. The others, *The Fairy Caravan, Little Pig Robinson,* and *Sister Anne,* published ten years later, and deliberately addressed to her American public, break away from her own tradition and are in that sense experimental; but they are not happy experiments [p. 129].

On October 14, 1913, a week after her marriage she wrote to Millie Warne: "I am sending you belated cake which I hadn't courage to do before! . . . I am very *happy* and in every way

301

satisfied with Willie. It is best now not to look back" (Lane, 1946, p. 111).

By Christmas time she wrote that she and her husband "do really well with roasts and vegetables. We cooked and ate a turkey and several other birds" (Lane, 1946, p. 112). The following April she wrote to Millie Warne: "I feel as if I have been married many years" (p. 112).

Her domesticity is evident in the following quotation from her letter to Barbara Ruxton[1] on December 31, 1913. "Mr. Heelis walks through the toes of his stockings so it is lucky I like darning!" (*Letters*, p. 215).

We get a clear picture of her marriage from her letter responding to Eleanor L. Choyce (Louie)[2] who had applied for a job working for the Heelises. Beatrix Potter's letter is dated March 15, 1916. In it she wrote: "I am fifty this year—very active and cheerful; but I am afraid I & my farm housekeeper are both going to be overworked. I must explain at once that I don't depend on the farm for a living. . . ." Following her description of the nature of the farm, its location, and the animals on it she states:

> My husband is a solicitor; and there are all sorts of people in the world. I may say he is a very quiet gentleman and I am a total abstainer!! We have been 2 years married, no family. We live very quietly in a cottage separate from the old farm house. . . . I don't go out much, haven't time; & the little town seems nothing but gossip and cards. I'm afraid our own special sin is not attending church regularly, not loving the nearest parson; & I was brought up a Dissenter. There is a good church at Hawkshead [*Letters*, p. 224].

After an exchange of letters Beatrix Potter hired Eleanor Choyce and her brother. A warm friendship developed between the two women, and after Eleanor Choyce left Beatrix

---

[1]Barbara Ruxton was about thirteen or fourteen years old at this time. She and her sixteen year-old cousin, Augusta Burn, stayed with Beatrix Potter at Castle Cottage in 1913 (see *Children*, pp. 152–154).

[2]A governess, Eleanor Choyce went to work for Beatrix Potter as a helper "during the First World War when most of the men from the farms were called up to fight." At the end of the war, she resumed her career (*Children*, p. 179).

Potter's employment she visited Hill Top occasionally in the summer. They continued to write to one another throughout the years. Beatrix Potter's last known letter to her is dated November 30, 1943.

It must not be thought that her marriage and change of name erased from Beatrix Potter's mind the memory of Norman Warne. In 1918, during World War I, she wrote the following to Millie Warne:

> This might have been a sorry and ashamed letter. I lost Norman's ring in the cornfield—pulled off while lifting wet sheaves with my fingers slipped under the bands; but it turned up amongst the remains of some wet stuff thrown down for the hens. I had untied many on the threshing floor in hopes of finding it. I am glad I was spared that last crowning distress. . . . I should have had just one consolation, it was a pretty, quiet, sheltered field to lie in, if it had not been found. My hand felt very strange and uncomfortable without it [Lane, 1946, p. 143].

In a letter dated May 2, 1925, she wrote to Miss Choyce about a child that she had not seen for a long time saying that she wanted "to see what she is like since she grew out of child." She writes: "You have had more experience and judgment of young persons than I have" (unpublished, NJ).

In this letter Beatrix Potter freely admits to her friend her own real ignorance about children. While she had a feeling for children and children's problems, as witnessed by the kind of books she had written for them, her admission that she had little experience with them is not surprising because of her restricted and isolated childhood. Taylor writes:

> One of the Sawrey children then was Willow Burns, now Willow Taylor, whose parents William and Margaret Burns kept *The Tower Bank Arms*, the village inn which nestles up against Hill Top. To Willow Beatrix Potter—or Mrs. Heelis as she was always known—was a crotchety old lady who interrupted her play and found fault with her appearance. "I doubt whether she ever knew any ball games or skipped, played hop-scotch or hide-and-seek when she was a child. She was not the sweet old grandmotherly type which a lot of people imagine her to be. I sometimes

wonder whether she resented the fact that we were enjoying the kind of childhood she had longed for? . . . It isn't that Mrs. Heelis disliked children, it is just that she didn't understand their ways" [*Children*, p. 10].

To this we may add that it could be that not only did she not understand children's "ways" but also, because she did not have children of her own, her resentment about her childless state manifested itself in her gruff attitude toward other people's children who misbehaved or infringed upon her domain.

We have some confirmation of her not really understanding *small* children. In her letter to Ivy Hunt Steel on November 13, 1926, she wrote:

> I must tell June [Ivy's daughter] about my very little littlest lamb called Dumple. He had a mother, but he got lost when he was only a month old—His mother was a careless old sheep—she went off to the high hills with the rest of the sheep and lambs and poor Dumple was left behind calling baa! baa! baa! The shepherd found him all alone; but the shepherd could not tell which was Dumple's mother, because she was not calling baa, baa! she had forgotten all about him. So he just walked about by himself all summer, and ate grass like an old sheep, and he has strong straight legs, like June; and as lively as can be; but he is hardly any bigger than a pussy cat! [Potter, 1977, p. 15].

Considering that June at this time in her life was only two years old, we may question Beatrix Potter's sensitivity in wishing to tell a very young child such a story. Perhaps we may understand this as further evidence of her own feeling about neglectful mothers as we have seen in some of her stories (e.g., *Fairy Clogs, Llewelyn's Well*).

Although Beatrix Potter lived in London with her parents until she married William Heelis, she spent as much time as possible at Hill Top. Her active participation in the daily operation of her farms left little time or energy for her literary work. After her marriage, the demands on her time were even greater. In a letter to Fruing Warne dated May 6, 1915, she wrote: "Somehow when one is up to the eyes in work with real live animals it makes one despise paper-book-animals—but I mustn't say that to my publisher! [as she was saying it!]" (*Letters*, p. 248). While her stories decreased in number, what she wrote about after her marriage, in her letters, and in *The Fairy Caravan*, was based on some of her own experiences with animals.

Farm life brought about many changes. Beatrix Potter found herself in a situation familiar to people who live on farms, and especially children, who have a close empathic relationship to their animal pets. At the same time, they are constantly confronted with the reality of farm life: that even though they may be pets, animals are slaughtered for food.

In a letter to Miss Choyce dated December 13, 1922, eight years before she completed *The Tale of Little Pig Robinson*, she wrote about sorting out her turkeys for sales to customers, and sending rabbits as Christmas presents to a friend. She writes:

> The men are trapping such fat ones. If you please I am a *butcher*! We have been butchering on the quiet for a long time, and someone reported (one of the professional butchers as a matter of fact). He did nobody any harm but himself. We had always been careful to kill in the open air. The Council have now licensed the hull next to the wash house at Hill Top. We find that a sheep or lamb home killed makes about 20/ more than market price and we can sell good meat for less than the butcher after all. Which the Council approves of, for once showing a little common sense [NJ].

Farming practices being what they are, it is not surprising that Beatrix Potter was involved in such an activity as butchering rabbits, lambs, or sheep. What is of special interest is that in the early printed versions of *Peter Rabbit* she pictured herself as the farmer's wife (see chapter 4). Now, almost three decades after writing that story, she freely admitted in her letter to Miss Choyce that she was as objective about the butchering of animals as any farmer's wife would have been.

From comments in Beatrix Potter's correspondence during this time, it is apparent that gradually she had begun to be troubled by changes in her eyesight. For her, a person who had been involved in drawing and painting since childhood, the changes in the acuity of her vision must have been very traumatic. She made many references to her handicap in her letters, repeatedly indicating that she was troubled with her eyes. We may quote some of these comments.

On May 18, 1915, she mentioned her problems with her eyesight in a letter to Harold Warne:

> I tried a little drawing in winter, but could not stick to it, also could not *see*, my eyes are gone so long sighted & not clear nearby. They are alright for general purposes, like poultry & outdoor work—I suppose I shall have to take to spectacles, but I had better get properly fitted in London—a place I have no wish to go to at present! [*Letters*, p. 221].

Evidently she was fitted with glasses but was not too pleased with the result as in her letter about a year later (July 6, 1916), she indicated that she was: "writing this in spectacles confusedly" (*Letters*, p. 226). After several weeks (on August 12th) she wrote: "[Y]ou will have to get used to the idea that my eyes are giving way, whether you like it or not" (*Letters*, p. 227).

Beatrix Potter had been fitted with "spectacles" again in July 1918 but on August 5, 1919, she wrote:

> I also send an idea for a cover though I fear you did not take to the title of the Birds and Mr. Tod [the new title for *Jenny Crow*]? The whole thing is rather a mess! I am not willing to get stronger glasses after only one year's wear. The oculist said that there was nothing wrong with my eyes, beyond 53 years of rather unmerciful usage. They will last my time I hope; but you must *not* count on my going on doing books of coloured illustrations. Find someone else [*Letters*, p. 258].

The impairment to her eyesight continued to distress her and on April 7, 1923, she wrote in an unpublished letter to Fruing Warne: "As usual I cannot see. My drawing days are over" (FW).

To abandon the artistic work that had given her so much pleasure, albeit involving such painstaking, detailed efforts, must have been a wrenching prospect for Beatrix Potter. After all, while her stories were interesting, their appeal was greatly enhanced by the pictures she painted to accompany the text. Lane (1946) puts it this way:

> The writing of her stories had always been inseparable from their illustration; the flavour of the books is tasted equally and indistinguishably in pictures and text; and it is a curious fact that from the moment when her eyes began to fail and she lost her power of fine drawing, her stories lost their shape, their emotional concentration and their poetry [p. 115].

As time went on Beatrix Potter became increasingly aware of the changes in her body as a result of aging. She was approaching seventy when she wrote to Bertha Mahony Miller on December 13, 1934: "I think time slips away faster and faster as one grows older; partly because this person when tired falls asleep; which is not conducive to writing letters, or any thing else" (*Letters*, p. 370). And, in the same letter, she continues: "I am 'written out' for story books, and my eyes are tired for painting; but I can still take great and useful pleasure in old oak—and drains—and old roofs—and damp walls—oh the repairs! And the difficulty of reconciling ancient relics and modern sanitation?" (*Letters*, p. 371).

While she was still interested in writing as an outlet for her creativity, her interest in other matters gradually took precedence. Probably the most important practical change in Beatrix Potter's way of life came about when she committed herself to the conservation and preservation of the Lake District. Inspired by her friend, Canon Hardwicke Rawnsley, she endeavored to prevent the demolition of traditional cottages and the exploitation of the land by real estate developers for commercial purposes.

Taylor, Whalley, Hobbs, and Battrick (1987) write that:

Beatrix was a realist who saw clearly that open countryside does not look after itself, the Lake District landscape in particular being almost entirely man-made, and she did not agree that the general public should be allowed to roam at will. She saw the preservation of her small farms and cottages as being essential for the protection of the way of life and, as a result, the landscape of the valleys, but was not yet altogether sure that the Trust, with its idealistic outlook, would be the best guardian. Farms needed a knowledgeable owner and responsible tenants who kept hikers to the footpaths [pp. 187–189].

Over the years, after her marriage to William Heelis, Beatrix Potter acquired a great deal of land. She began by purchasing small farms around her beloved Hill Top but eventually her acquisitions became more ambitious and included estates and farms of several thousand acres. In the event of her death, she intended that every farm that she possessed would go to the National Trust.[1] She followed up her intentions by willing over 5000 acres to that organization and stipulated in her will that the property she willed to her husband should be turned over to the National Trust after his death.

While the purchase of land for the National Trust was made possible by Beatrix Potter's own funds, it is evident that her husband concurred with her philosophy. Her correspondence reveals that she consulted him frequently about her plans, and that he made every effort professionally and personally to further her project. The results are evident today as we may see how a masterpiece of careful planning in managing the land has enabled people to enjoy the beauty of the fells. From her correspondence with the National Trust it is evident that she took great pains in making sure that the property was properly maintained. She had specific opinions about what trees should be cut down, and how the roads and trails should be improved, what fences should be mended, where they

---

[1]The National Trust for Places of Historic Interest or National Beauty. This organization works for the preservation of places of historic interest or natural beauty in England, Wales, and Northern Ireland. Formed in 1895, it is a registered charity, independent of the government, with a membership of over two million, making it one of the world's largest conservation bodies.

should be installed, and what signs should be made. All of this, while protecting the natural beauty of the area, enhanced the enjoyment of people walking over the fells.

Determined that matters concerning her project should be handled efficiently, Beatrix Potter demonstrated very little patience with errors and incompetence. As her letters reveal, she was extremely critical of any mistakes that were made, and in some instances she was openly aggressive, even to the point of being blunt. For example, in a letter to Samuel A. Hamer,[2] dated October 16, 1929, she had written: "The typical agent has the faults of the idle rich, with bumptiousness added" (NT). On June 10, 1932, she wrote to Mr. Hamer: "It's disagreeable to seem to be wiser than other people but I cannot help saying what I think" (NT).

When the National Trust was attempting to purchase land, Beatrix Potter tried to get her mother to contribute some money for the project and evidently had discussed this possibility with Mr. Hamer. In several letters to him she comments frankly about her mother's personality and her continuing frustration with her. On October 21, 1929, she wrote to him: "My mother is known to be so wealthy that nobody would subscribe to help *me*! She is hopeless. I tried in vain to *borrow* money from her. . . ." Then, later that year (December 12th) she wrote to Mr. Hamer again:

> I have not yet asked my Mother point blank and she has steadily taken no interest whatever! She will have to do something with her bank balance about New Year and I will try then; though it is some risk. Once when I pointed out the unwisdom of saving—she startled me by making a large unnecessary gift to a relative-in-law! . . .
> I take it if I do get anything from my mother it had better go into the general subscription—unless it were a big amount for an example, but I'm afraid she won't [*Letters*, p. 326].

---

[2]Secretary of the National Trust. Beatrix Potter wrote to him regularly—almost weekly.

On January 27th of the following year, she made further re-marks about her mother to Mr. Hamer informing him about her mother's attitude about contributing to buy more property.

> I asked my mother soon after you were here. She refused to give anything, & was annoyed at being asked. So I dropped it hastily. But she had a very great deal at her acct in two banks. And when it came to investing it, she consented to put it in my name. I am sorry I cannot give it to you, for 3 reasons. (1) She is quite capable of inquiring for the interest!! (2) She would be very angry if she heard I had given it away at once (3) I want it myself for the dividends! [NT].

Beatrix Potter was quite outspoken about how difficult her mother was about money in a letter to her cousin Caroline Clark on December 13, 1930: "It is annoying that she is so difficult about money—a regular miser in reluctance to spend money, which will simply be wasted in death duties when she has hoarded it up" (*Letters*, p. 336).

It was not only her mother's attitude about money that Beatrix Potter disapproved of. On January 15, 1931, she wrote to Joseph Moscrop. After writing about the colds that she and her husband had had, she stated that: "There are not so many like my mother who seems just the same at 91 as she did at 81—but then she has never exerted herself to work, in her life. I would rather keep going till I drop—early or late—never mind what the work is, so long as it is useful and well done" (*Letters*, p. 338).

Then, on April 19, 1931, Beatrix Potter wrote to Mr. Hamer from Lindeth How:

> My mother is coming to the end of her long life—92—last Wednesday. I think she must have had influenza. She sits before her fire and is quite smiling and peaceful—which in a perverse way is distressing—now that the end is in sight I would like to see her cross again! She may last some weeks, or even pick up; but she has turns with her heart and she may sleep away some night [NT].

Well over a year later, on December 18, 1932, she wrote to Alexander McKay:

> My old mother is refusing to die. She was unconscious for 4 hours yesterday, and then suddenly asked for tea. She cannot possibly recover, and she suffers a lot of pain at times, so we hope it will soon be over; but she has wonderful vitality for any age—let alone 93 [*Letters*, p. 352].

Helen Potter died on December 20, 1932. Her death certificate gives her age as 93 at the time of her death and indicates the cause of her death as "cardiovascular degeneration." On January 31, 1933, Beatrix Potter wrote to Joseph Moscrop informing him of her mother's death a little over a month earlier.

> I wish I could say my Mother had not suffered. She was happy and cheerful, like a child, the last week. But she had a long struggle, and it is very sad to see an old person sick and cross. She was too strong, she lived on after her works were worn out inwardly [*Letters*, p. 353].

In the past she had made many negative comments about her mother. With her death Beatrix Potter was able to express some of her affectionate feelings toward her as well.

In addition to her dedication to preserving the land and the buildings in the Lake District for posterity, Beatrix Potter's letters demonstrate her sense of social consciousness and ongoing concern for public affairs. She created almost single handedly the Hawkshead and District Nursing Association (Taylor, Whalley, Hobbs, and Battrick, 1987, p. 187). She was also able to provide suitable housing for the care of patients and even a house for the visiting nurse to live in.

Her interest, long abandoned, in having a child of her own became extended to an interest in children with whom she corresponded and to utilizing her name for the benefit of children's causes. Even though Beatrix Potter may not have had a comfortable relationship with all of the children she encountered, her concerns about them were real. From 1924 on she

*311*

was very active in the development of the Invalid Children's Aid Association. The aim of that organization was " 'to help, to supervise, and if possible to cure the seriously-invalided and crippled children of [the] poor by obtaining for them the best medical treatment and continued after-care, and finding for them when possible a means of earning a livelihood in the future' " (*Children*, p. 206).

Beatrix Potter began to breed Herdwick sheep in 1906 and by 1924 had several thousand of the animals on her farms. Her own creative energies, although hampered by the physical changes of aging, found increasing gratification in the management of this large herd. Breeding and showing Herdwick sheep became her primary interest. To help her in this endeavor she engaged Tom Storey to work at her farms and to take charge of the breeding. His knowledge, experience, and dedication proved to be eminently successful. The sheep they bred won prizes and Beatrix Potter herself was elected president of the Herdwick Sheep Breeders Association. She described some of her experiences with the sheep in stories in *The Fairy Caravan*.

In 1939, it was evident that Beatrix Potter was seriously ill. She wrote to Marian Frazer Harris Perry on March 30th from Women's Hospital in Liverpool:

I was in last Nov. for what seemed a trivial matter. There was some disquieting symptoms of bleeding a fortnight ago, so I came again and the surgeon is somewhat serious. I don't suppose it will be worse anything than "curetting," but anything in the womb is apt to be the beginning of the end. I am in no pain or discomfit, but awfully worried about my husband. You might have noticed, I am the stronger minded of the pair, also the money is mine; death duties would make it awkward for him and the servants. He belongs to a family who have the privilege of dying suddenly—in their sleep. I have always hoped to survive! At all costs I hope he will remarry happily and sensibly. I have felt very tired and aged the last two years. Maybe the surgeon will put me right—but he cannot put me young again [*Americans*, p. 94].

A hysterectomy was performed at that time. It is evident from her subsequent letters that she already had developed metastases from cancer. The symptoms that she referred to as "bronchitis" may have been a pulmonary involvement of the malignancy.

Later that year, on May 10th, Beatrix Potter reported to Miss Choyce that she had come home by road on "Sunday week" and could "now hobble about with a stick which I am told is good progress." She had been pleased with the care that she had received at the hospital, writing: "There could not be a pleasanter place to be ill in. I have been twice in Catharine Street hospital, and both times I have been heartily sorry to leave! Only it is selfish to want to hold up a bed." Further in her letter, she writes that she is in the upstairs sitting room and can now get in and out of bed.

> I have always sneered at married people requiring 2 beds! but now don't know what to do. W. H. is an uneasy bedfellow, in the habit of rolling up the whole of the bedclothes—so much so that the last three winters I have hit on the plan of having a thick separate rug. There is not room for 2 beds in our old bedroom and the spare room is bitterly cold in winter, perhaps it will be better to sleep in the piano. It is a pleasant outlook [NJ].

Things did not work out too well for on July 19th of that year she was back in the hospital again "for a thorough overhaul." Yet Beatrix Potter managed to heal, and while not in the best of health, suffering from bouts of influenza, bronchitis, and the complication of a heart condition, she was able to lead an active life around her farms.

Beatrix Potter's last known letter, written in a shaky handwriting nine days before her death, was addressed to Joe Moscrop. She wrote on December 13, 1943: "Very far through, but still some kick in me. Am not going right way at present. I write a line to shake you by the hand, our friendship has been entirely pleasant. I am very ill with bronchitis. Best wishes for New Year" (*Letters*, p. 465).

Up until the last day of her life, she and Tom Storey continued to discuss plans for work to be done on her estate. He reported that he had " 'been talking to her an hour or more the night before [her death] about the farm, and everything' " (Taylor, Whalley, Hobbs, and Battrick, 1987, p. 202). She died on December 22, 1943, and Tom Storey kept his promise to her to scatter her ashes, "telling only his son where they had been scattered" (p. 202).

Her death certificate, giving her name as Helen Beatrix Heelis, was registered in Ulverston in the subdistrict of Broughton West, in the county of Lancester, was signed by F. Wilson, acting deputy registrar, and lists her occupation simply as "wife of William Heelis, a solicitor." The cause of her death is given as "acute bronchitis, myocarditis, and carcinoma of uterus," and was certified by A. Brownlee, M.B.

In spite of her fame it cannot be said that Beatrix Potter lived her life as a public figure. During her lifetime people knew her name but little about her. Many people did not even know her married name and knew virtually nothing of her multifaceted interests: her serious work in mycology, her interests in archaeology and paleontology, and, for that matter, very much if anything about her personal life. Except in England, her unselfish dedication to preserving the beauty and the character of the fells through her generous gift of land to the National Trust, and her thoughtful counsel as to its management, is scarcely known. Partly this is because she wished it that way, and after her marriage had deliberately concealed the name by which she became famous, using her married name exclusively in her private life. It was as Mrs. Heelis that she wanted to be known by her neighbors and friends in the Lake District. She wanted to be known as a farmer and breeder of Herdwick sheep not as the author of *Peter Rabbit*, and certainly not as having come from a wealthy London family. She refused to be personally involved in any type of publicity to promote the sales of her books or the manufactured items relating to her characters. So it is indeed impressive that she has had such a lasting influence on children's literature, really based on a few stories written during the short space of a few years.

From what we learned about her life, we know that she was a very troubled person in her early years. She was depressed and anxious. We also know that she was able to triumph over life's adversities, to move away from disappointments, and to rise above them by dint of her own efforts and indomitable strength. Most importantly, what she was able to convey in her writings, from the initial story of *Peter Rabbit* on, were her own struggles to overcome her anxieties and childhood conflicts, her unconscious wishes and fantasies about which she felt guilty. She did this in such a skillful manner that the reader is lured into identifying not only with the conflicts but also with their resolution, thus enabling him to believe that ultimately all would turn out well. She invites the reader (or the listener) to identify with the hero and to participate with just enough anxiety, *almost* bordering on the intolerable, but yet permitting a degree of pleasure knowing that the anxiety-producing situation will be mastered and he will be triumphant in the end. Hers is the technique that elicits the kind of thrill people derive from frightening movies or stories that end well. It is the same anxiety that children have when they are tossed into the air and scream with delight as they are caught by a fond parent or relative.

While many writers of children's books have attempted to utilize this method, apparently few have been able to achieve such a high degree of artistry that their writings continue to capture the imagination of both children and adults for so many years and in so many different cultures. Her books have become a touchstone by which other works of literature for children can be judged. We must emphasize also the degree to which her stories were enhanced by her wonderful illustrations. It was the combination of the story and the pictures that brought about the popularity of her works. It is highly unlikely that when Beatrix Potter wrote her initial letter to the ailing Noel Moore in 1893 she had any idea of how powerful this letter would become. Nor was the essence of its success that she was writing the story for a particular "real" child, but rather that anyone, child or adult, could respond to its message. Her ability to do this was a remarkable achievement of a truly remarkable woman.

# References

*Note:* Abbreviations for frequently cited works appear in parentheses at the end of the reference.

Aesop, *Fables of Aesop*, tr. S. A. Handford. New York: Penguin books, 1954.

Austen, J. (1818), *Persuasion*. New York: Viking Books, 1985.

*A Beatrix Potter Photograph Album* (1993), text J. I. Whalley. London: The Beatrix Potter Society.

Bettelheim, B. (1975), *The Uses of Enchantment: The Meaning and Importance of Fairy Tales*. New York: Alfred A. Knopf.

Burney, F. (1778), *Evelina, or A Young Lady's Entrance into the World*. London: Thomas Lowndes.

—— (1782), *Cecilia; or Memoirs of an Heiress*. London: T. Payne & Son & T. Cadell.

—— (1796), *Camilla: or A Picture of Youth*. London: T. Payne, T. Cadell, jun., & W. Davies.

—— (1842–1846), *Diary and Letters of Madame d'Arblay*, ed. C. Barrett. London: Bickers & Son.

Chambers, R. (1842), *Popular Rhymes, Fireside Stories, and Amusements, of Scotland*. Edinburgh: William & Robert Chambers.

Crew, A. (1933), *London Prisons of Today and Yesterday*. London: Ivor Nicholson & Watson Ltd.

*Encyclopaedia Britannica*, Frances D'Arblay (Fanny Burney). In: *Encyclopaedia Britannica*, 7:50–51. 14th ed. Chicago: Encyclopaedia Britannica, 1954.

Freud, S. (1900), The Interpretation of Dreams. *Standard Edition*, 4 & 5. London: Hogarth Press, 1953.

———— (1905), Fragment of an analysis of a case of hysteria. *Standard Edition*, 7:3–122. London: Hogarth Press, 1953.

———— (1908), Creative writers and day-dreaming. *Standard Edition*, 9:142–153. London: Hogarth Press, 1959.

———— (1930), Address delivered in the Goethe House at Frankfurt. *Standard Edition*, 21:206–212. London: Hogarth Press, 1961.

Greene, G. (1933), Beatrix Potter. In: *The Lost Childhood and Other Essays*. London: Eyre & Spottiswoode, 1951, pp. 106–111.

Grimm, J., & Grimm, W. (1812, 1815), *The Complete Grimms' Fairy Tales*. New York: Pantheon Books Inc., 1944.

Jay, E., Noble, M., & Hobbs, A. S. (1992), *A Victorian Naturalist: Beatrix Potter's Drawings from the Armitt Collection*. London: Frederick Warne & Co.

Lane, M. (1946), *The Tale of Beatrix Potter*. London: Frederick Warne & Co., 1985.

———— (1978), *The Magic Years of Beatrix Potter*. London: Frederick Warne & Co.

Linder, L. (1971), *A History of the Writings of Beatrix Potter (Including Unpublished Work)*. London: Frederick Warne & Co., 1979.

Macaulay, T. B. (1843), Madame D'Arblay. In: *Critical Essays and Historical Essays*, Vol. 2, ed. A. J. Griere. New York: E. P. Dutton, 1907.

Moore, B. E., & Fine, B. D., Eds. (1990), *Psychoanalytic Terms and Concepts*. New Haven/London: American Psychoanalytic Association & Yale University Press.

Nunberg, H. (1961), *Curiosity*. New York: International Universities Press.

Opie, I., & Opie, P., Eds. (1951), *The Oxford Dictionary of Nursery Rhymes*. New York: Oxford University Press.

———— (1974), *The Classic Fairy Tales*. New York: Oxford University Press.

Perrault, C. (1697), *Perrault's Complete Fairy Tales*, tr. A. E. Johnson et al. New York: Dodd, Mead, 1961.

Petty, T. (1953), The tragedy of Humpty Dumpty. *The Psychoanalytic Study of the Child*, 8:404–412. New York: International Universities Press.

Potter, B. (1902), *The Tale of Peter Rabbit*. London: Frederick Warne & Co., 1987.

———— (1903a), *The Tailor of Gloucester*. London: Frederick Warne & Co., 1987.

———— (1903b), *The Tale of Squirrel Nutkin*. London: Frederick Warne & Co., 1987.

———— (1904a), *The Tale of Benjamin Bunny*. London: Frederick Warne & Co., 1987.

———— (1904b), *The Tale of Two Bad Mice*. London: Frederick Warne & Co., 1987.

—— (1905a), *The Tale of Mrs. Tiggy-Winkle.* London: Frederick Warne & Co., 1987.

—— (1905b), *The Tale of the Pie and the Patty-pan.* London: Frederick Warne & Co., 1987.

—— (1906a), *The Tale of Mr. Jeremy Fisher.* London: Frederick Warne & Co., 1987.

—— (1906b), *The Story of a Fierce Bad Rabbit.* London: Frederick Warne & Co., 1987.

—— (1906c), *The Story of Miss Moppet.* London: Frederick Warne & Co., 1987.

—— (1907), *The Tale of Tom Kitten.* London: Frederick Warne & Co., 1987.

—— (1908a), *The Tale of Jemima Puddle-Duck.* London: Frederick Warne & Co., 1987.

—— (1908b), *The Tale of Samuel Whiskers or The Roly-Poly Pudding.* London: Frederick Warne & Co., 1987.

—— (1909a), *The Tale of the Flopsy Bunnies.* London: Frederick Warne & Co., 1987.

—— (1909b), *The Tale of Ginger and Pickles.* London: Frederick Warne & Co., 1987.

—— (1910), *The Tale of Mrs. Tittlemouse.* London: Frederick Warne & Co., 1987.

—— (1911), *The Tale of Timmy Tiptoes.* London: Frederick Warne & Co., 1987.

—— (1912), *The Tale of Mr. Tod.* London: Frederick Warne & Co., 1987.

—— (1913), *The Tale of Pigling Bland.* London: Frederick Warne & Co., 1987.

—— (1917), *Appley Dapply's Nursery Rhymes.* London: Frederick Warne & Co., 1987.

—— (1918), *The Tale of Johnny Town-Mouse.* London: Frederick Warne & Co., 1987.

—— (1922), *Cecily Parsley's Nursery Rhymes.* London: Frederick Warne & Co., 1987.

—— (1929), *The Fairy Caravan*, new ed. London: Frederick Warne & Co., 1987.

—— (1930), *The Tale of Little Pig Robinson.* London: Frederick Warne & Co., 1987.

—— (1932), *Sister Anne.* Philadelphia: David McKay.

—— (1944), Wag-by-Wall. *The Horn Book*, Vol. 3. Boston: The Horn Book, pp. 199–202.

—— (1956), *The Tale of the Faithful Dove*, rev. ed. illus. M. Angel. London: Frederick Warne & Co., 1970.

—— (1966), *The Journal of Beatrix Potter 1881–1897*, rev. ed., foreword J. Taylor. London: Frederick Warne & Co., 1989. *(Journal)*

———— (1971), *The Sly Old Cat*. London: Frederick Warne & Co.

———— (1977), *Dear Ivy, Dear June: Letters from Beatrix Potter*. Toronto: Friends of the Osborn & Lillian Smith Collections/Other Press.

———— (1982), *Beatrix Potter's Americans: Selected Letters*, ed. J. C. Morse. Boston: The Horn Book. (*Americans*)

———— (1985), *Beatrix Potter: The V & A Collection: The Leslie Linder Bequest of Beatrix Potter Material*, catalogue compiled by A. Hobbs & J. Whalley. London: Frederick Warne & Co. and the Victoria and Albert Museum.

———— (1989), *Beatrix Potter's Letters*, sel. & intro. J. Taylor. London: Frederick Warne & Co. (*Letters*)

———— (1992), *Letters to Children from Beatrix Potter*, collected & intro. J. Taylor. London: Frederick Warne & Co. (*Children*)

———— Rawnsley, H. (1989), *Peter Rabbit's Other Tale*. London: The Beatrix Potter Society.

———— (1993), *"So I Shall Tell You a Story . . . " Encounters with Beatrix Potter*, sel. & ed. J. Taylor. London: Frederick Warne & Co.

———— (1994), *The Choyce Letters: Beatrix Potter to Louie Choyce 1916-1943*, ed. J. Taylor. London: The Beatrix Potter Society.

Rank, O. (1912), *Das Inzest-Motiv in Dichtung und Sage: Grundzüge einer Psychologie des dichterischen Schaffens* (The Incest Motif in Fiction and Saga: Fundamentals of a Psychology of Poetic Creation). Leipzig/Vienna: Deuticke.

Shakespeare, W. (1603), The Tragedy of Hamlet, Prince of Denmark. In: *Shakespeare: The Complete Works*, ed. G. B. Harrison. New York: Harcourt, Brace & World, 1968, pp. 884–934.

———— (1606), The Tragedy of Macbeth. In: *Shakespeare: The Complete Works*, ed. G. B. Harrison. New York: Harcourt, Brace & World, 1968, pp. 1184–1218.

———— (1607), The Tragedy of King Lear. In: *Shakespeare: The Complete Works*, ed. G. B. Harrison. New York: Harcourt, Brace & World, 1968, pp. 1140–1183.

Spence, L. (1948), *Minor Traditions of British Mythology*. London, New York: Rider.

Taylor, J. (1986), *Beatrix Potter: Artist, Storyteller and Countrywoman*, rev. ed. London: Frederick Warne & Co., 1987.

———— Whalley, J. I., Hobbs, A. S., Battrick, E. M. (1987), *Beatrix Potter 1866–1943: The Artist and Her World*. London: Frederick Warne & Co.

Westwood, J. (1985), *Albion: A Guide to Legendary Britain*. New York: Granada.

# Supplementary Reading

Bartlett, W., & Whalley, J. I. (1988), *Beatrix Potter's Derwentwater*. New York: Viking Penguin.

The Beatrix Potter Society (1984), *Beatrix Potter Studies I*. J. Pritchard & B. Riddle, eds. (Papers presented at The Beatrix Potter Lake District Study Conference July 1984). London: The Beatrix Potter Society.

———— (1987), *Beatrix Potter Studies II*. B. Riddle, ed. (Papers presented at The Beatrix Potter Society Lake District Study Conference July 1986). London: The Beatrix Potter Society.

———— (1989), *Beatrix Potter Before Peter Rabbit: Beatrix Potter Studies III*. B. Riddle, ed. (Papers presented at The Beatrix Potter Society Conference, Perth, July 1988). London: The Beatrix Potter Society.

———— (1991), *Beatrix Potter and Mrs. Heelis: Beatrix Potter Studies IV*. E. Bassom, R. Knox, & I. Whalley, eds. (Papers presented at The Beatrix Potter Society Conference, Lancaster, July 1990). London: The Beatrix Potter Society.

Davies, H. (1988), *Beatrix Potter's Lakeland*. New York: Viking Penguin.

Grinstein, A. (1983), *Uncle Tom's Cabin* and Harriet Beecher Stowe. Beating fantasies and thoughts of dying. *Amer. Imago*, 40:115–144.

Taylor, J. (1987), *That Naughty Rabbit: Beatrix Potter and Peter Rabbit*. London: Frederick Warne & Co.

Tucker, N. (1989), *Peter Rabbit and the Child Psychologist: Some Further Adventures*. Sixth Linder Memorial Lecture, 1986. London: Beatrix Potter Society.

# Index